Cisco Secure PIX Firewalls

Edited by:

David W. Chapman Jr. and Andy Fox

Cisco Press

Cisco Press
201 West 103rd Street
Indianapolis, IN 46290 USA

Cisco Secure PIX Firewalls

Edited by: David W. Chapman Jr. and Andy Fox

Copyright© 2002 Cisco Systems, Inc.

Published by:
Cisco Press
201 West 103rd Street
Indianapolis, IN 46290 USA

Printed in the United States of America 5 6 7 8 9 0

Library of Congress Cataloging-in-Publication Number: 2001086628

ISBN: 1-58705-035-8

Fifth Printing December 2002

Warning and Disclaimer

This book is designed to provide information about **Cisco PIX Firewalls**. Every effort has been made to make this book as complete and as accurate as possible, but no warranty or fitness is implied.

The information is provided on an "as is" basis. The authors, Cisco Press, and Cisco Systems, Inc., shall have neither liability nor responsibility to any person or entity with respect to any loss or damages arising from the information contained in this book or from the use of the discs or programs that may accompany it.

The opinions expressed in this book belong to the author and are not necessarily those of Cisco Systems, Inc.

The Cisco Press self-study book series is as described, intended for self-study. It has not been designed for use in a classroom environment. Only Cisco Learning Partners displaying the following logos are authorized providers of Cisco curriculum. If you are using this book within the classroom of a training company that does not carry one of these logos, then you are not preparing with a Cisco trained and authorized provider. For information on Cisco Learning Partners please visit:www.cisco.com/go/authorizedtraining. To provide Cisco with any information about what you may believe is unauthorized use of Cisco trademarks or copyrighted training material, please visit: http://www.cisco.com/logo/infringement.html.

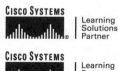

Trademark Acknowledgments

All terms mentioned in this book that are known to be trademarks or service marks have been appropriately capitalized. Cisco Press or Cisco Systems, Inc., cannot attest to the accuracy of this information. Use of a term in this book should not be regarded as affecting the validity of any trademark or service mark.

Feedback Information

At Cisco Press, our goal is to create in-depth technical books of the highest quality and value. Each book is crafted with care and precision, undergoing rigorous development that involves the unique expertise of members from the professional technical community.

Readers' feedback is a natural continuation of this process. If you have any comments regarding how we could improve the quality of this book, or otherwise alter it to better suit your needs, you can contact us through e-mail at feedback@ciscopress.com. Please make sure to include the book title and ISBN in your message.

We greatly appreciate your assistance.

Publisher	John Wait
Editor-In-Chief	John Kane
Cisco Systems Management	Michael Hakkert
	Tom Geitner
Executive Editor	Brett Bartow
Production Manager	Patrick Kanouse
Development Editor	Christopher Cleveland
Copy Editor	Doug Lloyd
Course Developers	Bob Du Charme
	Randy R. Rivera
	R. Eduardo Rivera
Technical Editors	Randy Ivener, Doug McKillip, David Ofsevit, Gilles Piché
Team Coordinator	Tammi Ross
Book Designer	Gina Rexrode
Cover Designer	Louisa Klucznik
Compositor	ContentWorks
Indexer	Larry Sweazy

CISCO SYSTEMS

Corporate Headquarters
Cisco Systems, Inc.
170 West Tasman Drive
San Jose, CA 95134-1706
USA
http://www.cisco.com
Tel: 408 526-4000
     800 553-NETS (6387)
Fax: 408 526-4100

European Headquarters
Cisco Systems Europe
11 Rue Camille Desmoulins
92782 Issy-les-Moulineaux
Cedex 9
France
http://www-europe.cisco.com
Tel: 33 1 58 04 60 00
Fax: 33 1 58 04 61 00

Americas Headquarters
Cisco Systems, Inc.
170 West Tasman Drive
San Jose, CA 95134-1706
USA
http://www.cisco.com
Tel: 408 526-7660
Fax: 408 527-0883

Asia Pacific Headquarters
Cisco Systems Australia,
Pty., Ltd
Level 17, 99 Walker Street
North Sydney
NSW 2059 Australia
http://www.cisco.com
Tel: +61 2 8448 7100
Fax: +61 2 9957 4350

Cisco Systems has more than 200 offices in the following countries.
Addresses, phone numbers, and fax numbers are listed on the
Cisco Web site at www.cisco.com/go/offices

Argentina • Australia • Austria • Belgium • Brazil • Bulgaria • Canada • Chile • China • Colombia • Costa Rica • Croatia • Czech Republic • Denmark • Dubai, UAE • Finland • France • Germany • Greece • Hong Kong • Hungary • India • Indonesia • Ireland • Israel • Italy • Japan • Korea • Luxembourg • Malaysia Mexico • The Netherlands • New Zealand • Norway • Peru • Philippines • Poland • Portugal • Puerto Rico Romania • Russia • Saudi Arabia • Scotland • Singapore • Slovakia • Slovenia • South Africa • Spain Sweden • Switzerland • Taiwan • Thailand • Turkey • Ukraine • United Kingdom • United States • Venezuela Vietnam • Zimbabwe

About the Authors

David W. Chapman Jr., CCSI, CCNP, CCDP, CSS-1, is a Cisco Security Instructor with Global Knowledge. As Course Director for the Cisco Secure PIX Firewall Course, David is charged with maintaining the integrity and quality of the course offering and mentoring instructors new to the course. David has been working with Cisco products in enterprise networks since 1994. Prior to joining Global Knowledge, he worked for a Cisco Gold Certified Partner in Portland, Oregon, where he spent the last year assisting Cisco SmartStart Customers prototype, test, and build secure e-commerce infrastructures. David recently passed the CCIE Security qualification exam and plans to challenge the lab.

Andy Fox, CCSI, CCNA, CCDA, CSS-1, is a Certified Cisco Systems Instructor with Global Knowledge. Andy has been teaching Cisco Certified Classes for more than five years and is the Course Director for the Managing Cisco Network Security course. After graduating from Purdue University in 1980, Andy began his career in computer science as a computer operator in the Air Force. Andy worked in various jobs during his five-year enlistment. One of the jobs he held was system administrator of a BBN C70 MINET host at Ramstein AFB in Germany. That job helped him get his next position as a network operations controller at Bolt Beranek and Newman in Cambridge, Massachusetts. Working in the Network Operations Center, Andy helped maintain many wide-area networks, including the ARPANET, MILNET, and MINET. Andy became an instructor in 1996 after working as a Systems Engineer at TYMNET (British Telecom) in New York City and RPR Pharmaceuticals in Collegeville, Pennsylvania.

About the Technical Reviewers

Randy Ivener is a Security and VPN specialist with Cisco Systems' Advanced Engineering Services team. He is a Cisco Certified Network Professional, Cisco Security Specialist-1, and ASQ Certified Software Quality Engineer. He has spent several years as a network security consultant helping companies understand and secure their networks. He has worked with many security products and technologies including firewalls, VPNs, intrusion detection, and authentication systems. Before becoming immersed in security, he spent time in software development and as a training instructor. Randy graduated from the U.S. Naval Academy and has an MBA.

Doug McKillip, P.E., CCIE #1851, is an independent consultant specializing in Cisco Certified Training in association with Global Knowledge. He has more than 13 years experience in computer networking and, for the past 9 years, has been actively involved in security and firewalls. Doug provided both instructional and technical assistance during the initial deployment of the MCNS Version 1.0 training class and has been the lead instructor and course director for Global Knowledge, a Training Parter of Cisco Systems. Doug holds bachelor's and master's degrees in chemical engineering from MIT, and a master's degree in computer science from the University of Delaware. He resides in Wilmington, Delaware.

David Ofsevit is a Technical Marketing Engineer for Cisco Systems, Inc. He currently works for Cisco's Enterprise Solutions Engineering group, concentrating on security components of network designs. This role builds on his prior experience in technical sales support, specializing in network security. He is a member of Cisco's Security Field Solutions Architecture Team as well as the Security and VPN Advisors Team.

David has been with Cisco since 1996, when it acquired TGV Software, Inc. Before working at TGV, David worked for Digital Equipment Corporation, the Mitre Corporation, and the U. S. Department of Transportation. He holds a combined S.B.-S.M. degree in electrical engineering from MIT.

Gilles Piché, CCSI, is a security consultant who has been working in the network security field in Canada for over five years. Prior to that, he did contract work with the Canadian government in a network engineering capacity. Gilles is also a Cisco Certified Security Instructor and has been teaching Cisco Security courses for Global Knowledge Network (Canada) for the last year and a half.

Dedications

David W. Chapman Jr.: I dedicate this book to Mom, Dad, and "Little Sister" for their love and encouragement. It has made all the difference.

Andy Fox: My thanks to my children, Zach and Jessica, and my wife Heidi. I owe a great deal of thanks to John Kinnaman the 3rd for his creative analysis and input.

Acknowledgments

We would first like to thank veteran Cisco Press author Catherine Paquet for helping this project find us. We would also like to extend a special thanks to the following fine folks at the Cisco VPN Security Business Unit in Austin, Texas:

Jessie Burke, Bob Du Charme, Bob Eckhoff, Steven Hanna, Jeanne Jackson, Leon Katcharian, Ed Rivera,Randy Rivera, Danny Rodriguez, Erin Stanley, Rick Stiffler, John Trollinger, Mike Wenstrom, Teresa Winget, and Cihan Yazicioglu.

Our thanks also to Brett Bartow and Christopher Cleveland from Cisco Press who got us over the inevitable hump faced by first-time authors.

We'd like to thank our Technical Editors: Randy Ivener, Doug McKillip, David Ofsevit, and Gilles Piché. They did a fantastic job helping the final shape of the book take form.

Finally, we'd like to acknowledge the many instructors (too many to name individually) who have taught us how to teach and brought us to where we are today.

Contents at a Glance

Contents

Foreword

The demand for qualified network security professionals has never been greater. Each day organizations find themselves engaged in a never-ending battle to keep their networks secure from those intent on damaging systems or gaining unauthorized access. Controlling firewalls is recognized as a critical skill for the network security professional responsible for securing access and controlling activities within the network.

Cisco Secure PIX Firewalls is a Cisco authorized, self-paced learning tool. This book teaches you how to describe, configure, verify, and manage the PIX Firewall product family and the Cisco IOS Firewall feature set within Cisco routers. Whether you are preparing to complete the Cisco Security certification or are interested in installing, configuring, and operating Cisco PIX Firewalls, this book will enhance your understanding of firewalls.

Cisco and Cisco Press present this material in text-based format to provide another learning vehicle for our customers and the broader user community in general. Although a publication cannot replace the instructor-led environment, we must acknowledge that not everyone responds in the same way to the same delivery mechanism. It is our intent that presenting this material via a Cisco Press publication will enhance the transfer of knowledge to our audience of networking professionals.

Cisco Press will present other books in the Certification Self-Study Series on existing and future exams to help achieve Cisco Internet Learning Solutions Group's principal objectives: to educate the Cisco community of networking professionals and to enable that community to build and maintain reliable, scalable networks. The Cisco Career Certifications and classes that support these certifications are directed at meeting these objectives through a disciplined approach to progressive learning.

In order to succeed with Cisco Career Certifications and in your daily job as a Cisco certified professional, we recommend a blended learning solution that combines instructor-led training with hands-on experience, e-learning, and self-study training. Cisco Systems has authorized Cisco Learning Partners worldwide, which can provide you with the most highly qualified instruction and invaluable hands-on experience in lab and simulation environments. To learn more about Cisco Learning Partner programs available in your area, please go to http://www.cisco.com/go/authorizedtraining.

The books Cisco creates in partnership with Cisco Press will meet the same standards for content quality demanded of our courses and certifications. It is our intent that you will find this and subsequent Cisco Press certification self-study publications of value as you build your networking knowledge base.

Thomas M. Kelly
Vice-President, Internet Learning Solutions Group
Cisco Systems, Inc.
November 2002

Introduction

This book is aimed at network engineers who need a strong understanding of the PIX Firewall and how it can be used to mitigate the enormous threat to their networks. Readers will have to know basic IP operation and security concepts to make full use of the information presented. For readers new to network security and the PIX Firewall, we recommend reading *Managing Cisco Network Security* by Michael Wenstrom and published by Cisco Press. Just as MCNS is the prerequisite for the Cisco Secure PIX Firewall course, the MCNS book provides the foundation material from which we built this book.

Not only network engineers will benefit from this book. Network designers will find the case studies presented invaluable to designing secure infrastructures. In addition, information systems auditors will gain the knowledge needed to properly evaluate complex configurations for compliance with confidence. Case studies will be provided with discussion of common configurations.

Motivation for the Book

This book is intended to fill the need of readers who want to refresh their knowledge of basic PIX operation and delve into advanced configurations. We have found no other book on the market that covers advanced PIX features at this level.

Goals of the Book

The purpose of this book is to take users with basic PIX skills and mentor them to a higher comfort level with advanced PIX Firewall options. By presenting readers with common, real-life scenarios and case studies, the book helps readers understand the benefits and caveats of making configuration decisions designing and deploying their own PIX security solutions.

Command Syntax Conventions

The conventions used to present command syntax in this book are the same conventions used in the Cisco IOS Software Command Reference. The Command Reference describes these conventions as follows:

- Vertical bars (|) separate alternative, mutually exclusive elements.
- Square brackets [ ] indicate optional elements.
- Braces { } indicate a required choice.
- Braces within brackets [{ }] indicate a required choice within an optional element.

- **Boldface** indicates commands and keywords that are entered literally as shown. In actual configuration examples and output (not general command syntax), boldface indicates commands that are manually input by the user (such as a **show** command).

- *Italics* indicate arguments for which you supply actual values.

Icons Used in This Book

Router

Bridge

Hub

DSU/CSU

Catalyst Switch

Multilayer Switch

ATM Switch

ISDN/Frame Relay switch

Communication Server

Gateway

Cisco 6732 Access Server

PIX Firewall

PC

PC with Software

Workstation

Mac

Terminal

File Server

Web Server

CiscoWorks Workstation

Printer

Laptop

IBM mainframe

Front End Processor

Cluster Controller

Line: Ethernet

Line: Serial

Line: Circuit-Switched

Frame Relay Virtual Circuit

Token Ring
Token Ring

FDDI ring

Network Cloud

This chapter covers the following topics:

- Why Network Security Is Necessary
- Secure Network Design Defined
- Categorizing Network Security Threats
- How Network Security Is Breached
- Network Security Policy and the Security Wheel

CHAPTER 1

Introduction to Network Security

Computers, networks, and the Internet affect our lives every day. The fast-paced, technologically savvy world we live in today is ever more dependent upon computers and networking. This did not happen overnight. Although the advances in computer technology are occurring at a very fast rate, computers have been around for quite some time.

In the beginning of this wave of computer technology, many were unsure how far the wave was going to go. Some were hesitant to place much time and effort into something that might have turned out to be a fad. The number of people who were working on the advancement of computer technology was relatively small, compared to today's widespread needs. In their small community, computer enthusiasts were comfortable working with each other, and they trusted each other. Participation was invited. In such a freewheeling environment, the security of computers and the software that ran those computers was not given a very high priority. Much of the time security was an afterthought.

Why Network Security Is Necessary

Today, the Internet is made up of tens of thousands of networks, interconnected without boundary. Network security is essential in this environment because any organizational network is accessible from any computer in the world and, therefore, potentially vulnerable to threats from individuals who do not require physical access to it.

In a recent survey conducted by the Computer Security Institute (CSI), 70 percent of the organizations polled stated that their network security defenses had been breached and that 60 percent of the incidents came from within the organizations themselves.

While it is difficult to measure how many companies have had Internet-related security problems and the financial losses due to those problems, it is clear that the problems do exist.

Secure Network Design Defined

An *internetwork* is made up of many networks that are connected. When accessing information in an internetwork environment, secure areas must be created. The device that separates each of these areas is known as a *firewall*. While it is true that a firewall usually separates a private network from a public network, that is not always the case. It is not unusual to use a firewall to separate network segments within a private network.

NOTE   A firewall, as defined in Cisco Press's *Dictionary of Internetworking Terms and Acronyms*, is a "router or access server, or several routers or access servers, designated as a buffer between any connected public networks and a private network. A firewall router uses access lists and other methods to ensure the security of the private network."

A firewall usually has at least three interfaces, although many early implementations had two interfaces. It is still common to install a two-interface firewall. When using a firewall that has three interfaces, at least three networks are created. The three areas that are created by the firewall are described as follows:

- **Inside**—The *Inside* is the *trusted* area of the internetwork. The devices on the Inside are the organization's private network (or networks). These devices share a common security policy relative to the Outside (the Internet) network. It is, however, a common practice to have a firewall to segment the trusted environment. If one department, such as Human Resources, needs to be protected from the rest of the trusted users, a firewall may be used.

- **Outside**—The *Outside* is the *untrusted* area of the internetwork. The firewall secures the devices on the Inside and DMZ from the devices on the Outside. In the course of doing business, organizations typically allow access to the DMZ from the Outside. If necessary, a firewall should be carefully configured for selective access from the Outside to hosts and services on the DMZ. If unavoidable, a firewall can be configured to allow access from a device on the Outside to a trusted device on the Inside. This is a much greater risk than permitting access from the Outside to the isolated DMZ.

- **DMZ (Demilitarized Zone)**—The DMZ is an isolated network, or networks, which is usually accessible to the Outside users. The firewall must be configured to allow access from the Outside or Inside to the DMZ. The creation of a DMZ allows an organization to make information and services available to Outside users in a secure and controlled environment. This permits access to Outside users, without allowing access to the Inside.

    The hosts or servers that reside on the DMZ are commonly referred to as *bastion hosts*. In this case, a bastion host is a host that is current with regard to its operating system and patches to that operating system. The action of being current will usually make it less vulnerable to attack because the vendor has fixed or "patched" any known security flaws. The bastion host is a host that is running only those services necessary to make it perform its application duties. Unnecessary (and sometimes more vulnerable) services are turned off or removed from the host.

Figure 1-1 illustrates this general network design.

Figure 1-1   *General Network Design Using a Firewall*

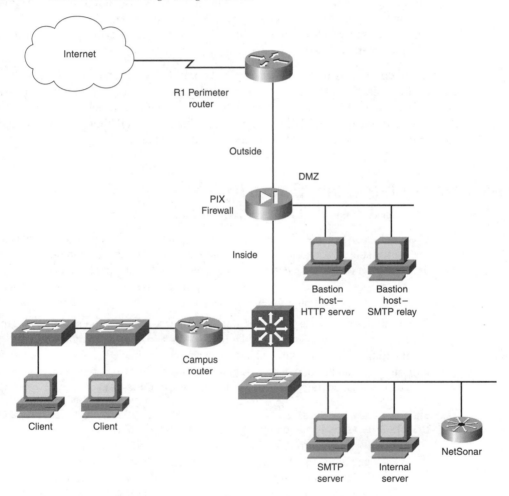

The baseline perspective for a firewall is to perform the following functions:

- Permit no access from the Outside to the Inside.
- Permit limited access from the Outside to the DMZ.

- Permit all access from the Inside to the Outside.
- Permit limited access from the Inside to the DMZ.

In many network designs there are exceptions to some or all of these rules. For example, it may be necessary to allow SMTP messages from the Outside directly to the Inside. If an environment does not have an SMTP server in the DMZ or does not have an SMTP mail relay host in the DMZ, then it would be necessary to allow SMTP directly to the SMTP server that physically resides on the Inside. Permitting this traffic will significantly increase the risk to the internal network.

Another exception may be that all traffic is not permitted to traverse from the Inside to the Outside. Potentially an IP address, a subnet, or the entire Inside network may be restricted from utilizing a particular application (port). Another restriction imposed upon Inside to Outside data traffic may be URL filtering. Establishing an HTTP filter, such as a WebSense filter, and other exceptions will be discussed in later chapters.

Categorizing Network Security Threats

Network security threats can be categorized into four broad themes:

- **Unstructured threats**—These originate mostly from inexperienced individuals using easily available hacking tools from the Internet. Some of the people in this category are motivated by malicious intent but most are motivated by the intellectual challenge and are commonly known as *script kiddies*. They are not the most talented or experienced computer operators, programmers, or users, but they have the time and motivation.

  Script kiddies pose a very serious threat to network security. Many times a script kiddie unleashes a virus or Trojan Horse without actually knowing the full ramifications. The virus they unleash may reach worldwide proportions and cause millions of dollars of damage. In some cases, a virus may be unleashed that contains information that actually points back to the author of the virus.

NOTE   A **virus** is malicious software that is attached to another trusted (or thought to be trusted) program to execute a particular unwanted function on a user's workstation. An example of a **virus** is a program that is attached to command.com (the primary interpreter for Windows systems) which deletes certain files and infects any other versions of command.com that it can find. A **Trojan horse** is different only in that the entire application was written to look like something else, when in fact it is an attack tool. An example of a **Trojan horse** is a software application that runs a simple game on the user's workstation. While the user is occupied with the game, the **Trojan horse** mails a copy of itself to every user in the user's address book. Then other users get the game and play it, thus spreading the **Trojan horse**.

Unstructured threats that are only executed with the intent of testing and challenging a script kiddie's skills can still do a lot of damage to a company. For example, if your company's external web site is hacked, your company's integrity is damaged. Even if your external web site is separate from your internal information that sits behind a protective firewall, the public does not know that. All they know is that if your web site was hacked, then it is an unsafe place to conduct business.

- **Structured threats**—These originate from individuals who are more highly motivated and technically competent than script kiddies. They usually understand network systems design and the vulnerabilities of those systems. They can understand as well as create hacking scripts to penetrate those network systems. An individual who presents a structured threat typically targets a specific destination or group. These threats are from groups that may be involved with the major fraud and theft cases reported to law enforcement agencies. Occasionally, these hackers are hired by organized crime, industry competitors, or state-sponsored intelligence organizations.

- **External threats**—These originate from individuals or organizations working outside your organization, who do not have authorized access to your computer systems or network. They usually work their way into a network from the Internet or dialup access servers.

- **Internal threats**—Typically, these threats originate from individuals who have authorized access to the network. These users either have an account on a server or physical access to the network. An internal threat may come from a disgruntled former or current employee or contractor. Some studies have shown that a majority of security incidents originate from Internal threats.

How Network Security Is Breached

The three types of network attacks are

- **Reconnaissance attacks**—An intruder attempts to discover and map systems, services, and vulnerabilities.

- **Access attacks**—An intruder attacks networks or systems to retrieve data, gain access, or escalate their personal access privileges.

- **Denial of Service attacks**—An intruder attacks your network in such a way that damages or corrupts your computer system, or denies you and other authorized users access to your networks, systems, or services.

Reconnaissance Attacks

Reconnaissance is an unauthorized user's attempt to discover and map network system devices, services available on those systems, and the vulnerabilities of those systems. It is also known as *information gathering* and, in most cases, precedes an actual *access* or *Denial of Service (DoS)* attack.

The malicious intruder typically ping sweeps the target network first to determine what IP addresses are active and responsive. This can lead to the intruder finding information about what services or ports are active on the live IP addresses. From the active IP address information, the intruder queries the application ports to determine the application type and version as well as the type and version of operating system running on the target host.

NOTE   A **ping sweep** is network reconnaissance technique that uses ping (ICMP echo and echo-reply) to map a known network.

Reconnaissance is somewhat analogous to a thief investigating a neighborhood for vulnerable homes to break into, such as an unoccupied residence, or an easy-to-open door or window. Just as a thief may rattle the door handle of a door without going in immediately if it is unlocked, the computer user on reconnaissance seeks to discover vulnerable services to be exploited at a later time, when there is less likelihood that anyone is paying attention.

Access Attacks

Access is a broad term that refers to the capability of a specific source (that is, a user on a computer, connected to a network that is connected to the Internet) to connect to a specific destination (that is, a computer on a network that is connected to the Internet). When a destination has been targeted, the attacker will attempt to use some software application to reach the destination. An access attack can come in the form of unauthorized data retrieval and manipulation, system access, or privileged escalation. Access attacks can also be used to gain control of a system and install and hide software that will be used later by the hackers.

Unauthorized Data Retrieval

Unauthorized Data Retrieval is simply reading, writing, copying, or moving files that are not intended to be accessible to the intruder. Sometimes this is as easy as finding share folders in Windows 9x or NT, or NFS exported directories in UNIX systems with read or read and write access to everyone. The intruder will usually have no problem getting to the files and, more often than not, the easily accessible information is highly confidential and completely unprotected to prying eyes, especially if the attacker is already an internal user. The intruder *will* have a problem if the file is encrypted and cannot be read.

Unauthorized System Access

A *System Access* attacker gains access to a system without authorization. An intruder may gain system access through any of a number of ways. Some systems may not be password protected, providing easy access to the intruder. Gaining access into systems that do have some form of security may involve running a script or using a software tool that exploits a known vulnerability of the system or application being attacked.

Operating system weaknesses can also be exploited to provide unauthorized system access. Some aspects of an operating system were developed without security concerns in mind. Those security flaws may be patched in later operating system code, but if the patch is not installed, the flaw will exist.

Unauthorized Privilege Escalation

Legitimate users with a low level of access privilege perform this kind of attack. An intruder who simply gains a low level of access may also perform it. The intent is to get information or execute procedures that are not authorized at their lower level of access. In many cases, this involves gaining root access in a UNIX system and installing a sniffer to record network traffic. The ultimate goal is to find usernames and passwords that can be used to access another target.

In some cases, intruders only want to gain access without wanting to steal information—especially when the motive is intellectual challenge, curiosity, or ignorance.

DoS Attacks

DoS is when an attacker disables or corrupts networks, systems, or services in order to deny the service to its intended users. It usually involves crashing the system or slowing it down to the point that it is unusable. DoS attacks can also be as simple as wiping out or corrupting information necessary for business. In most cases, performing the attack simply involves running a hack, script, or tool. The attacker does not need prior access to the target, only a path to the target. Once the path is realized, great paralyzing damage can be caused. Because many DoS attacks are relatively easy to initiate and can be performed anonymously, it is the most feared attack on the Internet.

A *Distributed* Denial of Service (DDoS) attack is one in which the source of the attack is many computers (usually spread across a large geographic area) making it very difficult to find and stop the source(s).

Network Security Policy and the Security Wheel

Network security is a continuous process. It is necessary because of the continuous advancement in computer technology and use of that technology. With an understanding of the potential threats to network security, security for a system or group of systems should be built around a security policy.

According to RFC 2196, "Site Security Handbook":

A security policy is a formal statement of the rules by which people who are given access to an organization's technology and information assets must abide.

A security policy needs to accomplish the following tasks:

- Identify the organization's security objectives. Determine what you want to protect and how to do it. Understanding weak points in a network and how they can be exploited is a step toward strengthening those weak points.

- Document the resources to be protected. Learn how systems normally function so that you understand how devices are used and how data flows.

- Identify the network infrastructure with current maps and inventories. Consider the physical security of your network and how to protect it. Physical access to a device may give a user control over that device.

A continuous security policy is most effective because it promotes re-testing and reapplying of updated security measures on a continuous basis. The Security Wheel graphically represents this continuous security process. Figure 1-2 illustrates the four steps of the Security Wheel.

Figure 1-2 *The Security Wheel*

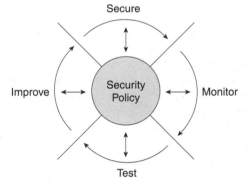

The security policy is the hub around which the four steps of the Security Wheel are based:

Step 1 *Secure* the system. Implement security devices and/or systems, with the intent to prevent unauthorized access to network systems:

(a) *Identification Authentication Systems*, such as One-Time Passwords (OTP), give access to authenticated and authorized users. Some examples of Identification Authentication Systems are Cisco Secure Access Control Server (CSACS), Windows Dial-up Networking, S/Key, CrytpoCard, and SecurID.

(b) *Encryption* can disguise traffic. Encrypting traffic can prevent unwanted disclosure to unauthorized or malicious users. This can ensure the confidentiality of the data traffic. IP Security (IPSec) is the standard encryption used on the Internet (The main RFC covering IPSec is RFC 2401) and will be covered in Chapter 11, "Configuring IPSec for Cisco PIX Firewalls."

(c) *Firewalls* can permit and deny specific data to allow only valid traffic and services.

(d) *Vulnerability Patching* is the act of applying fixes or measures to stop the exploitation of known vulnerabilities. This includes turning off services that are not needed on every system; the fewer services that are enabled, the harder it is for hackers to gain access.

(e) *Physical Security* is a very important, and sometimes overlooked aspect of securing the system. If someone is able to walk away with system hardware, all other security is moot. It is also important to protect unauthorized installation of promiscuous mode devices that could capture important data.

Step 2 *Monitor* the network for violations and attacks against the corporate security policy. Violations can occur within the secured perimeter of the network from a disgruntled employee or from the outside of the network from a hacker. A real-time intrusion detection system, such as the Cisco Secure Intrusion Detection System (CSIDS) can discover and prevent unauthorized entry. CSIDS can ensure that the security devices in Step 1 have been configured properly. Logging is an important aspect of monitoring. Keeping track of the data traffic that is flowing into a network can be the difference between discovering an attack and acting on it before it becomes a problem, and not discovering an attack and having the attack disable the network.

Step 3 *Test* the effectiveness of the security safeguards in place. Validation is a necessity. You may have a very sophisticated network security system, but if it is not configured or working properly, your network can be compromised. One tool that may be used to identify the security posture of the network is Cisco Secure Scanner.

Step 4 Continuously *Improve* the corporate security policy. Collect and analyze information from the monitoring and testing phases to make security improvements.

New network vulnerabilities and risks are created every day. In order to keep your network as secure as possible, all four steps—secure, monitor, test, and improve—should be repeated on a continuous basis and should be incorporated into updated versions of the corporate security policy.

Summary

Computers and networks are integrated into our everyday lives in many ways. Understanding data flow and security is necessary when working with networks. When security is an issue, being informed is essential. Network design, the applications used, traffic flow, and understanding of security threats are just some of the topics that should be known.

When the issue is sending data to, or receiving data from an untrusted environment, a firewall should be the centerpiece of your security solution. The focus of this book is using the Cisco Secure PIX Firewall as a part of the solution to network security. The next chapter details the Cisco Secure PIX Firewall software and hardware.

Review Questions

To test what you have learned in this chapter, answer the following questions and then refer to Appendix F for the answers.

1 I want to install a web server and allow Internet users access, but I don't want those users inside my network. How can I accomplish this?

2 A script kiddie poses what type of network security threat?

3 Of all of the different types of threats that exist, which one should I fear most?

4 What is used to allow only specified users access to a network?

This chapter covers the following topics:

- The Three Types of Firewall Technology
- Features of the PIX Firewall
- The Software Within the Hardware
- PIX Firewall Models

CHAPTER 2

Cisco PIX Firewall Software and Hardware

In the building construction industry, a firewall is a wall built using fireproof material. A firewall on the inside of a building can help prevent the spread of fire from one room to an adjoining room. Firewalls in building construction are very common and in many circumstances mandatory.

When applying the term *firewall* to a computer network, a firewall is a computer or group of computers that enforces an access control policy between two or more networks. When referring to a firewall as a single computer, it may simply be a device at the edge of a network that permits or denies traffic based on some specified criteria. Typically a firewall is a part of the perimeter security within an overall network security policy.

In a more elaborate scheme, the firewall itself is a single computer, but the firewall security system is a group of computers that provides for the security of a network or internetwork. In this type of scenario, the firewall is a part of an overall network security implementation.

Types of Firewalls

Firewall technology has existed since the need for security in the computer industry was first realized. A computer that filtered traffic based on packet information was the first firewall. It was a relatively simple way to categorize data traffic. Filtering the data was based upon where that data came from and where it was going. Once some specified information was determined to be within a particular packet, it was permitted or denied based upon the traffic filter rule.

If the type of data traffic that is flowing in a network is a known, standard protocol, then that data can be filtered. This is one example of the need for standardization. If the data traffic is following a standard (such as TCP/IP, IPX, AppleTalk, DECNET, and so on), the data has to follow specific guidelines so it can be understood and interpreted by both the source and the destination. As long as the data flowing in a particular network is based on a standard, it can be filtered, providing the filtering device has the capability to filter the given protocol stack.

Filtering data traffic in this way is just one example of how a firewall can operate. Firewalls can be defined as being in one of three categories:

- Packet filter
- Proxy filter
- Stateful packet filter

The sections that follow describe these three categories of firewall in greater detail.

Packet Filters

A firewall that is a TCP/IP packet filter typically analyzes network traffic at the transport layer or the Internet (network) layer of the TCP/IP protocol stack. As long as the data flowing in a particular network is based on the standard TCP/IP protocol stack (or any other standard protocol stack), it can be filtered. The fields within each packet of data that is flowing in the network are known (examples are source IP address, destination IP address, source port, and destination port). The information that is analyzed by a packet filter is the static packet header information.

When configuring a packet filter, rules are created using some specified source and/or destination criteria. As illustrated in Figure 2-1, a packet filter may permit or deny information based upon one or more of the following:

- Source IP address
- Destination IP address
- Protocol
- Source port
- Destination port

A Cisco router configured with an Access Control List (ACL) to filter traffic flowing through it is an example of a packet filter. A Cisco router can be configured with an ACL to filter traffic flowing through it. Native to Cisco IOS Software is the capability to create an ACL and filter data on a packet-by-packet basis.

An important aspect of a packet filter is that it doesn't retain stateful information. When the packet filter receives a packet, a decision is made to permit or deny the packet based upon the packet filter list. Once the packet filter has processed the packet, no information about that particular packet is retained. The next packet is received and the decision process is repeated.

The following are some disadvantages with a packet filter:

- Arbitrary packets can be sent that fit the ACL criteria and therefore pass through the filter.
- Packets can pass through the filter by being fragmented.

- Complex ACLs are difficult to create, implement, and maintain correctly.

- Some services cannot be filtered (port numbers can be specified, but with some applications—especially newer multimedia applications—the port numbers are unknown until after the session starts).

Figure 2-1   *Testing Packets with Access Lists*

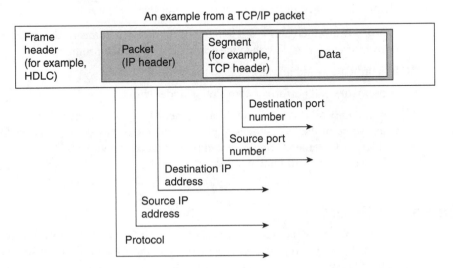

Proxy Filters

A proxy filter is a firewall device that examines packets at higher layers of the Open Systems Interconnection (OSI) model (usually Layers 4 through 7 of the OSI model). Looking at this much detail of the session makes a proxy filter very strong, but end-to-end throughput suffers. This device hides valuable data by requiring users to communicate with a secure system by means of a proxy. Users gain access to the network by going through a process that establishes session state, user authentication, and authorized policy. This means that users connect to outside services via application programs (proxies) running on the gateway connecting to the outside unprotected zone.

One possible way for a proxy filter firewall to work is to require the user on the inside (trusted side) of the firewall to first build a session to the firewall itself (the proxy is the destination for the session). The user must then authenticate. Based upon the user ID and password, the user is permitted specific access to the outside. When using a proxy firewall such as this, two unique sessions are built (one from the user to the proxy and one from the proxy to the destination).

Another way for a proxy firewall to work is for the user (on the trusted inside) to build the session directly to the destination (on the untrusted outside). At least that is what appears to the user. What actually happens is that the proxy intercepts the session and based upon some information (such as the source IP address) performs authentication and builds two unique sessions (one from the user to the proxy, and one from the proxy to the destination). This second way for a proxy firewall to work is much more transparent to the user.

Possible problems encountered with a proxy filter include the following:

- A proxy firewall creates a single point of failure, which means that if access to the firewall is compromised, then the entire network is compromised
- It is difficult to add new services to the firewall.
- A proxy firewall performs more slowly under stress.
- A proxy firewall is typically built on a general-purpose operating system, since it has to use some of the OS services to perform the proxy processes. This has the twin problems of overhead and decreased performance and vulnerability of the OS to attack since it is well known.

Stateful Packet Filters

The third type of firewall combines the best of packet filtering and proxy filter technologies. A stateful packet filter keeps complete session state information for each session built through the firewall. Each time an IP connection is established for an inbound or outbound connection, the information is logged in a stateful session flow table. Stateful packet filtering is the method used by the Cisco PIX Firewall.

The stateful session flow table contains the source and destination addresses, port numbers, TCP sequencing information, and additional flags for each TCP/UDP connection associated with that particular session. As a session is initiated through the firewall, it creates a connection object and, consequently, all inbound and outbound packets are compared against session flows in the stateful session flow table. Data is permitted through the firewall only if an appropriate connection exists to validate its passage.

This method is effective because it:

- Works on individual packets and compares individual packets to established connections.
- Operates at a higher performance level than packet filtering or using a proxy filter.
- Records data in a table for every connection or connectionless transaction. This table serves as a reference point to determine if packets belong to an existing connection or are from an unauthorized source.

The PIX Firewall Logic

The Cisco Secure PIX Firewall is a key element in the overall Cisco end-to-end security solution. It is a dedicated hardware/software firewall that delivers high-level security with less impact on network performance than other firewalls. It is considered a hybrid system because it features packet filter, proxy filter, and stateful packet filter technology.

The Cisco PIX Firewall provides the following benefits and features:

- **Secure, real-time, embedded system**—Unlike typical proxy filters that perform extensive processing on each data packet, the PIX Firewall uses a secure, real-time, embedded system that enhances the security of the network. The PIX operating environment is a proprietary, well-protected environment that is not subject to any known operating system vulnerabilities.

- **Adaptive Security Algorithm (ASA)**—This implements stateful connection control through the Cisco PIX Firewall. This stateful packet filtering is a secure method of analyzing data packets that places extensive information about a data packet into a table. In order for a packet to be considered "established" (the response to the request), information in that packet must match the information in the table.

- **Cut-through proxy**—A user-based authentication method of both inbound and outbound connections, providing low overhead processing and therefore improved performance in comparison to that of a proxy filter.

- **Stateful failover/hot standby**—The Cisco PIX Firewall enables you to configure two Cisco PIX Firewall units in a fully redundant topology.

The heart of the PIX Firewall is the ASA. The ASA is the part of the proprietary operating system that provides stateful packet inspection and retention of session flow and maintains the secure perimeters between the networks controlled by the firewall. The stateful, connection-oriented ASA design creates session flows based on source and destination addresses. The PIX can allow one-way (inside to outside) connections without an explicit configuration for each internal system and application.

Stateful packet filtering is a secure method of analyzing data packets that places extensive information about a data packet into a table. Each time a TCP connection is established for inbound or outbound connections through the PIX Firewall, the information about the connection is logged in a stateful session flow table. In order for a session to be established, information about the connection must match information stored in the table. With this methodology, the stateful filters work on the connections and not the packets, making it a more stringent security method with its sessions nearly immune to hijacking.

Using the ASA, the PIX performs the following stateful packet filtering processes:

- It obtains the session identifying parameters, such as IP addresses, and ports for each TCP connection.

- It logs the data in a stateful connection table and creates a session object.

- It compares the inbound and outbound packets against session objects in the connection table.
- It allows data packets to flow through the PIX Firewall only if an appropriate connection exists to validate their passage.
- When the connection is terminated, the connection information and session object(s) eventually get deleted.

The cut-through proxy feature of the Cisco PIX Firewall is a patented method of transparently verifying the identity of the users at the firewall and permitting or denying access to any TCP- or UDP-based applications. This is known as user-based authentication of inbound or outbound connections. Unlike a proxy filter that analyzes every packet at the application layer of the OSI model, the Cisco PIX Firewall first challenges a user at the application layer. After the user is authenticated and the policy is checked, the Cisco PIX Firewall shifts the session flow to a lower layer of the OSI model (Layer 3) for dramatically faster performance. This allows security policies to be enforced on a per-user-ID basis.

When using authentication with the PIX Firewall, connections must be authenticated with a user ID and password before they can be established. The user ID and password is entered via an initial HTTP, Telnet, or FTP connection. The user is authenticated against a database based on the Terminal Access Controller Access Control System (TACACS+) or Remote Authentication Dial-In User Service (RADIUS) and policy is checked. The PIX Firewall then shifts the session flow, and all traffic thereafter flows directly and quickly between the two parties while maintaining session state. The cut-through proxy method of the PIX Firewall may leverage the authentication, authorization, and accounting services of CiscoSecure Access Control Server.

Models of PIX Firewall

The following are the five models of PIX Firewalls currently available:

- **The Cisco Secure PIX 506**—The smallest of the five models, the 506 is intended for high-end, small office/home office (SOHO) organizations and has throughput measured at 10 Mbps.
- **The Cisco Secure PIX 515**—Intended for small/medium business and remote office deployments, it has throughput measured at 120 Mbps with the ability to handle up to 125,000 simultaneous sessions.
- **The Cisco Secure PIX 520**—This is intended for large enterprise organizations and complex, high-end traffic environments. It has throughput of up to 370 Mbps with the ability to handle 250,000 simultaneous sessions.
- **The Cisco Secure PIX 525**—Intended for enterprise and service provider use, it has throughput of 370 Mbps with the ability to handle as many as 280,000 simultaneous sessions.

- **The Cisco Secure PIX 535**—The latest and largest addition to the PIX 500 series, the 535 is intended for enterprise and service provider use. It has a throughput of 1 Gbps with the ability to handle up to 500,000 concurrent connections.

Table 2-1 lists the specifications and features of the PIX product line.

Table 2-1   *PIX Product Line Specifications and Features*

	Cisco Secure PIX 506	Cisco Secure PIX 515	Cisco Secure PIX 520	Cisco Secure PIX 525	Cisco Secure PIX 535
Size (RU [rack unit] = 1.75 inches)	1	1	3	2	3
Intel Pentium Processor (MHz)	200	200	350	600	1 GHz
Maximum Interfaces	2	6	6	8	10
Failover	No	Yes	Yes	Yes	Yes
Connections	400	125,000	250,000	280,000	500,000

Controls, Connectors, and Front/Back Panel Features

The connectors and controls of the PIX vary from model to model. They have the same naming convention between the models, but because of the difference in size and layout, the physical design is different.

Cisco PIX Firewall Model 506

The PIX 506 was designed for a small remote/branch office environment. It has two fixed 10BaseT interfaces and a console port for local management. The USB port next to the console port is currently not used. This model has no user-customizable access to the inside of the chassis. The 506 contains 32 MB of RAM and 8 MB of Flash memory. It is not rack mountable.

The 506 has the following LEDs on the front panel:

- **POWER**—On when the unit has power.
- **ACT**—Active indicator is on when the software image has been loaded on the PIX 506 unit.
- **NETWORK**—On when at least one network interface is passing traffic.

The LED indicators on the back panel, next to the interfaces, display the following transmission states:

- **ACT**—Shows network activity.
- **LINK**—Shows that data is passing on the network to which the connector is attached.

The PIX 506 also supports 56-bit DES and 168-bit 3DES. The 506 does not support failover.

Cisco PIX Firewall Model 515

The back panel features of the PIX 515 include RJ-45 Ethernet connectors, a console port, a failover connection, LEDs, and the power switch. Figure 2-2 shows the back panel of the 515-R PIX Firewall.

Figure 2-2   *The PIX 515*

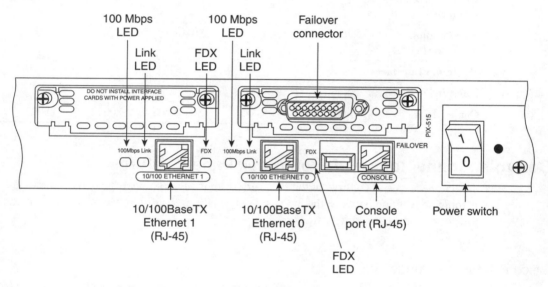

The list that follows details the back panel features of the PIX 515 called out in Figure 2-2:

- **Ethernet connections**—Ethernet 1 is the inside network connection. Ethernet 0 is the outside network connection.

NOTE   Beginning with software release 5.2X: Ethernet 0 is not required for the Outside interface and Ethernet 1 is not required to be the Inside interface. Any of the fixed or expansion ports can be configured to be the Inside or Outside network ports. For backward compatibility, the default configuration will still show Ethernet 0 as the Outside and Ethernet 1 as the Inside port.

- **Console port**—Used to connect a terminal (for example a PC running Windows using the Hyperterm application) to the PIX Firewall for console operations.

- **Failover connection**—Used to attach failover cable between two PIX Firewalls.
- **100 Mbps LED**—100 Mbps, 100BaseTX communications for the respective connector. If the light is off, the PIX Firewall 515 uses 10 Mbps data exchange.
- **LINK LED**—Indicates that data is passing on the network to which the connector is attached.
- **FDX LED**—Indicates that the connection uses full duplex data exchange: Data can be transmitted and received simultaneously. If the light is off, half duplex is in effect.
- **Power switch**—Controls the power to the PIX Firewall.

Note that the USB port to the left of the console port and the detachable plate above the Ethernet 1 connector, as illustrated in Figure 2-2, are for future PIX Firewall enhancements.

The following are the indicator LEDs on the front of the PIX 515. They indicate the same information as the 506 except for the **ACT** LED.

- **POWER**—When the PIX Firewall has power, the light is on.
- **ACT**—When the PIX Firewall is used in a standalone configuration, the light shines. When the PIX Firewall is configured for failover operations, the light shines on the active PIX Firewall (ACT stands for Active Failover Unit. Failover is discussed in Chapter 10, "Cisco PIX Firewall Failover").
- **NETWORK**—The light shines when at least one network interface is passing traffic.

There are two slots available for expansion on the PIX 515. The maximum number of interfaces allowed is six. In order to achieve the maximum of six ports, a single four-port card is inserted in the upper slot (see Figure 2-3). When upgrading the PIX to a six-port firewall, the software license must also be upgraded. The basic PIX 515 firewall is sold with a restricted license (PIX-515-R-BUN). The restricted license can be used with a three-interface PIX also. When upgrading to a six-port firewall, the license used must be a 515-UR or unrestricted.

NOTE   When upgrading some features of the PIX Firewall including increasing the number of connections, installing failover, installing IPSec, or adding additional interfaces, it may be necessary to upgrade from a restricted license to an unrestricted license.

When you connect the perimeter network cables to this card, you begin with the leftmost connector and move to the right. For example, Ethernet port 2 will go in the leftmost connector, Ethernet port 3 in the second connector from the left, and so on. Because the maximum number of interfaces allowed is six, any additional cards are not recognized.

The number of slots may be expanded from two to three or from two to four. If your PIX 515 Firewall has one or two additional single-port Ethernet cards installed in the auxiliary assembly on the left of the PIX Firewall at the rear, the cards are numbered top to bottom so that the top card is Ethernet 2 and the bottom card is Ethernet 3.

Figure 2-3 *Adding a Four-Port Expansion Card*

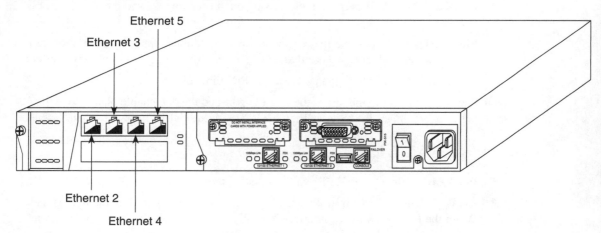

To configure and manage the PIX locally, a connection is made between the PIX and a computer terminal via the console port. To install the serial cable between the PIX and your console computer, you need to use the serial cable that was shipped with the PIX. This cable is one of the hardware components within your accessory kit. The entire serial cable assembly consists of a null modem cable with RJ-45 connectors, two separate DB-9 connectors, and a separate DB-25 connector.

To install the serial cable between the PIX Firewall 515 and your console computer, complete the following steps:

Step 1   Locate the serial cable assembly from the accessory kit shipped with your PIX Firewall.

Step 2   Connect one of the RJ-45 connectors to the PIX console port.

Step 3   Connect the other RJ-45 connector and either a DB-9 or DB-25 connector to the appropriate connector on your terminal interface.

Cisco PIX Firewall Model 520

The network cable connectors are in the front of the PIX 520 Firewall. The PIX 520 also comes with a 3.5-inch floppy disk drive. The power switch is on the rear panel. The height of the PIX 520 is 5.21 inches. Three RU (rack unit) spaces are needed to mount a PIX 520 Firewall (one RU is equivalent to 1.75 inches).

There are four interface slots on the PIX 520. When connecting network cables with four single-port interface cards on the PIX 520, the outside interface card must be in slot 0, which is the leftmost available slot. Within the configuration this slot is known as Ethernet 0.

The first card to the right of the outside interface is seen by the PIX Firewall as the inside interface card, regardless of location. This is known as Ethernet 1.If more than four Ethernet interfaces are needed, the assignment of interface sequence numbers is determined by the position of the necessary quad card. Figure 2-4 shows a quad card installed in slot 0. The figure also shows quad cards in slot 1 and slot 2. The quad card can be installed in any one of the three slots, as illustrated. Notice the difference in the numbering sequence.

Figure 2-4   *The PIX Firewall 520 Quad Card*

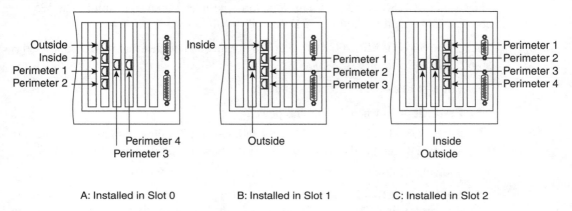

A: Installed in Slot 0   B: Installed in Slot 1   C: Installed in Slot 2

Example A shows that the quad card is numbered from top to bottom. The topmost connector is the outside interface. This would be indicated as Ethernet 0 in the configuration of the PIX.

Example B shows how the slots are numbered if a single-port interface card is in slot 0 and a quad card is in slot 1. The top port of the quad card would be Ethernet 1 in the configuration file.

Example C shows how the slots are numbered if a single-port interface card is in slot 0 and slot 1, and a quad card is installed in slot 3. The top port would be Ethernet 2 in the configuration of the PIX.

To connect to the console port of the PIX 520, install the serial cable between the PIX and your terminal. To make this connection, complete the following steps:

Step 1   Connect one end of the null modem cable to a DB-9 serial connector.

Step 2   Connect the DB-9 serial connector to the PIX Firewall console connector.

Step 3   Connect the other end of the null modem cable with the RJ-45 connectors to either a DB-9 or DB-25 connector.

Step 4   Connect this end to the communication port (either DB-9 or DB-25) of your computer terminal.

Cisco PIX Firewall Model 525

The Cisco PIX Firewall 525 is a large, enterprise perimeter firewall solution. The 525 delivers full firewall protection in a large-scale environment.

The 525 supports 10-MB, 100-MB, and Gigabit Ethernet interface cards. Also supported is 56-bit DES and 168-bit 3DES encryption.

There are two LEDs on the front panel of the 525:

- **POWER**—On when the unit has power.
- **ACT**—On when the unit is the Active failover unit. If failover is present, the light is on when the unit is the Active unit and off when the unit is in Standby mode.

The following LEDs are on the rear panel, next to the 100BaseTX interfaces:

- **100 Mbps LED**—This indicator is on the rear panel next to the port. If the LED is on, the port is using 100 Mbps. If the light is off during network activity, that port is using 10 Mbps for data exchange.
- **ACT**—This indicator is on the rear panel next to the port. This shows network activity.
- **LINK**—This indicator shows that data is passing through the interface. It is on the rear panel next to the port.

The fixed connectors on the rear panel are the RJ-45 Ethernet 0 interface, RJ-45 Ethernet 1 interface, RJ-45 console, DB-15 failover cable connector, and the unused USB interface.

Cisco PIX Firewall Model 535

Currently, the largest PIX Firewall is the Model 535. The Model 535 delivers carrier-class performance to meet the needs of large enterprise networks as well as service providers.

The 535 supports 10-MB, 100-MB, and Gigabit Ethernet interface cards. Also supported is 56-bit DES and 168-bit 3DES encryption.

The front panel has the same **POWER** and **ACT** LED indicators as on Model 525.

There are three separate buses for the eight interface slots in the rear of the PIX 535. The slots and buses (illustrated in Figure 2-5) are configured as follows:

- Slots 0 and 1—64-bit/66 MHz Bus 0
- Slots 2 and 3—64-bit/66 MHz Bus 1
- Slots 4 to 8—32-bit/33 MHz Bus 2

Figure 2-5   *The PIX Firewall 535*

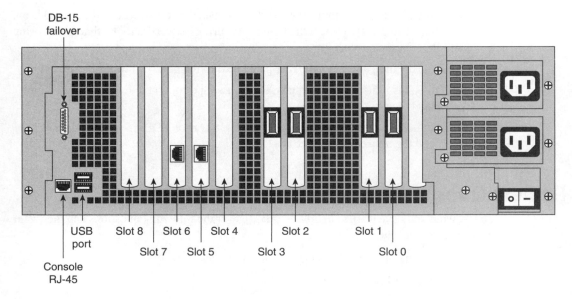

For optimum performance and throughput for the interface circuit boards, you must use the following guidelines:

- A total of six interface circuit boards are configurable with the restricted license and a total of eight are configurable with the unrestricted license.

- PIX-1 GE-66 (66 MHz) circuit boards can be installed in any slot but should be installed in the 64-bit/66 MHz Bus first. Up to eight PIX-1 GE-66 circuit boards can be installed.

- The FE circuit board (33 MHz) can be installed in any bus or slot (32-bit/33 MHz or 64-bit/66 MHz). Up to eight single-port FE circuit boards or up to two four-port FE circuit boards can be installed.

NOTE   The four-port FE circuit board should only be installed in the 32-bit/33 MHz Bus.

- Do not mix the 33-MHz circuit boards with the 66-MHz GE circuit boards on the same 64-bit/66 MHz bus (Bus 0 or Bus 1). The overall speed of the bus will be reduced by the lower-speed circuit board.

- The VPN Accelerator should be installed only in the 32-bit/33 MHz Bus.

The following LEDs are on the rear panel, next to the 100BaseTX interfaces:

- **100 Mbps LED**—This indicator is on the rear panel next to the port. If the LED is on, the port is using 100 Mbps. If the light is off during network activity, that port is using 10 Mbps for data exchange.

- **ACT**—This indicator is on the rear panel next to the port. It shows network activity.

- **LINK**—This indicator shows that data is passing through the interface. It is on the rear panel next to the port.

The fixed connectors on the rear panel are the RJ-45 console, DB-15 failover cable connector, and the unused USB interface.

Review Questions

To test what you have learned in this chapter, answer the following questions and then refer to Appendix F for the answers.

1 What are the three kinds of Firewall technologies?

2 What type of firewall is a Cisco router?

3 Briefly describe the function Adaptive Security Algorithm (ASA).

4 What is the maximum number of Ethernet interfaces on a PIX model 506?

5 What is the maximum number of Ethernet interfaces on a PIX model 535?

6 When installing a four-port expansion interface card on a PIX 515, which is the lowest interface number?

7 True or false. The PIX Model 506 supports gigabit Ethernet interfaces.

8 When installing a four-port expansion card on a PIX 520, which is the lowest interface number?

This chapter covers the following topics:

- Interaction with the Command-Line Interface
- Configuring, Maintaining, and Testing the PIX Firewall
- Upgrading the PIX OS
- Performing Password Recovery

CHAPTER 3

Working with and Upgrading the Cisco PIX Firewall Software Image

When working with any Cisco device, the command-line interface (CLI) is the primary user interface for configuring, monitoring, and maintaining that device. The interactive CLI is the most frequently used user interface for all Cisco products. The basic administrative modes used by Cisco devices are user EXEC, privileged EXEC, and various configuration modes. When in user EXEC mode, you can perform some basic queries, but no changes can be made. When in privileged EXEC mode, you can make more detailed queries. Configuration EXEC mode can be accessed only from privileged mode. Changes to the system configuration can be made from Configuration EXEC mode.

NOTE   Currently, you can use two graphical user interface products to configure the PIX Firewall. PIX Firewall Manager (PFM) and PIX Device Manager (PDM) are both available as of this writing. PFM is going to be obsolete in the near future. PDM is available with PIX OS 6.0 and later.

The PIX Command-Line Interface

The PIX Firewall contains a command set similar but not identical in syntax to the Cisco IOS command set. When accessing a specific command, you must be in the proper mode (for that particular command) to access that particular command. The PIX provides four administrative access modes:

- **Unprivileged Mode**—This mode is available when first accessing the PIX Firewall. This mode is frequently referred to as user EXEC mode. The > prompt is displayed. This mode lets you view a subset of all commands available. A user cannot make configuration changes if unprivileged mode is the only mode accessible.

- **Privileged Mode**—This mode displays the # prompt and enables you to change the current settings. Any unprivileged command also works in privileged mode. Once you have access to privileged mode, you have access to configuration mode.

- **Configuration Mode**—This mode displays the **(config)#** prompt and enables you to change system configurations. All privileged, unprivileged, and configuration commands work in this mode.

- **Monitor Mode**—PIX Firewalls have a special mode called the monitor mode that permits you to perform special tasks that could otherwise not be performed. One of those tasks is updating an image over the network. While in monitor mode, you enter commands in order to specify the location of the TFTP server and the binary image to download. Some PIX Firewalls do not have monitor mode and accomplish these tasks in other ways, which will be discussed later.

The mode that a user must be in for a particular command may be found in the *Command Reference* documentation (see the *Cisco PIX Firewall Command Reference* at: http://www.cisco.com/univercd/cc/td/doc/product/iaabu/pix/pix_v53/config/commands.htm). Within the *Command Reference*, the required mode is found in parentheses after the definition of the command, which comes directly below the command itself. Table 3-1 demonstrates the unique prompt that is associated with each administrative mode.

Table 3-1 *Distinctive PIX Prompt for Administrative Modes*

Mode	Prompt
Unprivileged mode	pixfirewall>
Privileged mode	pixfirewall#
Configuration mode	pixfirewall(config)#
Monitor mode	monitor>

Within each access mode, you can abbreviate most commands down to the minimum length needed to make them unique. For example, you can enter **wr t** to view the configuration instead of entering the full command, **write terminal**. Additional examples are to enter **en** instead of **enable** to start privileged mode and **co t** instead of **configuration terminal** to start configuration mode.

Help information is available from the PIX Firewall command line by entering **help** or **?** to list all commands. If you enter **help** or **?** after a command (for example, **route?**), the command syntax is listed. The number of commands listed when using the **help** (**?**) command differs by access mode so that unprivileged mode offers the least commands and configuration mode offers the greatest number of commands. In addition, you can enter any command by itself on the command line and then press Enter to view the command syntax.

NOTE   A configuration file may be created offline using a text editor. A user may then copy and paste it into the PIX configuration.

NOTE   The PIX allows an entire configuration to be input this way or one line at a time. You should always check the configuration after pasting information to be sure everything has been copied correctly. Another option when configuring the PIX is to use a TFTP server as will be discussed later in the chapter.

Maintaining and Testing the PIX Firewall

When working with PIX there are many general maintenance configuration commands. To move from unprivileged mode to privileged mode and then to configuration mode, enter the following sequence of commands:

```
pixfirewall> enable
Password:******
pixfirewall# config t
pixfirewall(conf)#
```

The commands that follow are used to configure, maintain, and test.

- **enable**—If the password is known, the **enable** command allows a user to enter privileged mode. After entering **enable**, the PIX Firewall will prompt the user for the privileged mode password. To exit and return to the previous mode, use the **disable**, **exit**, or **quit** commands. The command to set this password is **enable password** *password*. The password is encrypted within the configuration file.

- **configure terminal**—If you want to interactively change the configuration of the PIX, issue the **configure terminal** command. Any added configuration parameters are merged with the existing running configuration. When making a configuration change to the PIX, the change takes effect immediately and is saved in the running configuration in RAM.

- **enable password**—This configuration parameter sets the password that gives you access to privileged mode. You are prompted for this password after entering the **enable** command. There is no default password assigned to the **enable password** command. When accessing privileged mode for the first time (before an enable password has been created), you are prompted for a password. Because a password has not been set, simply pressing a carriage return will allow access to privileged mode. The password is case-sensitive and can be up to 16 alphanumeric characters. You can use any character, with the exceptions of the question mark, space, and colon. If a password is changed, it is good practice to store it (for example, written in a log and stored in a secured area) in a manner consistent with the site's security policy. Because the **enable password** is encrypted (by default), it cannot be viewed in clear text within the configuration once it has been created or changed. The **show enable** command displays the encrypted form of the password. When setting **enable password,** you may optionally type in the encrypted form of the password. This is done by entering the option **encrypted** after entering the **password** (see the *Cisco PIX Firewall Command Reference* at: http://www.cisco.com/univercd/cc/td/doc/product/iaabu/pix/pix_v53/config/commands.htm).

- **passwd**—The **passwd** command enables the user to set the password for inbound Telnet access to the PIX Firewall. The default password value is **cisco**. The password value is a case-sensitive, 16 character, alphanumeric string. Any character may be used except a question mark or a space. It is important to note that if a Telnet password is not set, an encrypted string will still appear in the configuration. The **clear passwd** command sets the Telnet password to **cisco**. When setting **passwd** a user may optionally type in the encrypted form of the password. This is done by entering the optional **encrypted** after entering the password (see the *Cisco PIX Firewall Command Reference* at: http://www.cisco.com/univercd/cc/td/doc/product/iaabu/pix/pix_v53/config/commands.htm).

- **show configure**—This displays the configuration that is stored in Flash memory (sometimes called the "startup configuration") on the terminal. Because Flash is non-volatile, the configuration that is stored there is not removed if the PIX loses power or is reloaded. The startup configuration is what the PIX loads to RAM during bootup.

- **write terminal**—Displays the running configuration (sometimes called the *current configuration*) on the terminal. This configuration is stored in RAM.

- **write net**—Stores the running configuration file on a TFTP server. It is good practice to keep a backup of all configuration files offline. When a server IP address and a file path are assigned, the running configuration is stored to a specific location. See the *Cisco PIX Firewall Command Reference* at: http://www.cisco.com/univercd/cc/td/doc/product/iaabu/pix/pix_v53/config/commands.htm.

- **write erase**—This clears the configuration file that is in Flash memory.

- **write memory**—Any change that is made to the PIX takes effect immediately. The change is written to the running configuration in RAM. If a change is meant to be kept on the PIX, it should be saved to Flash memory using the **write memory** command. The use of this command will replace the existing configuration in Flash with the configuration in RAM. The configuration in RAM remains unchanged. Processing continues during the **write memory** command, but the **write memory** command is not disruptive to the processing of the PIX. You cannot make changes to the configuration while the **write memory** command is executing.

- **write floppy**—This stores the running configuration on diskette (the PIX Firewall 520, 510, and earlier models have a 3.5-inch floppy disk drive). The floppy must be a DOS-formatted diskette. When formatting a floppy disk from a Windows operating system, choose the full-format type and not the quick-erase selection. The diskette that is created can only be read or written by the PIX Firewall. If using the **write floppy** command with a diskette that is not a PIX Firewall boot disk, do not leave it in the floppy drive because it will prevent the firewall from rebooting and coming up into a running state in the event of a power failure or system reload. Only one copy of the configuration can be stored on a single diskette. All current models of the PIX (PIX 506, PIX 515, PIX 525, and PIX 535) do not support the use of the *write floppy* command.

- **write standby**—Writes the configuration stored in RAM on the active failover PIX Firewall, to the RAM on the standby PIX Firewall. When the active PIX Firewall boots, it automatically writes the configuration to the standby PIX Firewall. Use this command to force the active PIX Firewall's configuration to the standby PIX Firewall. PIX Firewall models that do not support failover do not support the use of this command.

NOTE	When using failover, all commands entered on the active (primary) unit are automatically written to the standby unit without the use of the **write standby** command.

NOTE	It is important to remember that if the PIX loses power or is reloaded, the running configuration in RAM is lost. Use the **write memory** command to save the running configuration in RAM to Flash memory (non-volatile RAM).

- **configure net**—The **configure net** command merges the current running configuration with a TFTP configuration stored at a specified IP address and in a specified file. For example, if you specify **configure net 10.1.1.1:/backup/ topsfield1.txt**, the configuration parameters within the file topsfield1.txt in the /backup folder at the server with the IP address 10.1.1.1 will be merged with the existing running configuration in RAM.

NOTE	It is important to note that communication with the TFTP server is clear text and transferring firewall configurations should be done in accordance with the existing security policy.

- **configure memory**—Merges the running configuration with the configuration in Flash memory (also referred to as the startup configuration). **configure memory** does not replace the Flash memory configuration but adds the differences between the running configuration and the Flash configuration to the Flash memory configuration.
- **show history**—Displays previously entered command lines. Previous commands may be examined individually with the up and down arrows. Another option is to enter **Ctrl-p** to view previously entered lines or **Ctrl-n** to view the next line.

- **show interface**—The **show interface** command enables users to view information about the interface. Ethernet, Token Ring, and FDDI information is displayed, depending on which is installed on the PIX Firewall. This is one of the first commands to input when trying to establish connectivity.

  The following are explanations of the information that is displayed after entering the **show interface** command:

  — **Ethernet, FDDI,** or **Token Ring**—Indicate that a user has used the **interface** command to configure the interface. The statement indicates whether the interface is either inside or outside (or any other interface name) and whether the interface is available ("up") or not available ("down").

NOTE   Product Bulletins (Bulletin Numbers 1340 and 1341) released by Cisco have announced the "End-of-Sale" of the Token Ring interface (August 25, 2001) and the "End-of-Sale" of the FDDI interface (June 23, 2001). Gigabit Ethernet is now available in some models.

  — **line protocol up**—A working cable is plugged into the network interface. (Layer 1 connectivity)

  — **line protocol down**—Either the cable plugged into the network interface is incorrect or it is not plugged into the interface connector.

  — **network interface type**—Identifies the network interface.

  — **interrupt vector**—It is acceptable for interface cards to have the same interrupts because PIX Firewall uses interrupts to get Token Ring information but polls Ethernet cards.

  — **MAC address**—The MAC address is displayed in the output. The MAC appears after "address is" is displayed.

  — **IP address**—The assigned IP address is displayed.

  — **subnet mask**—The subnet mask is displayed.

  — **MTU** (maximum transmission unit)—The size in bytes that data can best be sent over the network.

  — **line speed**—10BaseT is listed as 10,000 kbps; 100BaseTX is listed as 100,000 kbps.

  — **line duplex status**—Indicates whether the PIX Firewall is running full-duplex (simultaneous packet transmission) or half-duplex (alternating packet transmission).

— **packets input**—If the input counter is incrementing, this indicates that packets are being received in the PIX Firewall.

— **input bytes**—A count of the bytes input is indicated.

— **packets output**—If the output counter is incrementing, this indicates that packets are being sent from the PIX Firewall.

— **output bytes**—A count of the bytes output is indicated.

The **show interface** output may also indicate errors or problems. The following are some potential interface problems:

— **no buffer**—Indicates the PIX Firewall is out of memory or slowed down due to heavy traffic and cannot keep up with the received data.

— **Received broadcast**—The number of Ethernet broadcasts received.

— **runt**—A frame that is less than the minimum allowable frame size.

— **giant**—A frame that is greater than the maximum allowable frame size.

— **CRC** (cyclic redundancy check)—Packets that contain corrupted data (checksum error).

— **frame errors**—Indicates Layer 2 framing errors.

— **ignored and aborted errors**—This information is provided for future use but is not currently checked; the PIX Firewall does not ignore or abort frames.

— **underruns**—These occur when the PIX Firewall is overwhelmed and cannot get data to the network interface card quickly enough.

— **overruns**—Occur when the network interface card is overwhelmed and cannot buffer received information before more needs to be sent.

— **output errors** (maximum collisions)—The number of frames not transmitted because the configured maximum number of collisions was exceeded. This counter should only increment during heavy network traffic

— **collisions** (single and multiple collisions)—The number of messages retransmitted due to an Ethernet collision. This usually occurs on an overextended LAN (Ethernet or transceiver cable too long, more than two repeaters between stations, or too many cascaded multiport transceivers). A packet that collides is counted only once by the output packets.

— **interface resets**—The number of times an interface has been reset. If an interface is unable to transmit for three seconds, the PIX Firewall resets the interface to restart transmission. During this interval, connection state is maintained. An interface reset can also happen when an interface is looped back or shut down

— **babbles**—Unused. "Babble" means that the transmitter has been on the interface longer than the time taken to transmit the largest frame.

— **late collisions**—The number of frames that were not transmitted because a collision occurred outside the normal collision window. A late collision is a collision that is detected late in the transmission of a packet. Normally, this should never happen. When two Ethernet hosts try to talk at once, they should collide early in the transmission and both back off, or the second host should see that the first one is talking and wait. If you get a late collision, a device is jumping in and trying to send the packet on the Ethernet before the PIX Firewall is finished sending the packet. The PIX Firewall does not resend the packet, because it may have freed the buffers that held the first part of the packet. This is not a real problem because networking protocols are designed to cope with collisions by resending packets. However, late collisions indicate that a problem exists in your network. Common problems are large repeated networks and Ethernet networks running beyond the specification.

— **deferred**—The number of frames that were deferred before transmission due to activity on the link.

— **lost carrier**—The number of times the carrier signal was lost during transmission.

- **show ip address**—The **show ip address** command enables a user to view which IP addresses have been assigned to the network interfaces. In the displayed output, the current IP addresses are the same as the system IP addresses on the failover active unit.

When the **show ip address** command is executed on the standby unit, the *System IP Addresses* are the failover IP addresses configured for the standby unit and the *Current IP Addresses* are the active IP addresses configured for the active unit.

Example 3-1 shows the output of the **show ip address** command if issued on the standby unit.

Example 3-1 **show ip address** *Command Output on the Standby Unit*

```
pixfirewall# show ip address
System IP Addresses:
        ip address outside 209.165.201.1 255.255.255.224
        ip address inside 192.168.2.1 255.255.255.0
        ip address failover 192.168.71.1 255.255.255.0
        ip address perimeter 192.168.70.3 255.255.255.0
Current IP Addresses:
        ip address outside 209.165.201.4 255.255.255.224
        ip address inside 192.168.2.4 255.255.255.0
        ip address failover 192.168.71.2 255.255.255.0
        ip address perimeter 192.168.70.4 255.255.255.0
```

If the primary unit fails, the Current IP Addresses become those of the standby unit.

- **show memory**—Displays a summary of the maximum physical memory and current free memory available to the PIX Firewall.

- **show version**—Enables a user to view the version of the operating system that is currently running on the PIX. The output also shows the time that the PIX has been operational since the last reboot. The output also shows

  — Hardware Type

  — Onboard Memory

  — Processor Type

  — Flash Memory Type

  — BIOS Flash Information

  — Interface Boards

  — Licensed Features (including whether failover, 56-bit DES, and 168-bit 3DES is enabled and the maximum number of interfaces)

  — Serial Number (BIOS ID)

  — Activation Key

Example 3-2 shows a sample output from the **show version** command.

Example 3-2   **show version** *Command Output*

```
pixfirewall#  show version
Cisco Secure PIX Firewall Version 5.1(1)
Compiled on Fri 01-Oct-99 13:56 by pixbuild

pix515 up 4 days 22 hours 10 mins 42 secs

Hardware: PIX-515, 64 MB RAM, CPU Pentium 200 MHz
Flash i28F640J5 @ 0x300
BIOS Flash AT29C257 @ 0xfffd8000

0: ethernet0: address is 00aa.0000.0037, irq 11
1: ethernet1: address is 00aa.0000.0038, irq 10
2: ethernet2: address is 00a0.c92a.f029, irq 9
3: ethernet3: address is 00a0.c948.45f9, irq 7

Licensed Features:
Failover: Enabled
VPN-DES: Enabled
VPN-3DES: Disabled
Maximum Interfaces: 6

Serial Number: 123 (0x7b)
Activation Key: 0xc5233151 0xb429f6d0 0xda93739a 0xe15cdf51
```

- **show xlate**—Displays the translation slot information. These are IP addresses allocated for address translation for sessions built through the PIX. Example 3-3 shows sample output from the **show xlate** command.

Example 3-3   **show xlate** *Command Output*

```
pixfirewall# show xlate
Global 209.165.201.10 Local 209.165.201.10 static nconns 1 econns 0
Global 209.165.201.30 Local 209.165.201.30 static nconns 4 econns 0
```

The output in Example 3-3 shows:

— **Global** *IP address*—the translated outside address

— **Local** *IP address*—the assigned inside address

— **static**—identifies this as an address translated with the **static** command

— **nconns**—number of connections for this local/global pair

— **econns**—number of embryonic (half-open) connections

- **exit**—Used to exit an access mode. For example, if a user is in config mode and enters and executes the **exit** command, that user will then be in privileged mode. If the user then enters and executes **exit**, that user will then be in unprivileged mode.

- **reload**—When this command is issued, the user is prompted with "Proceed with reload?" If the user responds with anything other than "n," the PIX reboots and reloads the configuration from a bootable floppy disk (with a model of PIX that has a disk drive) or, if a diskette is not present, from Flash memory.

- **hostname**—The **hostname** command changes the host name label on the command line prompt. Modifying the host name changes the fully qualified domain name. The host name can be up to 16 alphanumeric characters and uppercase or lowercase. The default hostname is **pixfirewall**.

- **ping**—The **ping** command determines if the PIX Firewall has connectivity to a specified destination or if a host is available (visible to the PIX Firewall) on the network. When the **ping** command is issued, an *echo-request* is sent out by the PIX. The destination should respond with an *echo-reply*. The command output shows if the echo-reply was received. If the echo-reply was received, then the host exists and is reachable on the network. If the echo-reply was not received, the command output displays "No response received." (At this time, a user may use the **show interface** command to ensure that the PIX Firewall is connected to the network and is passing traffic.) The **ping** command transmits three echo-requests to reach an IP address. If you want internal hosts to be able to ping external hosts, you must create an ICMP **conduit** or **access list** to permit the echo-reply. This will be discussed in another chapter. If pinging through the PIX Firewall between hosts or routers and the pings are not successful, use the **debug icmp trace** command to monitor the success of the ping. In older versions of the PIX operating system the interface the echo-request passed out had to be specified.

NOTE   After a PIX Firewall is configured and operational, a user will not be able to ping the inside interface of the PIX Firewall from the outside network or from the outside interfaces of the PIX Firewall. If you can ping the inside networks from the inside interface and if you can ping the outside networks from the outside interface, the PIX Firewall is functioning normally and your routes to the Firewall are correct.

- **telnet**—Enables you to specify which hosts can access the PIX Firewall console via Telnet. Prior to PIX OS 5.0, only internal hosts could be specified to access the PIX via Telnet. With PIX OS 5.0 and later, a user may enable Telnet to the PIX Firewall on all interfaces. However, the PIX Firewall enforces that all Telnet traffic to the outside interface be IPSec protected. Therefore, to enable a Telnet session to the PIX, a user needs to configure the PIX to establish an IPSec tunnel to either another PIX, a router, or a VPN client. That tunnel would then have to be encrypted for specific traffic, including the Telnet traffic to the individual host or network defined with the **telnet** command (not necessarily all traffic generated by the PIX). Up to 16 hosts or networks are allowed access to the PIX Firewall console with Telnet, five simultaneously.

  The following are commands which are typically used in conjunction with **telnet**:

  — **show telnet**—Displays the current lists of IP addresses authorized to access the PIX Firewall via Telnet.

  — **clear telnet** and **no telnet**—Removes Telnet access from a previously authorized IP address.

  — **telnet timeout**—Sets the maximum time in minutes that a console Telnet session can be idle before being logged off by the PIX Firewall.

  — **kill**—Terminates a Telnet session. When you kill a Telnet session, the PIX Firewall lets any active commands terminate and then drops the connection without warning the user.

  — **who**—Enables you to view which IP addresses are currently accessing the PIX Firewall console via Telnet.

Installing a New OS on the PIX Firewall

Installing a new operating system on a PIX Firewall will vary slightly, depending upon the model of the PIX and the version of the OS. There are some very important considerations when migrating to a new operating system. It is always important to read the release notes associated with the new version of the OS that is being installed. If the new PIX OS being installed is more than one version forward (for example migrating from version 5.1 to version 5.3, skipping over version 5.2), it is also a very good idea to read the release notes of all versions in between.

NOTE   The OS required for the PIX model 506 is 5.1x or greater, the PIX model 525 needs 5.2x or greater, and the PIX model 535 needs 5.3x or greater.

When installing a new OS it may be necessary to upgrade the PIX RAM or Flash or both. Table 3-2 shows the minimum system requirements for PIX OS versions 4.4 through 6.0.

Table 3-2   *Minimum System Requirements*

PIX Software Version	Flash Memory	RAM
P4.4(x)	2 MB	16 MB
P5.0(x)	2 MB	32 MB
P5.1(x)	2 MB	32 MB
P5.2(x)	8 MB	32 MB
P5.3(x)	8 MB	32 MB
P6.0(x)	8 MB	32 MB

Upgrading to a Different Version of PIX Software

If the PIX Firewall is running PIX software version 5.1.1 or later, you can use the **copy tftp flash** command to download a software image with TFTP (with the PIX model 515, use the monitor mode described later in the chapter). The image you download is made available to the PIX Firewall on the next reload (reboot).

Before beginning the upgrade, the PIX OS file must be on the TFTP server.

The following steps are taken to perform the upgrade:

Step 1   Issue the **copy tftp flash** command and enter the appropriate information when prompted.

Step 2   Enter the IP address of the TFTP server.

Step 3   Enter the source filename (the PIX OS .bin file).

Step 4   Enter **yes** to continue.

Example 3-4 demonstrates the PIX OS upgrade process.

Example 3-4   *Upgrading the PIX OS*

```
copy tftp flash
Address or name of remote host [127.0.0.1]? 10.1.1.1
Source file name [cdisk]? pix531.bin
copying tftp://10.1.1.1/pix531.bin to flash
[yes|no|again]? yes
!!!!!!!!!!!!!!!!!!!!!!!!!!!!!!!!!!!!!!!!!!!!!!!!!!!!!!!!!!!!!!!!!!!!!!!!!!!!!!!!!!!!
Received 2138112 bytes.
Erasing current image.
Writing 2048056 bytes of image.
!!!!!!!!!!!!!!!!!!!!!!!!!!!!!!!!!!!!!!!!!!!!!!!!!!!!!!!!!!!!!!!!!!!!!!!!!!!!!!!!!!!!
Image installed.
pixfirewall#
```

Upgrading to a Different PIX OS using Monitor Mode

The following are the steps to take when upgrading all current PIX models, using monitor mode. The PIX OS file that is going to be loaded to the PIX must be on the TFTP server.

Step 1   Interrupt the boot process to enter monitor mode. To do this, power-cycle the PIX or issue the **reload** command and then press the Escape key or send a Break character. Once in monitor mode, you can get help with the question mark (**?**).

Step 2   Specify the PIX Firewall interface to use for TFTP. Enter the following command at the monitor prompt:

```
monitor> interface num
```

Step 3   Specify the PIX Firewall interface's IP address:

```
monitor> address ip_address
```

Step 4   Specify the default gateway (if needed):

```
monitor> gateway ip_address
```

Step 5   Verify connectivity to the TFTP server:

```
monitor> ping server_addres
```

Step 6   Specify the TFTP server:

```
monitor> server ip_address
```

Step 7   Name the image filename:

```
monitor> file name
```

Step 8   Start the TFTP process:

```
monitor> tftp
```

Step 9 After the image downloads, you are prompted to install the new image. Enter **y** to install the image to Flash.

Step 10 When prompted to enter a new activation key, enter **y** to enter a new feature-based activation key or **n** to keep your existing connection-based activation key.

Installing PIX OS 5.0 and Earlier

For the image upgrade of the PIX Classic and models 10,000, 510, and 520 (PIX with a floppy drive) to versions 5.0 and earlier, complete the following steps:

Step 1 Download the PIX OS version required to a personal computer. This file will be a .bin file. The filename is of the format pix*nnx*.bin, where the *nn* is the version number and *x* is the release number. Also download the rawrite.exe and the README.txt files.

Step 2 Execute the rawrite.exe file as follows and enter the appropriate information when prompted:

```
C:\> rawrite
RaWrite 1.2 - Write disk file to a floppy diskette

Enter the source file name: pixnnx.bin
Enter the destination drive: a:
Please insert a formatted diskette into drive A: and press -ENTER- :
<Enter>
Number of sectors per track for this disk is 18
Writing image to drive A:. Press ^C to abort.
Track: 78 Head: 1 Sector: 16
Done.
C:\>
```

Step 3 Reboot your PIX Firewall with the diskette you just created by inserting it into the PIX disk drive. The system automatically loads the new image into Flash memory. Remove the diskette after rebooting. You are finished with the upgrade.

Installing PIX OS 5.1 and Later

PIX Firewall systems with a disk drive (PIX 520, PIX 510, and older) must use the boothelper utility to upgrade from a version 5.0 or older to version 5.1 or later software. This is because before version 5.1, the PIX Firewall software did not provide a way to TFTP an image directly into the Flash. Starting with PIX Firewall software version 5.1, the **copy tftp flash** command was introduced to copy a new image directly into the PIX's Flash.

NOTE	The PIX Firewall Classic, 10,000, and 510 have been discontinued and cannot run PIX Firewall software 6.0 or later. The PIX 520 will no longer be available for sale after June 23, 2001. Contact Cisco or check the Cisco web site (www.cisco.com) to get information on currently supported PIX operating systems.

Follow the steps addressed in the sections that follow to perform the installation.

Create a Boothelper Diskette Using a Windows PC

Step 1 Acquire the boothelper file from www.cisco.com. The filename is bh*nnx*.bin, where the *nn* is the version number and *x* is the release number.

Step 2 Download the appropriate PIX OS .bin file from www.cisco.com.

Step 3 Download the rawrite.exe utility from www.cisco.com.

Step 4 Move the .bin file into the appropriate directory to be used by the TFTP server.

Step 5 Obtain a DOS formatted diskette. Use the **Start>Run** command to run rawrite.exe from the appropriate directory. Follow the instructions as prompted.

For example:

```
RaWrite 1.2 - Write disk file to raw floppy diskette

Enter source file name: bh512.bin
Enter destination drive: a:
Please insert a formatted diskette into drive A: and press -ENTER- :
Number of sectors per track for this disk is 18
Writing image to drive A:. Press ^C to abort.
Track: nn Head: n Sector: nn
Done.
```

Creating a Boothelper Diskette with a UNIX, Solaris, or Linux Workstation

The Boothelper installation procedure is only necessary for an upgrade to PIX Firewall version 5.1 and later with a PIX model 510, 520, or older.

Step 1 Use the **ps aux | grep inetd** command string to determine the process ID of the current inetd process.

Step 2 Use the **kill -HUP process_id** command to kill the process. The process will restart automatically.

Step 3 Log in to www.cisco.com and access the Cisco Secure PIX Firewall software. From www.cisco.com, download the following files:

— The boothelper file, bh*xxn*.bin.

— The .bin software image file; for example, pi*xxn*.bin.

Step 4 Prepare a boothelper diskette using the following command:

```
# dd bs=18k bhxxn.bin /dev/rfd0
```

(The rfd0 diskette drive name may differ between UNIX versions.)

Step 5 Locate the TFTP server that came with your operating system and configure it to point to the directory containing the software image .bin file.

Installing and Using Boothelper for a PIX Firewall with a Floppy Drive

Step 1 If you have not done so already, start the TFTP server.

Step 2 Before continuing, access the PIX Firewall console's configuration mode and use the **ping** command to ensure the TFTP server is accessible. If not, make sure all cables are connected correctly and the server is available before proceeding.

Step 3 Insert the boothelper diskette into the PIX Firewall unit's disk drive and reboot the system.

Step 4 Specify the PIX Firewall interface to use for TFTP.

```
monitor> interface num
```

NOTE The PIX Firewall cannot initialize a Gigabit Ethernet interface from monitor or boothelper mode. Use a Fast Ethernet or Token Ring interface.

Step 5 Specify the PIX Firewall interface's IP address using the following command at the monitor prompt:

```
monitor> address ip_address
```

Step 6 Specify the default gateway (if needed):

```
monitor> gateway ip_address
```

Step 7   Verify connectivity to the TFTP server:

    monitor> **ping** *server_address*

Step 8   Specify the TFTP server:

    monitor> **server** *ip_address*

Step 9   Name the image filename:

    monitor> **file** *name*

Step 10   Start the TFTP process:

    monitor> **tftp**

Step 11   After the image downloads, you are prompted to install the new image. Enter **y** to install the image to Flash (make sure the boothelper diskette has been removed from the floppy drive).

Step 12   The PIX Firewall then reboots and installs the new image.

Once the PIX has been upgraded to 5.1 or later, it is no longer necessary to use a floppy disk to load new images onto the PIX. Starting with PIX software version 5.1, the **copy tftp flash** command allows you to TFTP your new PIX image directly to the PIX from a TFTP server.

Password Recovery

Password recovery requires that a special file be transferred to the PIX that nullifies the configured passwords without modifying the configuration. Depending on what model PIX you own, there are two different procedures to perform password recovery. There is the floppy method for PIX models: PIX Classic, PIX 10,000, 510, and 520. The 506, 515, 525, and 535 models all use the monitor mode to transfer the file.

Floppy Password Recovery for PIX Classic, PIX 10,000, 510, and 520

The password recovery for the PIX Firewall 520 requires writing a special image to a floppy disk. You use this diskette to boot PIX Firewall Classic, 10,000, 510, or 520. To perform a PIX Firewall floppy password recovery, complete the following steps:

Step 1   Download the np*xx*.bin (where *xx* is the version of the OS running on the PIX) file for the PIX Firewall software version you are running from the Cisco Connection Online (each version requires a different file). The following URL contains the np*xx*.bin files:

http://www.cisco.com/warp/public/110/34.shtml

Step 2   Download the rawrite.exe file into the same directory as the password version you downloaded previously.

You can obtain the rawrite.exe file from:

http://www.cisco.com/warp/public/110/34.shtml

TIP   You can find the password-recovery procedures for nearly any
Cisco product at www.cisco.com/warp/public/474.

Step 3   After you have retrieved the two files, open an MS-DOS window and
execute the rawrite.exe file as follows and enter the appropriate
information when prompted:

```
C:\> rawrite
RaWrite 1.2 - Write disk file to a floppy diskette
Enter the source file name: npXX.bin
(where XX=version number)
Enter the destination drive: a:
Please insert a formatted diskette into drive A: and press -ENTER- :
<Enter>
Number of sectors per track for this disk is 18
Writing image to drive A:. Press ^C to abort.
Track: 78 Head: 1 Sector: 16
Done.
C:\>
```

Step 4   Reboot your PIX Firewall with the diskette you just created. When
prompted, press **y** to erase the password:

```
Do you wish to erase the passwords? [yn] y
Passwords have been erased
```

The system automatically erases the password and starts rebooting (it is
necessary to remove the password-recovery diskette after the Flash
password is erased). The Telnet password is reset to cisco.

TFTP Password Recovery for PIX 506, 515, 525, and 535

The password recovery for all current models of the PIX Firewall (those without a floppy
drive) requires a TFTP server. To perform a PIX Firewall password recovery, complete the
following steps:

Step 1   Download the file for the PIX Firewall software version you are running
from www.cisco.com (each version requires a different file):

www.cisco.com/warp/public/110/34.shtml

Step 2   Move the binary file you just downloaded to the TFTP home folder on your TFTP server.

Step 3   Reboot your PIX Firewall and interrupt the boot process to enter monitor mode. To do this, you must press the Escape key or send a Break character.

Step 4   Specify the PIX Firewall interface to use for TFTP. To use the Inside interface (Ethernet1), enter the following command at the monitor prompt:

```
monitor> interface 1
```

Step 5   To specify that the PIX Firewall interface's IP address is 10.10.10.1, enter the following command at the monitor prompt:

```
monitor> address 10.10.10.1
```

Step 6   Specify the default gateway (this usually isn't required). To do this, you must enter the following command at the monitor prompt:

```
monitor> gateway ip_address
```

Step 7   To specify the IP address of the TFTP server as 10.10.10.100, enter the following command at the monitor prompt:

```
monitor> server 10.10.10.100
```

Step 8   Verify connectivity to the TFTP server by entering the following command at the monitor prompt:

```
monitor> ping 10.10.10.100
```

Step 9   To specify the filename of the password-recovery file (for example version 5.3(1) in the following sample), enter the following command at the monitor prompt:

```
monitor> file np53.bin
```

NOTE   The np53.bin works with all of the PIX OS 5.3(x) releases (for example, np53.bin works for OS version 5.3(1) and 5.3(2)). This holds true for the np44.bin, np50.bin, np51.bin, and np52.bin.

Step 10 Start the TFTP process. To do this, you must enter the following command at the monitor prompt:

```
monitor> tftp
```

Step 11 When prompted, press **y** to erase the password.

```
Do you wish to erase the passwords? [yn] y
Passwords have been erased
```

The system automatically erases the password and starts rebooting.

Review Questions

To test what you have learned in this chapter, answer the following questions and then refer to Appendix F for the answers.

1 What are the administrative modes that are available to users of the PIX Firewall?

2 What must be done after changes to the configuration are made to keep those changes?

3 What is an Ethernet frame called that is less than the minimum frame size required?

4 What command is required to start the process of copying a new OS to Flash with a PIX running OS version 5.1.1 or later?

5 How does a PIX get into monitor mode?

6 What command shows a user how long the PIX has been operational since the last reboot?

7 What command will start the process of merging a file on a TFTP server with the running configuration in RAM?

This chapter covers the following topics:

- ASA Security Levels
- The Six Basic Commands for Cisco PIX Firewall Configuration

CHAPTER 4

Configuring the Cisco PIX Firewall

When configuring the Cisco Secure PIX Firewall, it is important to keep in mind that a two-interface PIX is configured in the same way a six-interface PIX is configured. This is because the ASA (Adaptive Security Algorithm) uses the concept of *security levels*. Between any two interfaces, one will be of a higher level and one will be lower. In a very real sense, any two of the interfaces of the PIX form a *virtual* firewall.

ASA Security Levels

The security level designates whether an interface is inside (trusted) or outside (untrusted) relative to another interface. An interface is considered inside in relation to another interface if its security level is higher than the other interface's security level and is considered outside in relation to another interface if its security level is lower than the other interface's security level.

The primary rule for security levels is this:

> Once the PIX is configured with the six basic commands, data may enter the PIX through an interface with a higher security level, pass through the PIX, and exit via an interface with a lower security level. Conversely, data that enters an interface with a lower security level cannot pass through the PIX and exit via an interface with a higher security level without a conduit or an access list (which is discussed later).

Security levels range from 0 to 100, and the following are more specific rules for these security levels:

- **Security level 100**—This is the highest security level for an interface. It is used for the inside interface of the PIX Firewall. This is the default setting for the PIX Firewall and cannot be changed. Because 100 is the most trusted interface security level, the organization's network should be set up behind that interface. This is so that no one can access the organization's network unless she or he is specifically given permission. That permission must be configured into the PIX. Also once configured (and in accordance with the site's security policy), every device behind this interface can have access outside the organization's network.

Note   In version 5.2 and higher, it is permitted to choose an interface other than Ethernet1 for the inside interface and an interface other than Ethernet0 for the outside. It *must*, however, use a security level of 100. Except in the case of a need to use a gigabit interface for inside and outside, there isn't any compelling reason to change them from the defaults.

- **Security level 0**—This is the lowest security level. This security level is used for the outside interface of the PIX Firewall. This is the default setting for the PIX Firewall and cannot be changed. Because 0 is the least trusted interface security level, the most untrusted network should be behind this interface. Devices on the outside are only permitted access through the PIX if it is configured to do so. This interface is typically used for connecting to the Internet.

- **Security levels 1–99**—These security levels can be assigned to the perimeter interfaces connected to the PIX Firewall. It is common to connect one of these perimeter interfaces to a network that acts as a demilitarized zone (DMZ). A DMZ is a device or network that is (usually) accessible to users from the untrusted environment. The DMZ is an isolated area, separate from the internal, trusted environment. Figure 4-1 is an example of a three-interface PIX Firewall.

Figure 4-1   *PIX Security Levels*

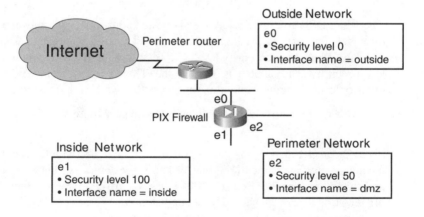

Table 4-1 explains the security levels depicted in Figure 4-1.

Table 4-1   *Figure 4-1 Explanation*

Interface Pair	Relative Interface Relationship for Ethernet 2 (DMZ) Interface	Configuration Guidelines
Outside security 0 to DMZ security 50	DMZ is considered inside	A static translation and a conduit or access list must be configured to enable sessions originated from the outside interface to the DMZ interface.
Inside security 100 to DMZ security 50	DMZ is considered outside	**Global** and **NAT** are typically configured to enable sessions originated from the inside interface to the DMZ interface. Another option is the **static** command to ensure the internal host has the same source address all the time.

The PIX Firewall can have up to four perimeter networks for a total of six interfaces.

With some basic configuration input, the following are examples of different interface connections between the PIX Firewall and other perimeter devices.

- **Data traveling from a more secure interface (higher security level) to a less secure interface (lower security level)**—A translation (either static or dynamic) is required to allow traffic from a higher security to a lower security interface. Once there is a translation, traffic originating from the inside interface of the PIX Firewall with a security level of 100 to the outside interface of the PIX Firewall with a security level of 0 is permitted, unless restricted by an **access list**, **authentication**, or **authorization**. This will be explained in much more detail.

- **Data traveling from a less secure interface (lower security level) to a more secure interface (higher security level)**—Two things are required for traffic to flow from a lower security to a higher security interface: a static translation and a conduit or an access list to permit the desired traffic. Traffic originating from the outside interface of the PIX Firewall with a security level of 0 to the inside interface of the PIX Firewall with a security level of 100 is not permitted, unless specifically allowed by the **conduit** command. If a **conduit** has been configured, a user may restrict the traffic if **authentication** and **authorization** are used.

- **Data traveling through two interfaces with the same security level**—No traffic flows between two interfaces with the same security level. While it is possible to configure two or more interfaces with the same ASA Security Level, it is *not* a TAC-supported configuration.

The Six Basic Commands for Cisco PIX Firewall Configuration

There are six basic configuration commands that are considered the foundations of the PIX Firewall. The **nameif**, **interface**, and **ip address** commands are necessary for the PIX to operate. The **nat**, **global**, and **route** commands are not required but are typically used. In order for traffic to flow through the PIX, it must be configured. The **nat** and **global** commands are what are used to provide access from a more trusted network (higher security level interface) to a less trusted network (lower security level interface).

nameif Command

The command **nameif** assigns a name to each interface on the PIX Firewall and specifies its security level (except for the inside and outside PIX Firewall interfaces, which are named by default).

NOTE   With a default configuration, Ethernet0 is named outside with a security level of 0 and Ethernet1 is named inside and is assigned a security level of 100.

Table 4-2 describes the options and arguments for the **nameif** command, the syntax of which is as follows:

```
nameif hardware_id if_name security_level
```

Table 4-2   **nameif** *Command Description*

nameif Command Argument/Option	Description
hardware_id	Specifies a perimeter interface and its physical location on the PIX Firewall. There are three types of interfaces that are supported: Ethernet, FDDI, or Token Ring. Each interface is represented by an alphanumeric identifier based on the physical position and type of the interface in the chassis. For example, an Ethernet interface is represented as ethernet1, ethernet2, ethernet3, and so on; an FDDI interface is represented as fddi1, fddi2, fddi3, and so on; and a Token Ring interface is represented as token-ring1, token-ring2, and token-ring3, and so on. Gigabit interfaces are referred to as gb-ethernet1, gb-ethernet2, and the like.
if_name	Assigns a name to the physical perimeter interface. This name is assigned by the user, and must be used in all future configuration references to the perimeter interface. By default, e1 is the "inside" and e0 is the "outside."
security_level	Indicates the security level for the perimeter interface. Enter a security level of 1–99.

NOTE	FDDI and Token Ring interfaces are no longer offered. Cisco announced they were End of Sale (EOS) August 31, 2001. The hardware will still be supported in existing networks until August 25, 2006. PIX OS greater than 5.3(x) will not have support for Token Ring or FDDI interfaces.

interface Command

The **interface** command identifies the type of hardware, sets the hardware speed, and enables the interface. When an additional Ethernet interface card is installed on the PIX Firewall, the PIX Firewall automatically recognizes the additional card. Table 4-3 describes the arguments and options for the **interface** command, the syntax for which is as follows:

```
interface hardware_id hardware_speed [shutdown]
```

Table 4-3   **interface** *Command Description*

interface Command Argument/Option	Description
hardware_id	Specifies an interface and its physical location on the PIX Firewall. This is the same variable that was used with the **nameif** command.
hardware_speed	Determines the connection speed. Enter **auto** so the PIX Firewall can sense the speed needed for the device.
	For network interface speed, possible Ethernet values are
	10baset—Sets 10 Mbps Ethernet half-duplex communications.
	10full—Sets 10 Mbps Ethernet full-duplex communications.
	100basetx—Sets 100 Mbps Ethernet half-duplex communications.
	100full—Sets 100 Mbps Ethernet full-duplex communications.
	auto—Sets Ethernet speed automatically.
	For network interface speed, possible Gigabit Ethernet (gb-ethernetX) values are
	1000sxfull—Sets full-duplex Gigabit Ethernet (default)
	1000basesx—Sets half-duplex Gigabit Ethernet
	1000auto—Auto negotiates full/half-duplex Gigabit Ethernet
	For network interface speed, **auto** is the only possible FDDI[1] (fddiX) value
	For network interface speed, possible Token Ring[1] (token-ringX) values include
	4—Sets ring speed at 4 Mbps
	16—Sets ring speed at 16 Mbps
shutdown	Administratively shuts down the interface.

[1] When an FDDI or Token Ring interface card is installed using the **interface** command, the FDDI or Token Ring interface card must be defined because the PIX Firewall does not automatically recognize them.

TIP	Avoid using the **auto** keyword for any Ethernet interface. Duplex mismatches might occur and lead to degraded performance. The best practice is to hard set the speed and duplex on the PIX and the switchport the interface connects to.

For those of you with Cisco IOS Software experience, an example of how the **shutdown** option is used is required. The default state of all interfaces is shutdown. Example 4-1 illustrates the default configuration of the interfaces of a PIX 506 and the command used to bring those interfaces up and shut them down.

Example 4-1   *Enabling and Shutting Down Interfaces on a PIX 506*

```
! Default configuration:
interface ethernet0 10baset shutdown
interface ethernet1 10baset shutdown
! Enable both interfaces as 10Mb, half duplex:
Pixfirewall#(config) interface ethernet0 10baset
Pixfirewall#(config) interface ethernet1 10baset
! Shut down both interfaces:
Pixfirewall#(config) interface ethernet0 10baset shutdown
Pixfirewall#(config) interface ethernet1 10baset shutdown
```

ip address Command

Each interface on the PIX Firewall must be configured with an IP address. After configuring the IP address and netmask, it is common to use the **show ip** command to view which addresses are assigned to the network interfaces. If a mistake is found, reenter the command with the correct information. Table 4-4 describes the arguments and options for the **ip address** command, the syntax of which is as follows:

```
ip address if_name ip_address [netmask]
```

Table 4-4   **ip address** *Command Description*

ip address Command Argument/Option	Description
if_name	Describes the interface. This name is assigned by the user and must be used in all future configuration references to the interface.
ip_address	The assigned IP address of the interface.
netmask	If a network mask is not specified, the *classful* network mask is assumed: Class A: 255.0.0.0 Class B: 255.255.0.0 Class C: 255.255.255.0

nat Command

Network Address Translation (NAT) enables the user to keep internal IP addresses (those behind the PIX Firewall) unknown to external networks. As an example, when connecting to the Internet or other foreign network, the **nat** command accomplishes this by translating the internal, unregistered IP addresses, which do not have to be globally unique, into registered, globally accepted IP addresses before packets are forwarded to the external network. With the exception of **nat 0**, the **nat** command is always used with the **global** command. Both **nat 0** and **global** will be discussed in detail.

Table 4-5 describes the arguments and options for the **nat** command, the syntax of which is as follows:

```
nat (if_name)nat_id local_ip [netmask]
```

Table 4-5   **nat** *Command Description*

nat Command Argument/Option	Description
(if_name)	Describes the internal network interface name that will use global addresses. Data will exit the PIX through the interface specified in the **global** command.
nat_id	Identifies the global pool and matches it with its respective **global** command.
local_ip	The IP address(es) assigned to the devices on the inside network. 0.0.0.0 may be used to allow all outbound connections to translate with IP addresses from the global pool.
netmask	Network mask for the local IP address.

When initially configuring the PIX Firewall, all inside hosts can be enabled to access outbound connections with the **nat 1 0.0.0.0 0.0.0.0** command. The **nat 1 0.0.0.0 0.0.0.0** command enables NAT and lets all inside hosts (specified as 0.0.0.0) access connections that are bound to the corresponding **global** command. The **nat** command can specify a single or range of hosts to make access more selective. When configuring, 0 can be used in place of 0.0.0.0. Use a single 0 to represent 0.0.0.0 as follows:

```
pixfirewall#(config) nat (inside) 1 0 0
```

This shortcut can be used on any PIX command where you need to specify 0.0.0.0.

global Command

When sending data from a trusted network to an untrusted network, the source IP address is often translated. The PIX can do this with two commands. The first command is **nat**, which defines the trusted source addresses to be translated. The command that is used to define the address or range of addresses that the source address will become is the **global** command. Table 4-6 describes the arguments and options for the **global** command, the syntax of which is as follows:

```
global (if_name)nat_id interface | global_ip [-global_ip] [netmask global_mask]
```

Table 4-6   **global** *Command Description*

global Command Argument/Option	Description
if_name	Describes the external network interface name where you will use the global addresses.
nat_id	Identifies the global pool and matches it with its respective **nat** command.
interface	Have the PIX translate all IP addresses specified by the **nat** command to the interface specified. Known as *interface PAT*. Port Address Translation (PAT) will be covered in detail later.
global_ip	Single IP addresses or the beginning IP address for a range of global IP addresses.
-global_ip	A range of global IP addresses.
netmask *global_mask*	The network mask for the global IP. If subnetting is in effect, use the subnet mask (for example, 255.255.255.128). If you specify an address range that overlaps subnets with the **netmask** command, this command will not use the broadcast or network address in the pool of global addresses. For example, if you use 255.255.255.128 and an address range of 192.150.50.20-192.150.50.140, the 192.150.50.127 broadcast address and the 192.150.50.128 network address will not be included in the pool of global addresses.

When an outbound IP packet that is sent from a device on the inside network reaches the PIX Firewall, the source address is extracted and compared to an internal table of existing translations. If the device's address is not already in the table, it is then translated. A new entry is created for that device and it is assigned a global IP address from a pool of global IP addresses. This is called a *translation slot*. After this translation occurs, the table is updated and the translated IP packet is forwarded. After a user-configurable timeout period, (this is configured with the **timeout xlate** *hh:mm:ss* command) or the default of three hours, during which there have been no translated packets for that particular IP address, the entry is removed from the table and the global address is freed for use by another inside device. Figure 4-2 illustratesNAT.

If the **nat** command is used, the companion command, **global**, must be configured to define the pool of translated IP addresses.

To delete a global entry, use the **no global** command. For example:

```
no global [outside] 1 192.168.1.10-192.168.1.254 netmask 255.255.0.0
```

Figure 4-2   *NAT with the PIX*

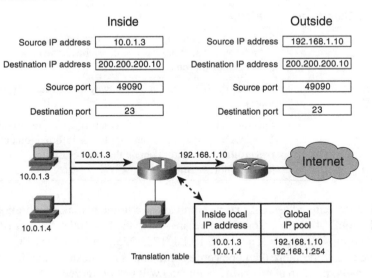

The PIX Firewall assigns addresses from the global pool starting from the low end to the high end of the range as specified in the **global** command.

The PIX Firewall uses the global addresses to assign a virtual IP address to an internal NAT address. After adding, changing, or removing a **global** statement, use the **clear xlate** command to clear all translation slots and make the IP addresses available in the translation table.

route Command

The **route** command defines a static route for an interface. The **route** statement may have a specific destination, or a default static route may be created. Table 4-7 describes the arguments and options for the **route** command, the syntax of which is as follows:

```
route if_name ip_address netmask gateway_ip [metric]
```

Table 4-7   **route** *Command Description*

route Command	Description
if_name	Describes the internal or external network interface name. Data will exit from the PIX through this interface.
ip_address	Describes the destination internal or external network IP address. Use 0.0.0.0 to specify a default route (all destination networks). The 0.0.0.0 IP address can be abbreviated as 0.

continues

Table 4-7   **route** *Command Description (Continued)*

route Command	Description
netmask	Specifies a network mask to apply to *ip_address*. Use 0.0.0.0 to specify a default route. The 0.0.0.0 netmask can be abbreviated as 0. It is common to have one default route.
gateway_ip	Specifies the IP address of the gateway router (the next-hop address for this route).
metric	Specifies the number of hops to *gateway_ip*. If you are not sure, enter 1. Your WAN administrator can supply this information or you can use a **traceroute** command to obtain the number of hops. The default is 1 if a metric is not specified.

All routes entered using the **route** command are stored in the configuration when it is saved. In Example 4-2, all outgoing packets are sent to the 192.168.1.1 router IP address. Because there is only one internal network, 10.1.1.0 255.255.255.0 and the PIX is directly connected to that network, more than one **route** command is not needed. If additional networks exist internally, more than one **route** command will be configured.

Example 4-2 provides a sample configuration of a PIX Firewall using the six basic commands, which are highlighted. The non-highlighted commands are system defaults.

Example 4-2   *PIX Firewall Configuration Using the Six Basic Commands*

```
nameif ethernet0 outside security0
nameif ethernet1 inside security100
nameif ethernet2 dmz security50
nameif ethernet3 pix/intf3 security15
nameif ethernet4 pix/intf4 security20
nameif ethernet5 pix/intf5 security25
enable password 8Ry2YjIyt7RRXU24 encrypted
passwd 2KFQnbNIdI.2KYOU encrypted
hostname pixfirewall
fixup protocol ftp 21
fixup protocol http 80
fixup protocol smtp 25
fixup protocol h323 1720
fixup protocol rsh 514
fixup protocol sqlnet 1521
names
pager lines 24
no logging timestamp
no logging standby
no logging console
no logging monitor
no logging buffered
no logging trap
logging facility 20
logging queue 512
interface ethernet0 100full
```

Example 4-2   *PIX Firewall Configuration Using the Six Basic Commands (Continued)*

```
interface ethernet1  100full
interface ethernet2  100full
interface ethernet3 auto shutdown
interface ethernet4 auto shutdown
interface ethernet5 auto shutdown
mtu outside 1500
mtu inside 1500
mtu pix/intf2 1500
mtu pix/intf3 1500
mtu pix/intf4 1500
mtu pix/intf5 1500
ip address outside 192.168.1.2 255.255.255.0
ip address inside 10.0.1.1 255.255.255.0
ip address dmz 172.16.1.1 255.255.255.0
ip address pix/intf3 127.0.0.1 255.255.255.255
ip address pix/intf4 127.0.0.1 255.255.255.255
ip address pix/intf5 127.0.0.1 255.255.255.255
no failover
failover timeout 0:00:00
failover ip address outside 0.0.0.0
failover ip address inside 0.0.0.0
failover ip address pix/intf2 0.0.0.0
failover ip address pix/intf3 0.0.0.0
failover ip address pix/intf4 0.0.0.0
failover ip address pix/intf5 0.0.0.0
arp timeout 14400
global (outside) 1 192.168.1.10-192.168.1.254 netmask 255.255.255.0
nat (inside) 1 0.0.0.0 0.0.0.0 0 0
no rip outside passive
no rip outside default
no rip inside passive
no rip inside default
no rip pix/intf2 passive
no rip pix/intf2 default
no rip pix/intf3 passive
no rip pix/intf3 default
no rip pix/intf4 passive
no rip pix/intf4 default
no rip pix/intf5 passive
no rip pix/intf5 default
route outside 0.0.0.0 0.0.0.0 192.168.1.1 1
timeout xlate 3:00:00 conn 1:00:00 half-closed 0:10:00 udp 0:02:00
timeout rpc 0:10:00 h323 0:05:00
timeout uauth 0:05:00 absolute
aaa-server TACACS+ protocol tacacs+
aaa-server RADIUS protocol radius
no snmp-server location
no snmp-server contact
snmp-server community public
no snmp-server enable traps
telnet timeout 5
terminal width 80
```

continues

Example 4-2   *PIX Firewall Configuration Using the Six Basic Commands (Continued)*

```
Cryptochecksum:d41d8cd98f00b204e9800998ecf8427e
: end
[OK].
```

Review Questions

To test what you have learned in this chapter, answer the following questions and then refer to Appendix F for the answers.

1 What is the default security level of the *inside* interface?

2 True or False. Two interfaces cannot have the same security level.

3 What is the syntax of the **route** command if I want to configure the PIX with a default route to my perimeter router (IP address 192.168.1.1) and static routes to three internal networks (10.1.1.0, 10.2.0.0, 10.3.0.0), all with a next hop router IP address of 10.1.1.5?

4 What must I also do if I configure the PIX using the **nat (inside) 1 0 0** command to translate all internal addresses when accessing the Internet?

5 How do I set the default gateway to 192.168.111.1? That IP address exists on the outside subnet.

This chapter covers the following topics:

- Transport Protocols
- PIX Firewall Translations

CHAPTER 5

Cisco PIX Firewall Translation

In order to understand any discussion of firewalls, firewall technology, or security in general, it is important to have a clear understanding of how traffic flows end to end. This is true with networking in general and is especially true with security. If there is an understanding of data traffic flow, then understanding how to secure that data traffic flow is easier.

Encapsulation occurs at the source of a session when application data is combined with transport layer information to create a segment. That, in turn, is encapsulated within network layer information, creating a packet. That data is encapsulated within some data-link information, creating a frame. The PIX searches for specific information within a frame to make important decisions about traffic flow.

Figure 5-1 illustrates the encapsulation of data to create a frame. The PC with the IP address of 10.0.0.3 initiates the session by issuing the command **telnet 172.30.0.50**.

To gain a deeper understanding of how the PIX Firewall processes inbound and outbound transmissions, a brief review of two primary TCP/IP transport protocols, TCP and UDP, is warranted.

Transport Protocols

A network session is frequently carried out over one of the following two transport layer protocols:

- TCP (Transmission Control Protocol), which is easy to inspect.
- UDP (User Datagram Protocol), which is difficult to inspect properly.

Examples of other protocols that may be inspected by the PIX are ICMP (Internet Control Message Protocol) and GRE (Generic Routing Encapsulation).

NOTE   As defined earlier, the term *outbound* means connections initiated from a more trusted side of the PIX Firewall to a less trusted side of the PIX Firewall. The term *inbound* means connections initiated from a less trusted side of the PIX Firewall to a more trusted side of the PIX Firewall.

Figure 5-1 *Encapsulation of a Telnet Session*

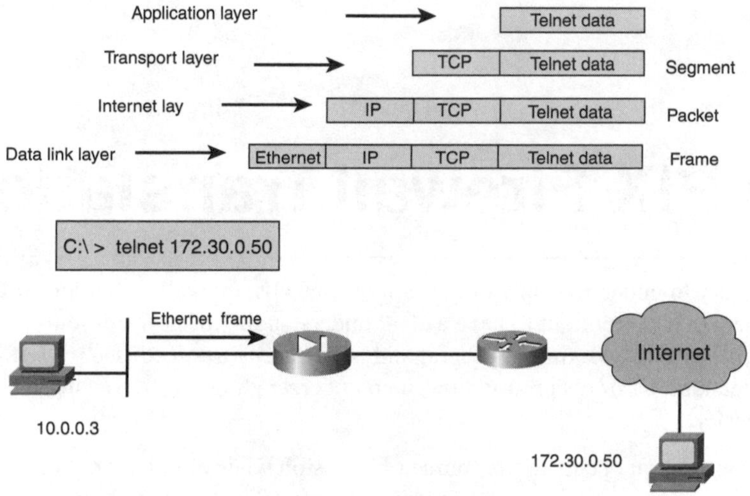

Transmission Control Protocol

TCP is a connection-oriented protocol. When a session is started from a host on the more secure interface of the PIX Firewall, the PIX Firewall creates an entry in its session state table. The PIX Firewall is able to extract network session information from the network flow and actively verify its validity in real time. This stateful filter maintains the parameters (or state) of each network connection and checks subsequent information (such as, but not limited to, source and destination port number and IP address) against its expectations. When TCP initiates a session through the PIX Firewall, the PIX Firewall records the network flow and looks for an acknowledgement from the destination device. The PIX Firewall then allows traffic to flow between the two devices based on the three-way handshake.

Figure 5-2 depicts what happens when a TCP session is established through the PIX Firewall.

The list that follows describes the sequence of events depicted in Figure 5-2.

1   When an IP packet is received by the PIX from the inside, the PIX checks for an existing translation slot. If there is not one, it creates one after verifying within the configuration that one should be created. A *translation slot* within the PIX is the inside IP address and the assigned globally unique IP address. This information is kept in memory so that it can be checked against subsequent packet flow. In the example, 10.0.0.3 is translated to 192.168.0.10. Then the embedded TCP information is used to create a *connection slot* (an active TCP connection) in the PIX Firewall.

2   The connection slot is marked as embryonic (not yet established).

Figure 5-2 *TCP Initialization, Inside to Outside*

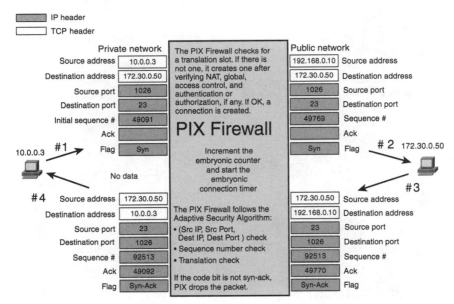

NOTE An embryonic connection is a half-open TCP session. It becomes a complete connection after the "three-way handshake" is completed by the inside host when it sends an ACK. The number of embryonic connections can be limited in a number of ways with the PIX, which can help reduce certain attacks against a network. Embryonic connections can be limited to a maximum number at a given time. Embryonic connections can also be timed to be completed within a given amount of time.

3 The PIX Firewall randomizes the initial sequence number (49091) of the connection and forwards the packet onto the outgoing interface.

4 The PIX Firewall now expects a SYN/ACK packet from the destination host. The PIX Firewall matches the received packet against the connection slot, computes the sequencing information, and forwards the return packet to the inside host. Any packets that match source and destination addresses and/or ports but do not match the proper step in the protocol are discarded and logged.

5 The inside host completes the connection setup (the three-way handshake) with an ACK (see Figure 5-3).

6 The connection slot on the PIX Firewall is marked as connected (active-established) and data is transmitted. The embryonic counter is then reset for this connection.

Figure 5-3 *TCP Initialization, Inside to Outside*

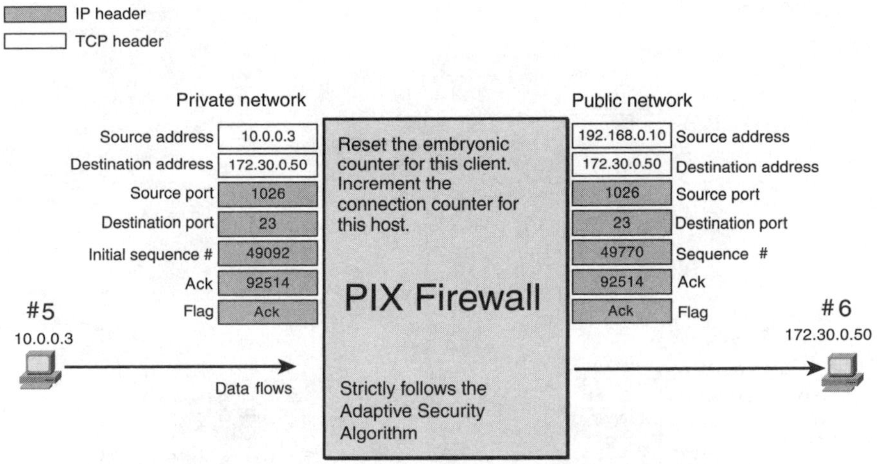

User Datagram Protocol

UDP is a connectionless protocol, so the PIX Firewall must take other measures to ensure the security of UDP. Applications using UDP are difficult to secure properly because there is no handshaking or sequencing. It is difficult to determine the current state of a UDP transaction (opening, established, or closing). It is also difficult to maintain the state of a session, as it has no clear beginning, flow state, or end. However, the PIX Firewall creates a UDP connection slot when a UDP packet is sent from a more secure interface to a less secure interface. All subsequent returned UDP packets matching the connection slot are forwarded to the inside network. The inherent problems of securing UDP mean that its applications (NFS, DNS, RPC, etc.) are often attacked, so it is important to use restrictive firewall rules for such applications. Figure 5-4 shows how the PIX works with a UDP session.

The PIX Firewall will accept inbound UDP packets after it has seen an outbound UDP packet from the same destination and source IP addresses. When the UDP connection slot is idle for more than the configured idle time (the default is two minutes), it is deleted from the connection table. The following are some UDP characteristics:

- UDP is an unreliable (connectionless) but efficient transport protocol.

- Spoofing UDP packets is very easy (no handshaking or sequencing). As there is no state machine, both the initiator of the transaction and the current state cannot be determined.

- UDP has no delivery guarantees.

- There is no connection setup and termination (application implements a state machine).

- UDP has no congestion management or avoidance.

Figure 5-4   *PIX Firewall UDP Session*

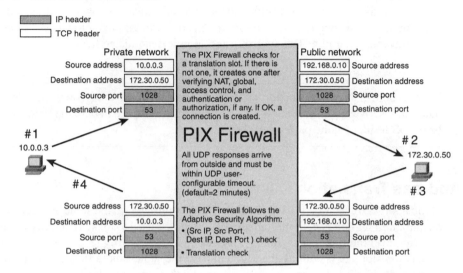

PIX Firewall Translations

The PIX Firewall may be used to translate all inside IP addresses, when data passes through from the inside. From a network security perspective, if a particular security policy is to permit only outbound traffic, translating internal addresses is a very secure action. If private addressing (RFC 1918) is used on the inside, the translated (source) addresses that connect to the Internet must be registered addresses.

If a user on the outside tries to make a connection to the inside, that [outside] user will not succeed. A session cannot be built from the Internet with the destination address being a private address unless it has been configured within the PIX to allow the session.

NOTE   RFC 1918 defines "Address Allocation for Private Internets."

The Internet Assigned Numbers Authority (IANA) has reserved the following three blocks of the IP address space for private internets:

    10.0.0.0   - 10.255.255.255 (10/8 prefix)

    172.16.0.0 - 172.31.255.255 (172.16/12 prefix)

    192.168.0.0 - 192.168.255.255 (192.168/16 prefix)

When setting up address translation with the PIX Firewall, there are two options. Inside addresses may translate to a specific global address, which is known as static address translation. The second option is translating inside addresses to a global pool of addresses when traversing the PIX. This type of translation is dynamic address translation.

NOTE   There is built-in NetBIOS support on the PIX Firewall. When a host on the inside builds an outbound NetBIOS session, the source IP address is translated in both the IP header and the NetBIOS header (in the payload of the packet).

Static Address Translation

Static address translation is used if a host is to be translated to the same address every time an outbound session is built through the PIX. It is also used to make IP addresses on higher-security level interfaces accessible to devices on lower-security level interfaces. The translation slot that is built by the PIX will have the same source IP address and the same translated address for every connection made by that source address.

When defining the syntax of commands on the PIX Firewall, the **local address** is defined as the assigned address to a host on the inside (for example, a host on a more trusted side of a session through the PIX). The **global address** is defined as the translated address that a **local address** becomes when a session is built through the PIX. A **foreign address** is defined as the IP address to a host on the outside (for example, a host on a less trusted side of a session through the PIX).

Table 5-1 describes the syntax for the **static** command, which is as follows:

```
static [(internal_if_name, external_if_name)] global_ip local_ip
[netmask network_mask] [max_conns [em_limit]] [norandomseq]
```

Table 5-1   **static** *Command Description*

static Command Argument/Option	Description
internal_if_name	The internal network interface name. The higher-security level interface you are accessing.
external_if_name	The external network interface name. The lower-security level interface you are accessing.
global_ip	A global IP address. This address cannot be a PAT (Port Address Translation) IP address. The IP address on the lower-security level interface you are accessing.
local_ip	The local IP address from the inside network. The IP address on the higher-security level interface you are accessing.

continues

Table 5-1   **static** *Command Description (Continued)*

static Command Argument/Option	Description
netmask	Reserve word required before specifying the network mask.
network_mask	The network mask pertains to both *global_ip* and *local_ip*. For host addresses, always use 255.255.255.255. For network addresses, use the appropriate class mask or subnet mask; for example, for Class A networks, use 255.0.0.0. An example mask is 255.255.255.224.
max_conns	The maximum number of connections per IP address, permitted through the static at the same time.
em_limit	The embryonic connection limit. Set this limit to prevent attack by a flood of embryonic connections. The default is 0, which means unlimited connections.
norandomseq	Do not randomize the TCP/IP packet's sequence number. Only use this option if another inline firewall is also randomizing sequence numbers and the result is scrambling the data.

In the example illustrated by Figure 5-5, the packet from 10.0.1.10 (local address) has a source address of 192.168.1.101 (global address) when a session is built through the PIX Firewall. The **static** command permanently maps the local address to the global address. The syntax of the required **static** command in Figure 5-5 is

```
pixfirewall(config)# static (inside, outside)192.168.1.101 10.0.1.10
```

Figure 5-5   *Permanently Mapping a Local Address to a Global Address*

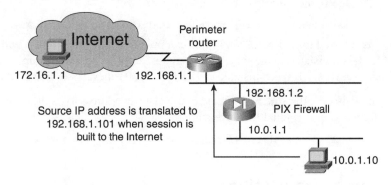

When permitting access to a specific inside host through the PIX, the IP address host must be defined to the users on the outside. The foreign address host must use the static global address (translated address) of the inside host as the destination IP address. The **conduit**

command is what permits access through the PIX and will be described in more detail in the next chapter. The syntax that follows shows the establishment of a Telnet session through the PIX with the **static** and **conduit** command for the network setup in Figure 5-6.

```
pixfirewall(config)# static (inside,outside)192.168.1.101 10.0.1.10
pixfirewall(config)# conduit permit tcp host 192.168.1.101 eq
   telnet host 172.16.1.1
```

In this Telnet session, the host with the foreign IP address of 172.16.1.1 is building a session to the inside host with a global IP address of 192.168.1.101. The PIX translates the global IP address of 192.168.1.101 to the local IP address of 10.0.1.10.

Figure 5-6 **static with conduit**

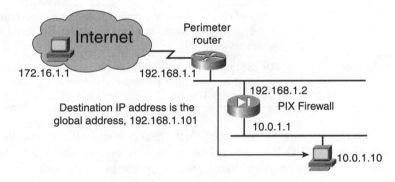

The **static** command can also be used to translate a range of addresses. If the Class A subnet of 10.1.1.0 255.255.255.0 is to be translated to the Class C network of 192.168.1.0 255.255.255.0, the syntax of the command is

```
pixfirewall(conf)# static (inside,outside) 192.168.1.0 10.1.1.0
```

This is referred to as a *netstatic*. In this example each specific address within the subnet 10.1.1.0 is translated to the same global address every time. For example, the host with the IP address 10.1.1.100 is translated to 192.168.1.100 for every session built through the PIX.

You can also use the **static** command to translate an address to itself. In that case, the local IP address and the global IP address are the same:

```
pixfirewall(conf)# static (inside,outside) 192.168.1.10 192.168.1.10
```

Dynamic Address Translation

Dynamic address translation is used to translate a range of local addresses to either a range of global addresses or a single global address. Translating a range of local addresses to a range of global addresses is referred to as Network Address Translation (NAT). Translating a range of local addresses to a single global address is referred to as Port Address Translation (PAT).

Network Address Translation

With dynamic address translation using NAT, the local hosts (which are to be translated) must be defined with the **nat** command. The address pool must then be defined with the **global** command. The pool for address allocation is chosen on the outgoing interface based on the *nat_id* selected with the **nat** command. A user may specify up to 256 global pools of IP addresses. An example of NAT is in Figure 5-7. The specific syntax for Figure 5-7 is as follows:

```
pixfirewall(config)# nat (inside) 1 0.0.0.0 0.0.0.0 0 0
pixfirewall(config)# global (outside) 1 192.168.1.10-192.168.1.254
   netmask 255.255.255.0
```

If the host 10.0.1.10 is the first outbound connection made though the PIX to the Internet, it translates to 192.168.1.10. Chapter 4, "Configuring the Cisco PIX Firewall," covered the syntax of the **global** and the **nat** commands.

Figure 5-7   *Network Address Translation*

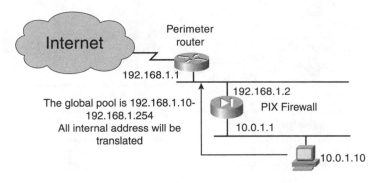

In Figure 5-7, the global pool of addresses assigned by the **global** command are 192.168.1.10 through 192.168.1.254, enabling up to 245 individual IP addresses (the range is inclusive). All local addresses are translated due to the use of 0.0.0.0 in both the network and mask portion of the **nat** command.

It is common to use the **static** command and the **global/nat** commands in the same configuration. It is important to keep the global IP address of the **static** command outside the global range. For example, the following example is incorrect because the **static** global address of 192.168.1.10 is within the range of the **global** command global address range of 192.168.1.10 through 192.168.1.254:

```
pixfirewall(conf)# nat (inside) 1 0.0.0.0 0.0.0.0 0 0
pixfirewall(conf)# global (outside) 1 192.168.1.10-192.168.1.254 netmask
   255.255.255.0
pixfirewall(conf)# static (inside,outside) 192.168.1.10 10.1.1.10
```

What follows is the correct configuration:

```
pixfirewall(conf)# nat (inside) 1 0.0.0.0 0.0.0.0 0 0
pixfirewall(conf)# global (outside) 1 192.168.1.11-192.168.1.254 netmask
  255.255.255.0
pixfirewall(conf)# static (inside,outside) 192.168.1.10 10.1.1.10
```

Port Address Translation

When using PAT, all local addresses are translated to a single global address. The configuration for PAT is similar to that of NAT. The one exception is that the **global** statement contains a single IP address instead of a range of IP addresses as demonstrated in Figure 5-8 and the following command syntax:

```
pixfirewall(config)# nat (inside) 1 0.0.0.0 0.0.0.0
pixfirewall(config)# global (outside) 1 192.168.1.10 netmask 255.255.255.255
```

Figure 5-8 *Port Address Translation*

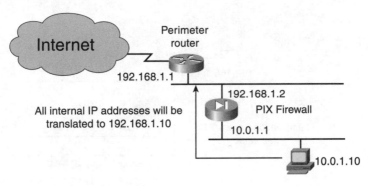

When connecting to the Internet, all internal IP addresses will be translated to the single IP address, 192.168.1.10.

Some important considerations with regard to PAT are as follows:

- PAT lets multiple outbound sessions appear to originate from a single IP address. With PAT enabled, the firewall chooses a unique port number from the PAT IP address for each outbound *xlate* (translation slot). This feature is valuable when an ISP cannot allocate enough unique IP addresses for your outbound connections.

- An IP address you specify for a PAT cannot be used in another global address pool.

- When a PAT augments a pool of global addresses, first the addresses from the global pool are used and then the next connection is taken from the PAT address. If a global pool address becomes free, the next connection takes that address. The global pool addresses always come before a PAT address is used. Augment a pool of global addresses with a PAT by using the same *nat_id* in the global command statements that create the global pools and the PAT. For example:

```
global (outside) 1 172.16.201.1-172.16.201.10 netmask 255.255.255.224
global (outside) 1 172.16.201.22 netmask 255.255.255.224
```

- PAT does not work with H.323 applications and caching name servers. Do not use PAT when multimedia applications need to be run through the firewall. Multimedia applications can conflict with port mappings provided by PAT.

- PAT does not work with the established command.

- PAT works with DNS, FTP and passive FTP, HTTP, e-mail, RPC, rshell, Telnet, URL filtering, and outbound traceroute.

Translations and Connections

There is a distinction made between translated sessions and connected sessions when discussing the PIX Firewall. Translations are at the IP layer of the TCP/IP protocol stack, and connections are at the transport layer. Connections are subsets of translations. You can have many connections open under one translation.

The **xlate** command allows you to show or clear the contents of the translation (xlate) slots. A translation slot is created when a session is built through the PIX. That translation slot can remain after configuration changes have been made. It is good practice to use the **clear xlate** after adding, changing, or removing **alias**, **conduit**, **global**, **nat**, **route**, or **static** commands in your configuration. Though it is more invasive, a **reload** or power-cycle of the PIX will also accomplish the same goal of clearing the translation slots.

The syntax for the **clear xlate** and **show xlate** commands are as follows:

```
show xlate [global | local ip1[-ip2] [netmask mask]] lport | gport port[-port]]
    [interface if1[,if2][,ifn]] [state static [,dump] [,portmap]
    [,norandomseq] [,identity]]

clear xlate [global | local ip1[-ip2] [netmask mask]] lport | gport port[-port]]
    [interface if1[,if2][,ifn]] [state static [,dump] [,portmap]
    [,norandomseq] [,identity]]
```

Table 5-2 describes the parameters for the **clear xlate** and **show xlate** commands.

Table 5-2   **show/clear xlate** *Command Description*

Command Parameter	Description
[**global** | **local** *ip1*[-*ip2*]] [**netmask** *mask*]	Display active translations by global IP address or local IP address using the network mask to qualify the IP addresses.
lport | **gport** *port*[-*port*]	Display active translations by local and global port specification.
interface *if1*[,*if2*][,*ifn*]	Display active translations by interface.
state	Display active translations by state; **static** translation (**static**), **dump** (cleanup), PAT **global** (**portmap**), a **nat** or **static** translation with the **norandomseq** setting (**norandomseq**), or the use of the **nat 0** identity feature (**identity**).

To display all active connections, issue the **show conn** command. This command will show the number of connections as well as the source and destination IP address and port number for each connection. Table 5-3 describes the **show conn** command, the syntax for which is as follows:

```
show conn [count] [foreign | local ip[-ip2] [netmask mask]] [protocol tcp |
   udp | protocol] [fport | lport port1[-port2]] [state up[,finin][,finout]
   [,http_get][,smtp_data][,smtp_banner][,smtp_incomplete][,nojava][,data_in]
   [,data_out][,sqlnet_fixup_data][,conn_inbound][,rpc][,h323][,dump]
```

Table 5-3   show conn *Command Description*

Command Parameter	Description
count	Display only the number of used connections. This feature is no longer supported and returns unreliable information.
**foreign	local** *ip*[*-ip2*]**netmask** *mask*	Display active connections by foreign IP address or local IP address. Qualify foreign or local active connections by a network mask.
**protocol tcp	udp**	*protocol*	Display active connections by protocol type. *protocol* is a protocol specified by number.
fport|lport *port1*[*-port2*]	Display foreign or local active connections by port.
state	Display active connections by their current state: up (**up**), FIN inbound (**finin**), FIN outbound (**finout**), HTTP get (**http_get**), SMTP mail data (**smtp_data**), SMTP mail banner (**smtp_banner**), incomplete SMTP mail connection (**smtp_incomplete**), an **outbound** command denying access to Java applets (**nojava**), inbound data (**data_in**), outbound data (**data_out**), SQL*Net data fix up (**sqlnet_fixup_data**), inbound connection (**conn_inbound**), RPC connection (**rpc**), H.323 connection (**h323**), dump cleanup connection (**dump**).

Review Questions

To test what you have learned in this chapter, answer the following questions and then refer to Appendix F for the answers.

1 What is the first thing created in the PIX when a user on the inside establishes an outbound session?

2 True or False. TCP and UDP are the only two protocols that are permitted through the PIX.

3 What is an embryonic connection?

4 True or False. If I configure a **static** statement, I must also configure a **conduit** statement.

5 What should I do after I make a change to the global range of the **global** command?

6 What command shows all active TCP connections through the PIX?

7 Assuming a NAT ID of 3, build the **global** command necessary to translate all intenal IP addresses to be 172.16.1.1.

8 What is a net static?

This chapter covers the following topics:

- Access Through the PIX Firewall
- Understanding Statics and Conduits
- Other Ways Through the PIX Firewall
- Configuring Multiple Interfaces

CHAPTER 6

Configuring Access Through the Cisco PIX Firewall

As discussed previously, the baseline configuration for a firewall is to permit all access from the inside to the outside, and permit no access from the outside to the inside. Given this configuration, it is then up to the security administrator to allow certain access from the outside to the inside as exceptions to the baseline within the constraints of the security policy.

The **nat** and **global** commands (defined in Chapter 5, "Cisco PIX Firewall Translation,") configured on the PIX can be used to define inside-to-outside access. The **static** command (defined in Chapter 5) may be used to allow access from inside to outside also. One focus of this chapter is defining how to configure access from the outside to the inside.

Configuring Access Through the PIX Firewall

There are only two ways through the PIX from a less trusted device (coming into the PIX through an interface with a low security level) to a more trusted device (exiting the PIX through an interface with a higher security level).

- **Response to Valid Request**—When a user on the inside builds a connection to a device on the outside, by default the response to that request is permitted through the PIX. All inside to outside connections will populate the translation table in the PIX. When an outside device responds to the request, the PIX Firewall checks the translation table to see if a translation slot exists for that particular request. If it exists, the PIX Firewall allows the response to continue. After the session is terminated, the idle timer for that particular translation slot starts. The default in version 5.1 is three hours.

- **Configure a Conduit**—Used for outside-to-inside communication. A **static** translation or **global** and **nat** is configured first (while it is true that the **nat/global** commands support connections that originate on the inside, if a user wants an echo-reply permitted back through the PIX, a **conduit** must be configured). A conduit is then configured that defines the address or group of addresses, source, and/or destination TCP/UDP port or range of ports that are allowed to flow through the PIX Firewall.

NOTE	Newer versions of the PIX Firewall OS allow two additional methods of access through the PIX from less trusted to more trusted. One method of access is the **access list** command. A second method is to utilize encryption and have the PIX act as the source or termination point of the encryption session. Both of these methods do not require a conduit.

Understanding the static and conduit Commands

Although most connections occur from an interface with a high security level to an interface with a low security level, there are circumstances that require connections from an interface with a lower security level to an interface with a higher security level. To do this, use the **conduit** command.

An example of when to use the **conduit** command is with testing connectivity through a PIX with ICMP messages. In order to permit an echo-request (ping) from the outside through the PIX, a **conduit** must be configured. Also, the user on the outside must have a destination IP address to use. That information can be mapped on the PIX using the **static** command.

The **static** command creates static mapping between a local (inside) IP address and a global (outside) IP address. Using the **static** command enables you to set a permanent global IP address for a particular inside IP address. This sets up the capability to create an entrance for the specified interfaces with the lower security level into the specified interface with the higher security level.

After creating a static mapping between a local IP address and a global IP address by using the **static** command, the connection from the outside to the inside interface is still blocked by the PIX Firewall's Adaptive Security Algorithm (ASA). The **conduit** command is used to allow traffic to flow between an interface with a lower security level to an interface with a higher security level. The **conduit** command creates the exceptions to the PIX Firewall's ASA.

The **static** command creates a permanent mapping (called a *static translation slot* or *xlate*) between a local and a global IP address. For outbound connections, use static to specify a global address that is always used for translation between the local host and that global address. For inbound connections, use **static** with the **conduit** command to identify addresses visible on the external network.

It is important to remember

* The **conduit** command allows connections from a lower security interface to a higher security interface. The **conduit** command is an exception in the ASA's inbound security policy for a given host.

* The **static** command is used to create a permanent mapping between a local and a global IP address.

static Command

The **static** command creates a permanent mapping (static translation slot) between a local and a global IP address. When connecting to the Internet, the global IP address must be a registered IP address. Chapter 5 defines the syntax for the **static** command. **static** statements take precedence over **nat** and **global** command pairs. Use the **show static** command to view **static** statements in the configuration.

The security level for each interface is set by the **nameif** command. When used with the **static** command, the **conduit** command allows traffic to originate from an interface with a lower security value through the PIX Firewall to an interface with a higher security value. For example, **static** and **conduit** must be configured to allow incoming sessions from the outside to the DMZ interface or from the outside to the inside interface.

conduit Command

The **conduit** command permits or denies connections from outside the PIX Firewall to access TCP, UDP, and other protocol services on hosts inside the network. The **conduit** statement may be used in a very general way or in a very specific way. For example, it is possible to allow HTTP access to a specific host.

In Example 6-1, the **static** command is used first to statically translate 10.0.1.10 to 192.168.1.101. The **conduit** command in the example will permit HTTP access only to host 10.0.1.10 (translated to 192.168.1.101).

Example 6-1   *Using the* **static** *and* **conduit** *Commands in Tandem to Permit HTTP Access Only*

```
pixfirewall(config)# static (inside,outside) 192.168.1.101 10.0.1.10 netmask
   255.255.255.255
pixfirewall(config)# conduit permit tcp any eq www host 172.16.1.1
```

Figure 6-1 illustrates the effect of the **conduit** command used in Example 6-1.

Figure 6-1   *The* **conduit** *Command*

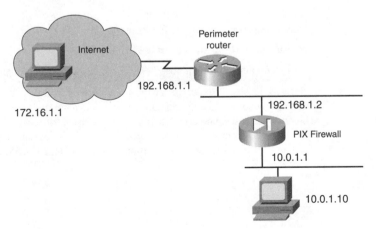

Table 6-1 describes the parameters of the **conduit** command, the syntax for which is as follows:

```
conduit permit|deny protocol global_ip global_mask[operator port[ port]]
    foreign_ip foreign_mask[operator port [ port]]
```

Table 6-1 **conduit** Command Description

Command Parameter	Description
permit	Permit access if the conditions are matched.
deny	Deny access if the conditions are matched.
protocol	Specify the transport protocol for the connection. Possible literal values are **icmp**, **tcp**, **udp**, or an integer in the range 0 through 255 representing an IP protocol number. Use **ip** to specify all transport protocols. If you specify the ICMP protocol, you can permit or deny ICMP access to one or more global IP addresses. Specify the ICMP type in the *icmp_type* variable or omit to specify all ICMP types.
global_ip	A global IP address previously defined by a **global** or **static** command. You can use **any** if the *global_ip* and *global_mask* are 0.0.0.0 0.0.0.0. The **any** option applies the **permit** or **deny** parameters to the global addresses. If *global_ip* is a host, you can omit *global_mask* by specifying the **host** command before *global_ip*. For example **conduit permit tcp host 209.165.201.1 eq ftp any** This example lets any foreign host access global address 209.165.201.1 for FTP.
global_mask	Network mask of *global_ip*. The *global_mask* is a 32-bit, four-part dotted decimal, such as 255.255.255.255. Use zeros in a part to indicate bit positions to be ignored. Use subnetting if required. If you use **0** for *global_ip*, use **0** for the *global_mask*; otherwise, enter the *global_mask* appropriate to *global_ip*.
foreign_ip	An external IP address (host or network) that can access the *global_ip*. You can specify **0.0.0.0** or **0** for any host. If both the *foreign_ip* and *foreign_mask* are 0.0.0.0 0.0.0.0, you can use the shorthand **any** option. If *foreign_ip* is a host, you can omit *foreign_mask* by specifying the **host** command before *foreign_ip*. For example **conduit permit tcp any eq ftp host 209.165.201.2** This example lets foreign host 209.165.201.2 access any global address for FTP.
foreign_mask	Network mask of *foreign_ip*. The *foreign_mask* is a 32-bit, four-part dotted decimal, such as 255.255.255.255. Use zeros in a part to indicate bit positions to be ignored. Use subnetting if required. If you use **0** for *foreign_ip*, use **0** for the *foreign_mask*; otherwise, enter the *foreign_mask* appropriate to *foreign_ip*. You can also specify a mask for subnetting—for example, 255.255.255.192.

Table 6-1   **conduit** Command Description *(Continued)*

Command Parameter	Description
operator	A comparison operand that lets you specify a port or a port range. Use without an operator and port to indicate all ports. For example, **conduit permit tcp any any** Use **eq** and a port to permit or deny access to just that port. For example, use **eq ftp** to permit or deny access only to FTP: **conduit deny tcp host 192.168.1.1 eq ftp 209.165.201.1** Use **lt** and a port to permit or deny access to all ports less than the port you specify. For example, use **lt 2025** to permit or deny access to the well-known ports (1 to 1024): **conduit permit tcp host 192.168.1.1 lt 1025 any** Use **gt** and a port to permit or deny access to all ports greater than the port you specify. For example, use **gt 42** to permit or deny ports 43 to 65535: **conduit deny udp host 192.168.1.1 gt 42 host 209.165.201.2** Use **neq** and a port to permit or deny access to every port except the ports that you specify. For example, use **neq 10** to permit or deny ports 1–9 and 11 to 65535: **conduit deny tcp host 192.168.1.1 neq 10 host 209.165.201.2 neq 42** Use **range** and a port range to permit or deny access to only those ports named in the range. For example, use **range 10 1024** to permit or deny access only to ports 10 through 1024. All other ports are unaffected. **conduit deny tcp any range 10 1024 any**
port	Service(s) you permit to be used while accessing *global_ip* or *foreign_ip*. Specify a service by the port that handles it, such as **smtp** for port 25, **www** for port 80, and so on. You can specify ports by either a literal name or a number in the range of 0 to 65535. You can specify all ports by not specifying a port value. For example, **conduit deny tcp any any** This command is the default condition for the **conduit** command in that all ports are denied until explicitly permitted.
icmp_type	The type of ICMP message. Table 6-2 lists the ICMP type literals that you can use in this command. Omit this option to mean all ICMP types. An example of this command that permits all ICMP types is: **conduit permit icmp any any**. This command lets ICMP pass inbound and outbound.

Table 6-2 *ICMP and Port Type Literals*

ICMP Type	Literal
0	echo-reply
3	unreachable
4	source-quench
5	redirect
6	alternate-address
8	echo
9	router-advertisement
10	router-solicitation
11	time-exceeded
12	parameter-problem
13	timestamp-reply
14	timestamp-request
15	information-request
16	information-reply
17	mask-request
18	mask-reply
31	conversion-error
32	mobile-redirect

NOTE   You can view valid protocol numbers at the following site: www.iana.org/assignments/ protocol-numbers. When specifying the foreign (source) port or global (destination) port, the port values from RFC 1700 are used. In many circumstances, the application name may be used. Table 6-3 lists the literal application name that can be used instead of the port number.

Table 6-3 *Application Names/Port Numbers*

Application Name	Protocol (TCP/UDP)	Port Number
bgp	TCP	179
biff	UDP	512
bootpc	UDP	68

Table 6-3   *Application Names/Port Numbers (Continued)*

Application Name	Protocol (TCP/UDP)	Port Number
bootps	UDP	67
chargen	TCP	19
cmd	TCP	514
daytime	TCP	13
discard	TCP/UDP	9
domain	TCP	53
dnsix	UDP	195
echo	TCP/UDP	7
exec	TCP	512
finger	TCP	79
ftp	TCP	21
ftp-data	TCP	20
gopher	TCP	70
hostname	TCP	101
nameserver	UDP	42
ident	TCP	113
irc	TCP	194
isakmp	TCP	500
klogin	TCP	543
kshell	TCP	544
lpd	TCP	515
Login	TCP	513
mobile-ip	UDP	434
netbios-ns	UDP	137
netbios-dgm	UDP	138
nntp	TCP	119
ntp	UDP	123
pim-auto-rp	TCP/UDP	496
pop2	TCP	109
pop3	TCP	110

continues

Table 6-3 *Application Names/Port Numbers (Continued)*

Application Name	Protocol (TCP/UDP)	Port Number
radius[1]	UDP	1645, 1646
rip	UDP	520
smtp	TCP	25
snmp	UDP	161
snmptrap	UDP	162
sqlnet[2]	TCP	1521
sunrpc	TCP/UDP	111
syslog	UDP	514
tacacs	TCP/UDP	49
talk	TCP	517
telnet	TCP	23
tftp	UDP	69
time	TCP	37
uucp	TCP	540
who	UDP	513
whois	TCP	43
www	TCP	80
xdmcp	UDP	177

[1] The PIX Firewall listens for RADIUS on ports 1645 and 1646. If your RADIUS server uses ports 1812 and 1813, you will need to reconfigure it to listen on ports 1645 and 1646.

[2] The PIX Firewall uses port 1521 for SQL*Net. This is the default port used by Oracle for SQL*Net; however, this value does not agree with IANA port assignments.

When using the **conduit** command it is best to be as specific as possible. Allowing all users on the outside to telnet to a host on the inside may be a breach of the security policy. Example 6-2 and Figure 6-2 illustrate the example of the intent to allow access to only one local host from one global host. The **static** command is also included in this example to complete the configuration.

Example 6-2 *Allowing Access to Only a Single Local Host from a Single Global Host*

```
pixfirewall(config)# static (inside,outside) 192.168.1.101 10.0.1.10
  netmask 255.255.255.255
pixfirewall(config)# conduit permit tcp host 192.168.1.101 eq www telnet
  host 172.16.1.1
```

Figure 6-2 *Static and Conduit Together*

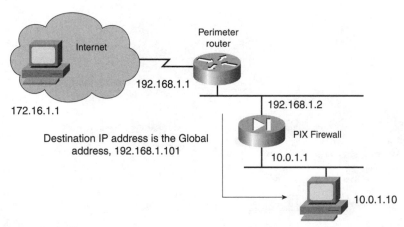

In Figure 6-2, the user on the outside with the IP address of 172.16.1.1 uses a destination IP address of 192.168.1.101. The PIX translates that address and sends the request on the inside to 10.0.1.10 due to the configured **static**. You can have up to 8000 conduits on the PIX. To look at the configured conduits, use the **show conduit** command (this also displays the number of "hits"or times the conduit has been utilized). To remove a conduit, use the **no conduit** command.

NOTE   If you want internal users to be able to ping external hosts, you must create an ICMP conduit to permit the echo-reply.

Additional Methods of Access Through the PIX

The most common method of access through the PIX from the inside to the outside is by using the **global** and **nat** pair. This is referred to as *Network Address Translation* (NAT). This allows a range of addresses on the inside (defined with the **nat** command) to be translated to a range of addresses (defined with the **global** command) when accessing devices on the outside. It is also possible to translate a range of inside addresses to a single global address. This is referred to as *Port Address Translation* (PAT).

PAT is a combination of an IP address and a source port number that creates a unique session. The PIX translates each local address to the same global address but assigns a unique source port greater than 1024. Figure 6-3 illustrates an example of PAT.

Figure 6-3   *Port Address Translation*

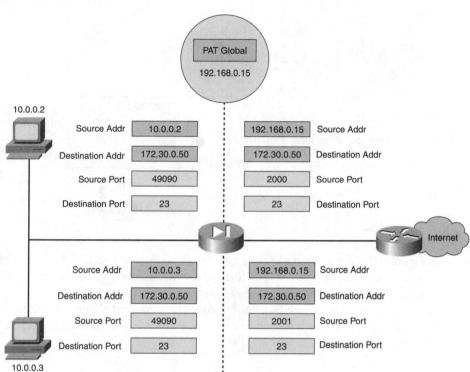

This example addresses the two clients, 10.0.0.2 and 10.0.0.3 (and any other local addresses) requesting connectivity to the Internet and is translated to the global address, 192.168.0.15. The PIX also translates the source port to a unique number greater than 1024. The source port is translated so that when the response comes back to the PIX from the host on the Internet, the PIX can then translate to the appropriate local address.

Configuring PAT

Configuring PAT is identical to configuring NAT with one exception—use a single IP address in the **global** statement instead of a range. Figure 6-4 shows a sample configuration of PAT. All local hosts on the 10.0.0.0 network will be translated to the global address of 192.168.0.15. All source ports will be changed to a unique port number greater than 1024. Example 6-3 shows a partial sample configuration of PAT for the network in Figure 6-4.

Example 6-3   *PAT Configuration for the Network in Figure 6-4*

```
pixfirewall(config)# ip address (inside) 10.0.0.1 255.255.255.0
pixfirewall(config)# ip address (outside) 192.168.0.2 255.255.255.0
pixfirewall(config)# route (outside) 0.0.0.0 0.0.0.0 192.168.0.1
pixfirewall(config)# global (outside) 1 192.168.0.15 netmask 255.255.255.0
pixfirewall(config)# nat (inside) 1 10.0.0.0 255.0.0.0
```

Figure 6-4   *Configuring Port Address Translation*

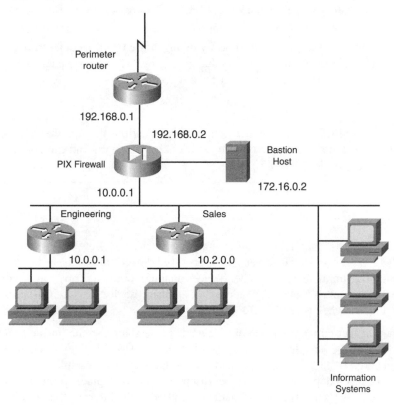

PAT provides the following additional features and advantages:

- **PAT and NAT can be used together**—There may be a situation where the local
  addresses to be translated outnumbers the global addresses. In that circumstance, PAT
  and NAT can be used together. With the following configuration, each local IP address
  will use NAT and be translated using the range of addresses 192.168.0.1 through
  192.168.0.9 until the global address range is completely used. The PIX would at that
  point start using PAT and translate any additional local addresses coming through it
  to 192.168.0.10.

  ```
  pixfirewall# global (outside) 1 192.168.0.1-192.168.0.9 netmask
    255.255.255.0
  pixfirewall# global (outside) 1 192.168.0.10 netmask 255.255.255.0
  pixfirewall# nat (inside) 1 0.0.0.0 0.0.0.0
  ```

- **One global IP address may be used for up to 64,000 inside hosts**—This is a
  limitation of the size of the port field. It is a 16-bit field, which creates 65,536 ports.
  The first 1023 are reserved, allowing for more than 64,000 possible translated local
  hosts. Bandwidth and other considerations will make a more realistic limit much less.

- **Maps port numbers to single IP address**—Using a single global address for all internal hosts will mean leasing fewer IP addresses from a service provider. This will lower network costs considerably.

- **Hides inside source address by using single IP address from the PIX Firewall**—Hiding the internal addresses due to NAT or PAT is a very secure act when connecting to the Internet—or any untrusted environment.

NOTE   Do not use PAT when running multimedia applications through the PIX Firewall. Multimedia applications may need to access specific ports and can conflict with port mappings provided by PAT.

Configuring nat 0

It is a common function of connecting to the Internet to allow access from the outside to an HTTP server or SMTP server. Those accessed devices must have registered addresses in order to communicate with other devices on the Internet. It is possible to configure the PIX so that the actual assigned IP address of an inside device is what is used as the destination IP address when accessing from the outside.

The **nat 0** command lets you disable address translation so that inside IP addresses are visible on the outside without address translation. Use this feature when InterNIC-registered IP addresses on the inside network are to be accessible on the outside network. Use of **nat 0** depends upon the security policy that is in place. If the policy allows for internal clients to have their IP address exposed to the Internet, then **nat 0** is the process to provide that service. The use of **nat 0** alone does not permit access from the outside to the inside. If the policy also allows access from outside to inside, then the **conduit** command should be used.

In Figure 6-5, the IP address 192.168.1.9 is not translated. The HTTP server on the DMZ has been assigned the IP address 192.168.1.9. With the **nat (DMZ) 0** command the PIX will not translate the IP address of the HTTP server. With the **conduit** command, the PIX will allow any port 80 request to 192.168.1.9 to be permitted.

Example 6-4 shows the configuration of the **conduit** and **nat** statements for Figure 6-5.

Example 6-4   *Disabling Address Translation so That Inside IP Addresses Are Visible on the Outside Without Address Translation for the Network in Figure 6-5*

```
pixfirewall(config)#conduit permit tcp host 192.168.1.9 eq www any
pixfirewall(config)#nat (DMZ) 0 192.168.1.9 255.255.255.255
```

In this example, the **nat 0** command ensures that 192.16.1.9 is not translated. All security aspects of PIX remain in place. It is the **conduit** command that will then permit WWW access to 192.168.1.9. Given the configuration of the network in Example 6-4, Example 6-5 shows the output of the **show nat** command.

Example 6-5   show **nat** *Command Output*

```
pixfirewall(config)#show nat
pixfirewall(config)#nat 0 192.168.1.9 will be non-translated
```

Figure 6-5   **nat 0** *Configuration*

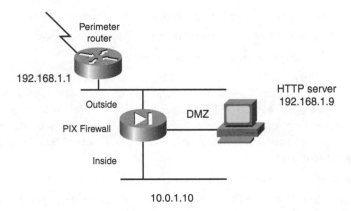

Configuring the FIXUP Protocol

The **fixup** command allows a user to view, change, enable, or disable the use of a service or protocol throughout the PIX Firewall. The ports that are specified by the **fixup** command are the services that the PIX Firewall listens for. You can change the port value for each service except RSH.

Some applications such as FTP require that the PIX Firewall understand special properties of the application so that connections that are legitimately part of the application are permitted. During an FTP transfer from inside to outside, the PIX Firewall needs to be aware of the second data channel that is opened from the server to the initiating workstation. The PIX identifies applications by the TCP or UDP port number contained in the IP packets (as defined in RFC 1700). For example, it recognizes FTP by port number 21, SMTP by port number 25, and HTTP by port number 80.

To enable the **fixup** command, enter the following:

```
pixfirewall(config)# fixup protocol ftp [port]
pixfirewall(config)# fixup protocol http [port[-port]]
pixfirewall(config)# fixup protocol h323 [port[-port]]
pixfirewall(config)# fixup protocol rsh [514]
pixfirewall(config)# fixup protocol smtp [port[-port]]
pixfirewall(config)# fixup protocol sqlnet [port[-port]]
```

To prevent web browsers from sending embedded commands in FTP requests, the optional parameter **strict** may be used. The **strict** parameter is added, as follows, with the **fixup protocol ftp** command:

```
pixfirewall(config)# fixup protocol ftp [strict] [port]
```

The use of **strict** with FTP will require each FTP command to be acknowledged before a new command is allowed. Connections sending embedded commands are dropped.

To remove the fixup protocol, use the following:

```
pixfirewall(config)# no fixup protocol protocol [port[-port]]
```

To display what has been configured with the fixup protocol, use the following:

```
pixfirewall(config)# show fixup [protocol protocol]
```

For the most part, there is no reason to change these port numbers, but in special circumstances you may have a service listening on a non-standard port number. For example, you could have an HTTP server listening on port 5000. The PIX Firewall would not recognize that port 5000 is being used for HTTP and will block the returned HTTP data connection from the server. This problem could be resolved by adding port 5000 to the **fixup protocol** command:

```
pixfirewall (config)# fixup protocol http 5000
```

This command allows the PIX to recognize that connections to port 5000 should be treated in the same manner as connections to port 80.

The PIX Firewall security features are based on checking and changing, or "fixing up" information in packets sent over a network. Different network protocols, such as SMTP for mail transfer, include protocol-specific information in the packets. Protocol fixup for SMTP packets includes changing addresses embedded in the payload of packets, checking for supported commands, replacing bad characters, and so on.

By default, the PIX Firewall is configured to fix up the following protocols: FTP, SMTP, HTTP, RSH, SQL*NET, and H.323.

The **fixup** commands are always present in the configuration and are enabled by default. You can add multiple commands for each protocol. You can specify multiple ports for one protocol. For example, for SQL*NET you can specify ports 1521 and 1523 and get SQL*NET to work with NAT on both of these ports as demonstrated in Example 6-6:

Example 6-6   *Specifying Multiple Ports for One Protocol*

```
Pixfirewall (config)# fixup protocol sqlnet 1521
Pixfirewall (config)# fixup protocol sqlnet 1523
```

Multimedia Support

Multimedia applications can be troublesome to a firewall because multimedia protocols dynamically open various ports for connection.

The PIX Firewall offers the following advantages with multimedia applications:

- Dynamically opens and closes UDP ports for secure multimedia connections. Other firewalls may require configurations that open a large range of UDP ports, creating security risks, or they may have to configure one port for inbound multimedia data requiring client reconfiguration.

- Supports multimedia with or without NAT. Some firewalls cannot simultaneously support NAT and multimedia, which limits multimedia usage to registered users, and requires exposure of inside addresses to the Internet.

The currently supported multimedia applications are as follows:

- Intel Internet Video Phone
- Microsoft NetMeeting (based on H.323 standards)
- White Pine Meeting Point
- Microsoft NetShow
- White Pines CuSeeMe
- VDOnet VDOLive
- RealNetworks RealAudio and RealVideo
- VXtreme WebTheatre
- Xing StreamWorks
- VocalTech Internet Phone

Configuring Multiple Interfaces

As a device providing security for a network, a firewall with two interfaces is often sufficient. In such a scenario, the firewall is acting simply as a secure gateway for traffic in and out of the network. Frequently, however, having only two interfaces is not enough.

The PIX Firewall model 535 now supports up to eight additional perimeter interfaces (for a total of 10) for platform extensibility and security policy enforcement on publicly accessible services. The multiple perimeter interfaces enable the PIX Firewall to protect publicly accessible web, e-mail, and DNS servers in a demilitarized zone (DMZ). Web-based and traditional Electronic Data Interchange (EDI) applications that link vendors and customers are also more secure and scalable when implemented on a physically separate network.

Once a user has configured two interfaces, configuring additional interfaces on a PIX is a relatively simple matter. It is a matter of adding the **nameif, interface,** and **ip address** commands for the additional interface(s). Example 6-7 shows a partial configuration for the PIX with four interfaces illustrated in Figure 6-6.

Example 6-7   *Configuring Multiple Interfaces on the PIX Firewall*

```
pixfirewall(config)# nameif ethernet0 outside sec0
pixfirewall(config)# nameif ethernet1 inside sec100
pixfirewall(config)# nameif ethernet2 dmz sec50
pixfirewall(config)# nameif ethernet3 partnernet sec20
pixfirewall(config)# interface ethernet0 auto
pixfirewall(config)# interface ethernet1 auto
pixfirewall(config)# interface ethernet2 auto
pixfirewall(config)# interface ethernet3 auto
pixfirewall(config)# ip address outside 192.168.0.2 255.255.255.0
pixfirewall(config)# ip address inside 10.0.0.1 255.255.255.0
pixfirewall(config)# ip address dmz 172.16.0.1 255.255.255.0
pixfirewall(config)# ip address partnernet 172.26.26.1 255.255.255.0
pixfirewall(config)# nat (inside) 1 10.0.0.0 255.255.255.0
pixfirewall(config)# global (outside) 1 192.168.0.15-192.168.0.254 netmask
   255.255.255.0
pixfirewall(config)# global (dmz) 1 172.16.0.10-172.16.0.254  netmask 255.255.255.0
pixfirewall(config)# static (dmz,outside) 192.168.0.11 172.16.0.2
pixfirewall(config)# conduit permit tcp host 192.168.0.11 eq http any
```

Figure 6-6   *Configuring Four Interfaces*

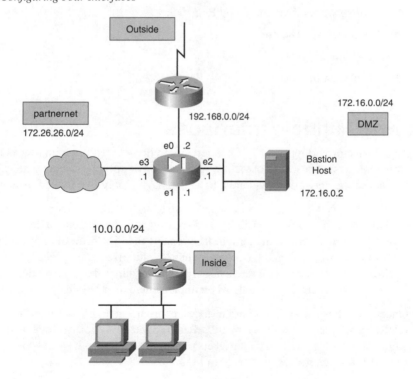

There is an inside (10.0.0.1/24), outside (192.168.0.2/24), DMZ (172.16.0.1/24), and partnernet (172.26.26.1/24) configured on the PIX. With the given configuration, users on the inside are permitted access to the outside and the DMZ. Users on the outside are permitted HTTP access to the bastion host 172.16.0.2, which is connected to the DMZ. Users on the outside use the destination IP address of 192.168.0.11 due to the **static** translation on the PIX.

When your PIX Firewall is equipped with three or more interfaces, use the following guidelines to configure it while employing NAT:

- Beginning with PIX OS version 5.2X, the outside interface can be renamed, but the default is **outside**. This interface cannot be given a different security level.

- An interface is always "outside" with respect to another interface, if it has a lower security level. Packets cannot flow between interfaces that have the same security level without the appropriate **static** and **conduit** or **access-list** commands.

- Use a single default route statement to the outside interface only. Set the default route with the **route** command.

- Use the **nat** command to let users on the respective interfaces start outbound connections. Associate the *nat_id* with the *global_id* in the **global** command statement. The valid ID numbers can be any positive number up to more than two billion.

- After you have completed a configuration in which you add, change, or remove a **global** statement, save the configuration, and enter the **clear xlate** command so that the IP addresses will be updated (when a new connection is made) in the translation table.

- One way to permit access to servers on protected networks is to use the **static** and **conduit** commands.

Table 6-4 is a quick reference guide for Figure 6-6, that explains when to use the **nat** and **static** commands for configuring various interfaces in the PIX Firewall.

Table 6-4   *Guide to Configuring Interfaces on the PIX Firewall*

From This Interface	To This Interface	Use Command
Inside	Outside	**nat/global**
Inside	DMZ	**nat/global**
Inside	Partnernet	**nat/global**
DMZ	Outside	**nat/global**
DMZ	Partnernet	**nat/global**
DMZ	Inside	**static/conduit**
Partnernet	Outside	**nat/global**

continues

Table 6-4 *Guide to Configuring Interfaces on the PIX Firewall (Continued)*

From This Interface	To This Interface	Use Command
Partnernet	DMZ	**static/conduit**
Partnernet	Inside	**static/conduit**
Outside	DMZ	**static/conduit**
Outside	Partnernet	**static/conduit**
Outside	Inside	**static/conduit**

Use of the name Command

The **name** command enables the PIX to resolve locally a list of name-to-IP mappings. This allows the use of names in the configuration instead of the IP address. The **names** command enables use of the **name** command. In other words, turn on the ability to use the **name** command with the **names** command. You can specify a name by using the following syntax (it may be necessary to issue **names** first):

```
names
name ip_address name
```

Table 6-5 describes the parameters for this command.

Table 6-5 **name** *Command Description*

name Command Parameter	Description
ip_address	The IP address of the host being named.
name	The name assigned to the IP address. Allowable characters are **a** to **z**, **A** to **Z**, **0** to **9**, a dash, and an underscore. The *name* cannot start with a number. If the name is over 16 characters long, the **name** command fails.
	The name is case-sensitive and must consist of alphanumeric characters. Use of an underscore is also supported, but the name cannot exceed 16 characters.

After a name is defined, it can be used in any PIX Firewall command references instead of an IP address. The names in the PIX Firewall configuration can be cleared by entering the command **no names**.

Review Questions

To test what you have learned in this chapter, answer the following questions and then refer to Appendix F for the answers.

1 What is required to allow an HTTP server on the DMZ to retain its assigned IP address when being accessed from the Internet?

2 What command is used to create a permanent mapping between a local IP address and a global IP address?

3 What is the maximum number of interfaces supported by the PIX Firewall model 515?

4 What does the **fixup** command do?

5 What are the two ways through the PIX that were discussed in this chapter?

6 It is good practice to issue what command after making a change to the range of addresses specified in the **global** command?

7 True or False. The **nat 0** command will permit access from the outside to the DMZ.

This chapter introduces you to the skills required to configure the PIX Firewall to send syslog messages to a syslog server.

- Configure the PIX to Generate Syslog Messages
- Upgrade Memory
- Install Interface Cards
- Perform Password Recovery
- New Syslog Messages by Version

CHAPTER 7

Syslog

Syslog Messages

The PIX Firewall generates syslog messages for system events, such as alerts and resource depletion. Syslog messages received by a syslog server may be used to create e-mail alerts and log files or displayed on the console of a designated syslog host. Higher-end syslog servers, such as Private-I from Open Systems, intelligently parse incoming messages and store them in a back-end SQL database. Private-I has powerful query tools to analyze current and historical data.

The PIX Firewall can send syslog messages to any syslog server. In the event that all syslog servers or hosts are offline, the PIX Firewall stores up to 100 messages in its memory. Subsequent messages that arrive overwrite the buffer starting from the first line. This feature is only available when the PIX is using TCP as the transport for syslog.

The PIX Firewall sends syslog messages to document the following events:

- **Security**—Dropped UDP packets and denied TCP connections
- **Resources**—Notification of connection and translation slot depletion
- **System**—Console and Telnet logins and logouts, and when the PIX Firewall reboots
- **Accounting**—Bytes transferred per connection

The sections that follow examine the syslog configuration commands and determine what effect they have on the behavior of how the PIX handles syslog messages.

Syslog Configuration

By default, all logging functions on the PIX are disabled. To enable logging, use the **logging on** command.

One of the most important concepts to grasp before you configure logging on the PIX is the *logging level* applied to the various logging commands. The logging level determines what level of detail you want reflected in your logs. This is a very important consideration, as syslog can generate tremendous amounts of data in busy networks. I had a student from a major federal financial institution who (at debug level) logged over 16 GB every day! You will need to monitor the size of the syslog file on your log server to ensure the log file doesn't consume too much disk space. Table 7-1 documents the logging levels.

Table 7-1   *Logging Levels*

Logging Level	Logging Level Description	System Condition
0	Emergencies	System unusable messages
1	Alerts	Take immediate action
2	Critical	Critical condition
3	Errors	Error message
4	Warnings	Warning message
5	Notifications	Normal but significant condition
6	Informational	Information message
7	Debugging	Debug messages and log FTP commands and WWW URLs

When a logging level number is set, any higher-level logging messages are suppressed. This is to say that if you set the logging level to 4, you will not see any syslog messages from levels 5, 6, or 7. When setting the logging level, you can use either the number or the name in the command, but the PIX translates the number to the name in the configuration.

The **logging** command is used to manage and configure all aspects of syslog on the PIX.

Table 7-2 illustrates the syntax of the various combinations of the **logging** command.

Table 7-2   *Logging Parameters*

Command Parameter	Explanation
on	Start sending syslog messages to all output locations. Stop all logging with the **no logging on** command.
buffered	Send syslog messages to an internal buffer that can be viewed with the **show logging** command. Use the **clear logging** command to clear the message buffer. New messages append to the end of the buffer.

Table 7-2   *Logging Parameters (Continued)*

Command Parameter	Explanation
level	Specify the syslog message level as a number or string. The *level* you specify means that you want that *level* and those less than the *level*. For example, if *level* is **3**, syslog displays **0**, **1**, **2**, and **3** messages. Possible number and string *level* values are **0** — **emergencies** — System unusable messages **1** — **alerts** — Take immediate action **2** — **critical** — Critical condition **3** — **errors** — Error message **4** — **warnings** — Warning message **5** — **notifications** — Normal but significant condition **6** — **informational** — Information message **7** — **debugging** — Debug messages and log FTP commands and WWW URLs
console	Specify that syslog messages appear on the PIX Firewall console as each message occurs. You can limit the types of messages that appear on the console with *level*. Cisco recommends that you do not use this command in production mode because its use degrades PIX Firewall performance.
facility	Specify the syslog facility. The default is 20.
facility	Eight facilities, LOCAL0(16) through LOCAL7(23); the default is LOCAL4(20). Hosts file the messages based on the *facility* number in the message.
history	Set the SNMP message level for sending syslog traps.
host	Specify a syslog server that will receive the messages sent from the PIX Firewall. You can use multiple **logging host** commands to specify additional servers that would all receive the syslog messages. However, a server can be specified to only receive either UDP or TCP, not both. PIX Firewall sends only TCP syslog messages to the PIX Firewall Syslog Server.
in_if_name	Interface on which the syslog server resides.
ip_address	Syslog server's IP address.
protocol	The protocol over which the syslog message is sent: either **tcp** or **udp**. PIX Firewall sends only TCP syslog messages to the PIX Firewall Syslog Server. You can view the port and protocol values you previously entered only by using the **write terminal** command and finding the command in the listing—the TCP protocol is listed as 6 and the UDP protocol is listed as 17.

continues

Table 7-2   *Logging Parameters (Continued)*

Command Parameter	Explanation
port	The port from which the PIX Firewall sends either UDP or TCP syslog messages. This must be the same port at which the syslog server listens. For the UDP port, the default is 514 and the allowable range for changing the value is 1025 through 65535. For the TCP port, the default is 1470, and the allowable range is 1025 through 65535. TCP ports work only with the PIX Firewall Syslog Server.
message	Specify a message to be allowed. Use the **no logging message** command to suppress a syslog message. Use the **clear logging disabled** command to reset the disallowed messages to the original set. Use the **show message disabled** command to list the suppressed messages. All syslog messages are permitted unless explicitly disallowed. The "PIX Startup begin" message cannot be blocked and neither can more than one message per command statement.
syslog_id	Specify a message number to disallow or allow. If a message is listed in syslog as %PIX-1-101001, use "101001" as the *syslog_id*. Refer to the *System Log Messages for the Cisco Secure PIX Firewall Version 6.0* guide for message numbers. You can view this document online at the following site: http://www.cisco.com/univercd/cc/td/doc/product/iaabu/pix/pix_v53/syslog/index.htm
disabled	Clear or display suppressed messages. You can suppress messages with the **no logging message** command.
monitor	Specify that syslog messages appear on Telnet sessions to the PIX Firewall console.
queue *queue_size*	Specify the size of the queue for storing syslog messages. Use this parameter before the syslog messages are processed. The queue parameter defaults to 512 messages, 0 (zero) indicates unlimited, and the minimum is one message. Use the **show logging queue** command to determine the number of messages in the queue.
standby	Let the failover standby unit also send syslog messages. This option is disabled by default. You can enable it to ensure that the standby unit's syslog messages stay synchronized should failover occur. However, this option causes twice as much traffic on the syslog server. Disable with the **no logging standby** command.
timestamp	Specify that syslog messages sent to the syslog server should have a time stamp value on each message.
trap	Set logging level only for syslog messages.
clear	Clear the buffer for use with the **logging buffered** command.
show	List which logging options are enabled. If the **logging buffered** command is in use, the **show logging** command lists the current message buffer.

logging host Command

The **logging host** command has the following syntax:

```
logging host [if_name] ip_address [protocol/port]
```

This logging command specifies the IP address of the syslog server and optionally, the protocol and port. When *protocol/port* aren't specified, the PIX defaults to UDP port 514. If you use Cisco's PIX Firewall Syslog Server (PFSS), WinSyslog, Kiwi Syslog, or Private-I, you can choose to use TCP for reliable transport of syslog messages.

NOTE   Please refer to Appendix E, "Security Resources," for the web sites of third-party syslog servers.

When set to use TCP transport, the PIX generates syslog messages on TCP port 1468. While this assures every message is received by the syslog server, there is increased transfer overhead. PFSS is available on CCO to users with PIXs under warranty or users who hold a valid SmartNet contract at

www.cisco.com/cgi-bin/tablebuild.pl/pix

NOTE   Multiple **logging host** commands are allowed for the PIX Firewall to send syslog messages to multiple servers, but only one protocol, UDP or TCP, is permitted for a specific syslog server. A subsequent command statement overrides the previous one. It is also important to understand that logging to additional syslog servers increases the load on the PIX.

logging trap Command

The **logging trap** command is used to determine what level syslog messages are sent to the syslog server. The syntax for this command is

```
logging trap level
```

NOTE   The **logging trap** command only sets the level for syslog entries. To set the level of SNMP traps, use the **logging history** command. For additional information on the **logging history** command, see Appendix B, "Configuring Simple Network Management Protocol (SNMP) on the PIX Firewall."

logging buffered Command

Use the **logging buffered** command to send syslog messages to an internal memory buffer on the PIX that can be viewed with the **show logging** command. The syntax for the **logging buffered** command is as follows:

```
logging buffered level
```

Use the **clear logging** command to clear the message buffer. New messages append to the end of the buffer.

NOTE   The logging buffer is a circular buffer limited to a fixed, non-configurable size of 4 KB (4096 bytes). Once the buffer is full, the oldest messages are overwritten by the newest.

Use the **show logging** command (demonstrated later in Example 7-1) to list the current message buffer.

Use the **clear logging** command to clear the message buffer. New messages append to the end of the buffer.

logging console Command

Use the **logging console** command to force the PIX to display syslog messages to the console port. Use **no logging console** to turn off console logging. The syntax for both forms of this command is as follows:

```
logging console level
no logging console
```

The number and type of syslog messages sent to the console will depend on the *level* set in the **logging console** command. Refer to *System Log Messages for the Cisco Secure PIX Firewall* documentation appropriate for the version of the PIX OS running on your PIX.

NOTE   Cisco recommends that you do not use this command in production because its use degrades PIX Firewall performance.

---

logging facility Command

The **logging facility** command has the following syntax:

```
logging facility facility
```

This command sets the *facility* number of syslog messages sent to the syslog server. There are eight facilities, LOCAL0(16) through LOCAL7(23); the default is LOCAL4(20). Older syslog hosts (primarily UNIX syslog) could only file incoming messages based on the facility number in the message. Most newer syslog implementations offer the flexibility to file messages based on the facility or the source IP address of the device. Because network devices share the eight facilities, filing messages by facility essentially limits you to monitoring eight devices per syslog server. In a network with numerous syslog sources, it's important that your syslog server be able to file incoming messages based on source IP address.

logging monitor Command

Use the **logging monitor** command to have the PIX send syslog messages to Telnet sessions on the PIX. The **no logging monitor** command stops the PIX from sending syslog messages to Telnet sessions. Both forms of the command are expressed as follows:

```
logging monitor level
no logging monitor
```

NOTE   Use of **logging monitor** in busy production networks can result in lost Telnet sessions.

logging standby Command

The **logging standby** command enables the failover standby unit to send syslog messages. The **standby** option (as with all logging options) is disabled by default. You can enable it to ensure that the standby unit's syslog messages stay synchronized should failover occur. However, this option causes twice as much traffic on the syslog server. Disable with the **no logging standby** command.

logging timestamps Command

The **logging timestamps** command forces the PIX to timestamp every syslog message using its internal clock. Be certain the time is correctly set on the PIX with the **show clock** command.

It is considered best practice to set the clock of the PIX to UTC (also known as Greenwich Mean Time) for consistency of log times across multiple time zones. If you ever need to use your syslog entries as evidence in a legal action, it is expected that all timestamps be in UTC.

NOTE   The PIX doesn't know to automatically account for Daylight Savings Time, so you will need to manually reset the time every six months. Network Time Protocol (NTP) would eliminate the need for manual time corrections, but the PIX doesn't currently support NTP. NTP is a means to have a network device synchronize its clock to a trusted time source. PIX support for NTP is rumored to be available in an upcoming release of the PIX OS.

NOTE	The **clock** and **logging timestamps** commands first appeared in PIX OS version 4.3. Before PIX OS 4.3, there was no way for the PIX to generate timestamps on syslog messages.

(no) logging message Command

The syntax for the **logging message** command and the **no** form (which is the one of interest here) is as follows:

```
logging message syslog_id
no logging message syslog_id
```

Use the **no logging message** command to specify syslog messages to be suppressed. All syslog messages are permitted unless explicitly disallowed. The "PIX Startup begin" message cannot be blocked and neither can more than one message per command statement. Specify a message number to disallow or allow. If a message is listed in syslog as %PIX-1-101001, use **no logging message 101001** to suppress the *syslog_id*. Suppressed syslog messages are added to the PIX configuration file. To view suppressed syslog messages in the running config, use the **write terminal** command. To view suppressed syslog messages in the startup config, use the **show config** command. Refer to *the System Log Messages for the Cisco Secure PIX Firewall guide* for message numbers. PIX Firewall documentation is available online at

www.cisco.com/univercd/cc/td/doc/product/iaabu/pix/pix_v53/index.htm

TIP	After perusing your syslog files, you will probably come to the conclusion that not all of the messages generated by the PIX are useful to your organization. Use the **no logging message** command to keep unnecessary entries from being logged.

show logging Command

The **show logging** command lists which logging options are enabled. If the **logging buffered** command is in use, the **show logging** command lists the current message buffer. Example 7-1 shows the output of the **show logging** command.

Example 7-1   show logging *Command Output*

```
pixfirewall(config)# show logging
Syslog logging: enabled
    Timestamp logging: disabled
    Standby logging: disabled
    Console logging: disabled
    Monitor logging: disabled
    Buffer logging: disabled
    Trap logging: level debugging, facility 20, 46498 messages logged
        Logging to inside 192.168.111.3
    History logging: level debugging, facility 20, 46498 messages logged
```

clear logging Command

The **clear logging** command clears the buffer used by the **logging buffered** command. Because PIX logs only 100 messages to the log buffer, it isn't usually necessary to clear the buffer. After the buffer is full, the oldest messages in the buffer are overwritten by the newest messages. In a production environment, there may be several hundred messages a minute or more. This command is used to initialize the local log buffer.

Now that you're familiar with the various logging options, Example 7-2 shows the configuration entries of a PIX configured to send a timestamped syslog message to a syslog server on the Inside interface. Syslog message 111001 "Begin configuration: console writing to memory" will be suppressed.

Example 7-2   *PIX Syslog Configuration Logging Using TCP Transport to the Cisco PIX Firewall Syslog Server*

```
logging on
logging host inside 10.10.1.10 tcp/1470
logging trap informational
logging timestamp
no logging message 111001
```

New Syslog Messages by Version

With each new version of the PIX OS, Cisco is continually updating, adding to, and improving the features of the PIX Firewall. As these improvements are incorporated into the OS, new syslog messages are added to provide forensic data for those features. For a compilation of new syslog messages and in what version they first appear, refer to the release notes appropriate to the version of the PIX OS in which you are interested. The PIX documentation for all available versions can be found at

www.cisco.com/univercd/cc/td/doc/product/iaabu/pix/index.htm

Review Questions

To test what you have learned in this chapter, answer the following questions and then refer to Appendix F for the answers.

1   What kind of system events does the PIX Firewall syslog generate messages for?

2   What protocol does the syslog use to send these messages?

3   What command is used to start generating syslog messages?

4   How many different levels of syslog messages are there? Can you name three?

5   What command is used to cause the PIX to send syslog messages to the console screen?

This chapter covers the following topics:

- AAA Defined
- Cut-Through Proxy
- Supported AAA Servers
- Installation of CSACS for Windows NT
- Authentication
- Authorization
- Accounting
- Troubleshooting the AAA Configuration

CHAPTER 8

AAA Configuration on the Cisco PIX Firewall

Most security policy implementations are designed around a layered approach. In other words, it is not just one security measure that makes for a successful security policy. A multifaceted approach, which is a more comprehensive approach, is one that uses many methods of security. One aspect of a security policy might be the requirement of a user to input a user ID and password for access to specific, if not all, services. This is called *user-based authentication*. Authentication may have nothing to do with a specific user at all, but rather with authenticating one network device to another. Authentication may be proving that a network entity (device, client, server) other than a user is indeed the entity it claims to be.

AAA Defined

Authentication determines a user's identity and verifies the information. Traditional authentication uses a name (or some unique identifier) and a fixed password. Accessing a device or network with a user ID defines who the user is. Once a user has authenticated, the authentication server may be configured to allow specific *authorization*, based upon the user ID and password. Authorization defines what the user can do. When a user has logged in and is accessing a service, host, or network, a record of what that user is doing may be kept. *Accounting* is the action of keeping track of what the user does. Having an accounting record of what is being accessed in a network can be very helpful. If problems arise in the network, having historical records can help to identify and eventually rectify those problems. Accounting records can also be used for billing, forensics, and planning.

Authentication, Authorization, and Accounting (AAA) is used by the PIX Firewall to identify who the user is, what the user can do, and what the user did. The basic access controls for the PIX itself are based on IP addresses and ports. These access controls do not provide a mechanism to identify individual users and then control traffic flow based upon that user. Authentication is valid without authorization. Authorization is never valid without authentication.

AAA, when used with the PIX, is generally processed in the following manner:

1   The client requests access to some service. The PIX, as a gateway between the client and the device the service is on, (based on the request and the configuration on the PIX) requires the client to forward a user ID and password.

2 The PIX receives that information and forwards it to an AAA server where it is confirmed to be permitted or it is denied. A server is defined as a logical entity that provides any of the three AAA functions. The AAA server can hold the user ID/password database for confirmation that a client can access the requested service.

Having a separate AAA server (those processes reside on a different device) will reduce the (CPU) load on the firewall, simplify configuration and management of the firewall, and increase scalability.

It is possible to allow only certain authenticated users access to a network. An example may be to allow only those with a valid user ID and password to access from the inside network, through the PIX Firewall, out to the Internet. It is also possible to restrict the authorization (the applications accessed) of those authenticated users. By configuring the PIX and the AAA server, an administrator can restrict the services accessed to be FTP, HTTP, Telnet, or any other application (or any combination of applications). An AAA server is an authentication server that can be configured with Cisco Secure Access Control Server (CSACS) software that authenticates and authorizes users by controlling access. The AAA server can also track accounting records.

Another scenario may be to allow a user to access only the FTP service through the PIX. The request is made by the end user, and the PIX intercepts the request and requires a username and password. When the information is input by the user, it is passed by the PIX to the AAA server. Once the user is authenticated by the AAA server, the user may make additional requests. Each request is received by the PIX and (transparent to the end user) passed to the AAA server for authorization.

A user can authenticate with the PIX Firewall using one of three services: FTP, Telnet, or HTTP. Each of these have inline authentication mechanisms within the service itself. This does not limit the applications the PIX can then permit. What a user will see depends upon what service is being accessed. Figure 8-1 illustrates what a user must input depending upon the service being accessed.

- **Telnet**—A prompt is generated by the PIX Firewall. Each user has up to four chances to log in. If the username or password fail after the fourth attempt, the PIX Firewall drops the connection. If authentication and authorization are successful, the user is prompted for a username and password if required by the destination server.

- **FTP**—A prompt is generated from the FTP program. If an incorrect password is entered, the connection is dropped immediately. If the username or password on the authentication database differs from the username or password on the remote host which is being accessed via FTP, enter the username and password in the following format (which is shown in Figure 8-1):

    — aaa_username@remote_username
    — aaa_password@remote_password

Figure 8-1   *What the User Must Input*

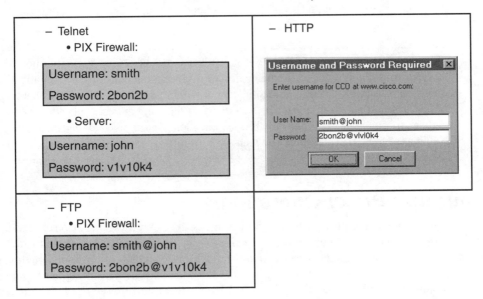

The PIX Firewall sends the aaa_username and aaa_password to the AAA server, and if authentication and authorization are successful, the remote_username and remote_password are passed to the destination FTP server.

- **HTTP**—The browser generates a username and password pop-up window. If an incorrect password is entered, the user is prompted again. An account may be disabled after some number (it is configurable) of failed attempts.

    If the username or password on the authentication database differs from the username or password on the remote host which is being accessed via HTTP, enter the username and password in the following format (which is shown in Figure 8-1):

    — aaa_username@remote_username

    — aaa_password@remote_password

    The PIX Firewall sends the aaa_username and aaa_password to the AAA server, and if authentication and authorization are successful, the remote_username and remote_password are passed to the destination HTTP server.

The PIX Firewall supports authentication (AAA) usernames up to 127 characters and passwords of up to 63 characters. Because of the special handling of logging in with FTP or HTTP while using AAA also, as described previously in this chapter, a password or username may not contain an "at" (@) character as part of the password or username string.

NOTE   Once authenticated with HTTP, a user never has to reauthenticate no matter how low the PIX Firewall configuration parameter **timeout uauth** (timeout of user authentication, a timer that can force a user to authenticate that will be discussed later in the chapter) is set. This is because the browser caches the authorization string in every subsequent connection to that particular site. This can only be cleared when the user exits all instances of Netscape Navigator or Internet Explorer and restarts. Flushing the cache is of no use.

Cut-Through Proxy Operation

Configuring authentication and authorization on the PIX Firewall is also referred to as setting up a process known as *cut-though proxy*. The PIX Firewall gains dramatic performance advantages because of cut-through proxy, which is a patented method of transparently verifying the identity of users at the firewall and permitting or denying access to any TCP- or UDP-based application. This method eliminates any negative impact that UNIX (and other operating) system-based firewalls impose in similar configurations, and can leverage the authentication and authorization services of the CSACS. One impact may be the expense incurred by the required purchase of the server hardware, the operating system, and the firewall application itself. Another impact is the overhead involved (once installed) with the operating system on the server where the firewall software resides.

The PIX Firewall cut-through proxy operates by determining that a session requires user-based authentication, providing an appropriate username/password challenge, and authenticating the user against a standard TACACS+ or RADIUS database. After the policy is checked, the PIX Firewall shifts the session flow and all traffic flows directly and quickly between the server and the client while maintaining session state information.

A typical design for using this technology is a user on the Internet accessing an HTTP server on a company DMZ. Shown in Figure 8-2, the user on the Internet enters the appropriate URL to get to the XYZ web server. The AAA requirement on the PIX forces the user to input a username and password. The user inputs the information, which is passed to the PIX in clear text, and the PIX forwards the information to the AAA server, in this case running CSACS software. If authenticated, the user is permitted to interact with the destination. If the destination web server also requires authentication, as in Figure 8-2, the remote username and password are passed on.

Figure 8-2   *Cut-Through Proxy Operation*

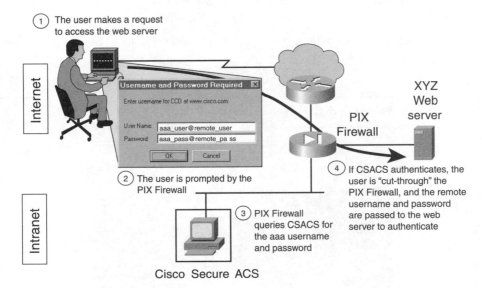

Supported AAA Servers

The PIX Firewall supports the following AAA protocols and servers:

- Terminal Access Controller Access Control System Plus (TACACS+)
    - Cisco Secure Access Control Server (CSACS) for Windows NT (CSACS-NT)
    - Cisco Secure ACS for UNIX (CSACS-UNIX)
    - TACACS+ Freeware
- Remote Authentication Dial-In User Service (RADIUS)
    - Cisco Secure ACS for Windows NT (CSACS-NT)
    - Cisco Secure ACS for UNIX (CSACS-UNIX)
    - Livingston (now a part of Lucent Technologies)
    - Interlink Network's Merit
    - Funk Software's Steel Belted Radius

Installation of CSACS for Windows NT

CSACS is an application that provides AAA services. CSACS provides centralized control for AAA from a web-based graphical interface. With ACS the administrator can manage and administer user access through the PIX Firewall.

To install CSACS for Windows NT, perform the following steps, beginning with the screen capture in Figure 8-3.

NOTE   Close all Windows programs before running Setup.

Figure 8-3   *Installation Wizard*

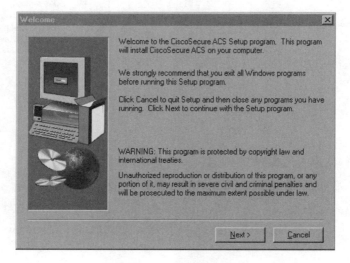

Step 1   Log into the NT Server as system administrator.

Step 2   Insert the CSACS CD-ROM into the CD-ROM drive. CSACS has an Autorun function; therefore, the installation window opens.

Step 3   Select **Install**. The Software License Agreement window opens.

Step 4   Read the Software License Agreement. Select **Accept** to agree to the licensing terms and conditions. The Welcome window opens.

Step 5   Select **Next**. The Before You Begin window opens.

Step 6   Verify that each condition is met, and then select the checkbox for each item. Select **Next**.

NOTE   If this is a new installation, skip to Step 9.

Step 7   *(Optional)* If CSACS is already installed, the Previous Installation window opens. The user is prompted to remove the previous version and save the existing database information. To keep the existing data, select **Yes, keep the existing database**, and select **Next**. To use a new database, deselect the checkbox and click **Next**. If keeping the existing database, Setup backs up the existing configuration and removes the old files. When the files are removed, select **OK**.

Step 8   If Setup finds an existing configuration, the user is given the option to import the configuration. To keep the existing configuration, select **Yes, import configuration**, and select **Next**. To use a new configuration, deselect the checkbox and select **Next**.

Step 9   The Choose Destination Location window opens. To install the software in the default directory, click **Next**. To use a different directory, click **Browse** and enter the directory to use. If the directory does not exist, the user is prompted to create one. Select **Yes**. The Authentication Database Configuration window opens.

Step 10   At this point, the user can select to authenticate against the CSACS database or against CSACS first and then check the Windows NT User Database. (Click **Explain** for more information on the listed items. If any condition is not met, select **Cancel** to exit Setup.)

To limit dial-in access to only those users specified in the Windows NT User Manager, select **Yes, reference Grant dialin permission to user** setting. Select **Next**. The Network Access Server Details window opens.

Step 11   Complete the following information within the Network Access Server Details window (see Figure 8-4):

— **Authenticate Users Using**—Type of security protocol to be used. TACACS+ (Cisco) is the default.

— **Access Server Name**—Name of the network access server (NAS) that will be using the CSACS services. When installing in conjunction with a PIX, the NAS name is the hostname of the PIX.

— **Access Server IP Address**—IP address of the NAS that will be using the CSACS services. When installing in conjunction with a PIX, the Access Server IP Address is the IP address of the PIX.

— **Windows NT Server IP Address**—IP address of this Windows NT server.

— **TACACS+ or RADIUS Key**—Shared secret of the NAS and Cisco Secure ACS. These passwords must be identical to ensure proper function and communication between the NAS and CSACS. Shared secrets are case-sensitive. Setup installs the CSACS files and updates the Registry. Select **Next**.

Figure 8-4 *NAS Detail Configuration*

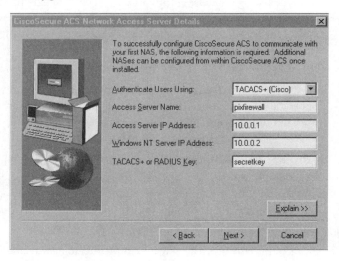

Step 12 The Advanced Options window opens. The Advanced Options options are disabled by default. Select the checkbox to enable any or all of the options listed. Select **Next**.

NOTE Configuration options for these items are displayed in the CSACS interface only if they are enabled. Any or all of these additional options may be disabled or enabled after installation, in the Interface Configuration: Advanced Options window.

Step 13 The Active Service Monitoring window opens. To enable the CSACS monitoring service, CSMon, select the **Enable Log-in Monitoring** checkbox, and then select a script to execute when the login process fails the test:

— **No Remedial Action**—Leave CSACS operating as is.

— **Reboot**—Reboot the system on which CSACS is running.

— **Restart All** (Default)—Restart all CSACS services.

— **Restart RADIUS/TACACS+**—Restart only RADIUS, TACACS+, or both protocols.

The option to develop and install scripts to be executed if there is a system failure is also available. See the online documentation for more information.

Step 14 To have CSACS generate an e-mail message when administrator events occur, check the **Enable Mail Notifications** checkbox, and then enter the following information:

— **SMTP Mail Server**—The name and domain of the sending mail server—for example, server1.company.com.

— **Mail account to notify**—The complete e-mail address of the intended recipient—for example, msmith@company.com.

Step 15 Select **Next**. The Cisco Secure ACS Service Initiation window opens. If not configuring a NAS from Setup, select **Next**. To configure a single NAS now, select **Yes, I want to configure Cisco IOS now**. Select **Next**.

Step 16 The Cisco Secure ACS Service Initiation window is next. The Administrator now has the option of starting the CSACS service, launching the CSACS administration browser, and reviewing the readme file.

Adding Users to CSACS-NT

The user database that is used by CSACS can reside within the application itself, or it can be an external database (such as the Windows NT user database). To add users to CSACS for NT, perform the following steps:

Step 1 In the navigation bar, select **User Setup**. The Select window opens. Figure 8-5 shows the User Setup window within CSACS.

Step 2 Enter a name in the **User** field.

> **NOTE** The username can contain up to 32 characters. Names cannot contain the following special characters: #?"*><. Leading and trailing spaces are not allowed.

Step 3 Click **Add/Edit**. The Edit window opens. The username being added or edited appears at the top of the window. Figure 8-5 shows the Edit window when adding a new user.

Figure 8-5 *How to Add Users to CSACS-NT*

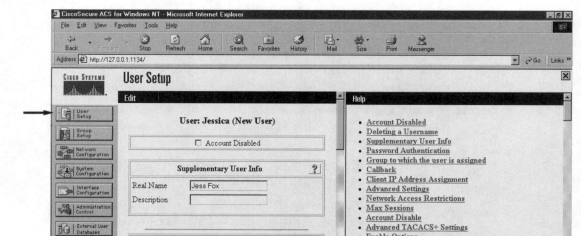

In the Edit window, the administrator may edit the following options:

- **Account Disable**—Select the **Account Disabled** checkbox to deny access for this user. Note that you must click **Submit** to have this action take effect.

- **Supplementary User Information** *(Optional)*—Enter the following information:

  — **Real Name**—If the username is not the user's real name, enter the real name here.

  — **Description**—Enter a detailed description of the user.

NOTE   This item can contain up to five user-configurable fields. The administrator may select **Interface Configuration** from the navigation bar. Select **User Data Configuration**. Put a check in **Field ID** numbers 3, 4, and 5. This will add three additional **User Fields** within the Edit window of the User Setup.

- **User Setup**—Edit or enter the following information for the user as applicable:
  - **Password Authentication**—Select the authentication type from the drop-down menu.
  - **Cisco Secure Database**—Authenticates a user from the local CSACS database.
  - **Windows NT**—Authenticates a user with an existing account in the Windows NT user database located on the same machine as the Cisco Secure server. There is also an entry in the CSACS database used for other CSACS services. This authentication type will appear in the user interface only if this external user database has been configured in External User Databases: Database Configuration.
- **Password and Confirm Password**—Enter and confirm the Password Authentication Protocol (PAP) password to be used.
- **Separate CHAP/MS-CHAP/ARAP**—This is not used with the PIX Firewall.

NOTE   The Password and Confirm Password fields are required for all authentication methods except for all third-party user databases.

- **Group to which the user is assigned**—From the drop-down menu, select the group to which to assign the user. The user inherits the attributes and operations assigned to the group. By default, users are assigned to the Default Group. Users who authenticate via the Unknown User method who are not found in an existing group are also assigned to the Default Group.
- **Callback**—This is not used with the PIX Firewall.
- **Client IP Address Assignment**—This is not used with the PIX Firewall.
- **Account Disable**—Define the circumstances under which this user's account will become disabled.

NOTE   The Account Disable field is not to be confused with account expiration due to Password Aging. Password Aging is defined for groups only, not for individual users.

- **Never**—Click to keep the user's account always enabled. This is the default.
- **Disable account if**—Click to disable the account under the circumstances specified in the following fields:
  - **Date exceeds**—From the drop-down menus, select the month, date, and year on which to disable the account. The default is 30 days after the user is added.

— **Failed attempts exceed**—Click the checkbox and enter the number of consecutive unsuccessful login attempts to allow before disabling the account. The default is five.

— **Failed attempts since last successful login**—This counter shows the number of unsuccessful login attempts since the last time this user logged in successfully.

— **Reset current failed attempts count on submit**—If an account is disabled because the failed attempts count has been exceeded, check this checkbox and click **Submit** to reset the failed attempts counter to 0 and reinstate the account.

NOTE   If using the Windows NT user database, this expiration information is in addition to the information in the Windows NT user account. Changes here do not alter settings configured in Windows NT.

Click **Submit** when all selections have been completed.

Configuring Authentication

Once the CSACS is configured, a corresponding entry for the AAA server must be entered into the PIX configuration. There are many different options an administrator can configure with regard to AAA and the PIX. First, an AAA group must be created and an authentication protocol must be specified. Next, the AAA server is created and assigned to be a part of the AAA group. Multiple AAA servers can be defined to be a part of the same AAA group. This allows for server access failure. If the first AAA server is not reachable (there is a configurable timer which is described later in the chapter), the request will be made to the next defined AAA server.

Use the **aaa-server** command to specify AAA server groups. With the PIX Firewall, an administrator may define separate groups of TACACS+ or RADIUS servers for specifying different types of traffic, such as one TACACS+ server for inbound traffic and a different TACACS+ server for outbound traffic. The AAA command references the group tag to direct authentication, authorization, or accounting traffic to the appropriate AAA server.

An administrator may have up to 16 tag groups and each group can have up to 16 AAA servers for a total of up to 256 TACACS+ or RADIUS servers. By specifying multiple AAA servers, an administrator can provide for a hot standby. When a user logs in, the servers are accessed one at a time, starting with the first server specified in the tag group, until a server responds.

The default configuration provides for two AAA server protocols. The following two configuration parameters will be in the configuration file by default:

* **aaa-server tacacs+ protocol tacacs+**
* **aaa-server radius protocol radius**

Older versions of the PIX OS did not require the creation of an AAA group. The benefit to having these two parameters as default parameters is that a default group is created. That means that when an older version is upgraded to a newer version (that requires the AAA group) the other AAA commands will not be discarded.

NOTE   The PIX Firewall uses ports 1645 and 1646 for RADIUS. If the RADIUS server uses ports 1812 and 1813, it will be necessary to reconfigure it to use ports 1645 and 1646.

The syntax for the **aaa-server** command is as follows:

```
aaa-server group_tag (if_name) host server_ip key timeout seconds
aaa-server group_tag protocol auth_protocol
```

Table 8-1 describes the syntax of the **aaa-server** command.

Table 8-1   **aaa-server** *Command Description*

aaa-server Command Parameter	Description
group_tag	An alphanumeric string which is the name of the server group. Use the *group_tag* in the **aaa** command to associate **aaa authentication** and **aaa accounting** command statements to an AAA server.
if_name	The interface name on which the server resides.
host *server_ip*	The IP address of the TACACS+ or RADIUS server.
key	A case-sensitive, alphanumeric keyword of up to 127 characters that is the same value as the key on the TACACS+ server. Any characters entered past 127 are ignored. The key is used between the client and server for encrypting data between them. The *key* must be the same on both the client and server systems. Spaces are not permitted in the key, but other special characters are. If the key is not specified, encryption does not occur.
timeout *seconds*	A retransmit timer that specifies the duration that the PIX Firewall retries access four times to the AAA server before choosing the next AAA server. The default is five seconds. The maximum time is 30 seconds. For example, if the timeout value is 10 seconds, the PIX Firewall retransmits for 10 seconds and if no acknowledgment is received, tries three times more for a total of 40 seconds to retransmit data before the next AAA server is selected.
protocol *auth_protocol*	The type of AAA server, either **tacacs+** or **radius**.

Example 8-1 demonstrates the **aaa-server** command. The first statement in the example creates the group and assigns the authentication protocol. The name of the group is

MYTACACS and the authentication protocol is TACACS+. The second statement in the example assigns the server to the group MYTACACS, assigns the interface the AAA server will communicate with the PIX through (inside), defines the IP address of the AAA server (10.0.0.2), assigns a key (secretkey), and defines a timeout period (10 seconds).

Example 8-1   *Specifying AAA Server Groups*

```
pixfirewall(config)# aaa-server MYTACACS protocol tacacs+
pixfirewall(config)# aaa-server MYTACACS (inside) host 10.0.0.2 secretkey timeout 10
```

Having configured the **aaa-server** command, it is now time for the administrator to configure **authentication**. The **aaa authentication** command enables or disables user authentication services. When a user initiates a connection via Telnet, FTP, or HTTP, the user is prompted for a username and password. An AAA server, designated previously with the **aaa-server** command, verifies whether the username and password are correct.

The **aaa authentication** command is not intended to mandate a security policy. The AAA servers determine whether a user can or cannot access a system, what services can be accessed, and what IP addresses the user can access. The PIX Firewall interacts with Telnet, FTP, and HTTP to display the prompts for logging. A PIX can be configured to specify that only a single service is required to use authentication, but this must agree with the AAA server to ensure that both the firewall and server agree.

The PIX Firewall permits only one authentication protocol type per network. For example, if one network connects inbound through the PIX Firewall using TACACS+, the same network cannot connect inbound through the PIX Firewall using RADIUS; however, if one network connects inbound through the PIX Firewall using TACACS+, a different network may connect inbound through the PIX Firewall using RADIUS.

The syntax for the **aaa authentication** command is as follows:

```
aaa authentication include | exclude authen_service inbound | outbound |
    if_name local_ip local_mask foreign_ip foreign_mask group_tag
```

Table 8-2 describes the syntax of the **aaa authentication** command.

Table 8-2   **aaa authentication** *Command Description*

aaa authentication Command Parameter	Description
authentication	Enable or disable user authentication, prompt user for username and password, and verify information with authentication server.
	When used with the **console** option, enables or disables authentication service for access to the PIX Firewall console over Telnet or from the console connector on the PIX Firewall unit.
	Use of the **aaa authentication** command requires that the **aaa-server** command has already been configured to designate an authentication server.

Table 8-2   **aaa authentication** *Command Description (Continued)*

aaa authentication Command Parameter	Description
include	Create a new rule with the specified service to include.
exclude	Create an exception to a previously stated rule by excluding the specified service from authentication to the specified host. The **exclude** parameter improves the former **except** option by allowing the user to specify a port to exclude to a specific host or hosts.
authen_service	The application with which a user is accessing a network. Use **any**, **ftp**, **http**, or **telnet**. The **any** value enables authentication for all TCP services. To have users prompted for authentication credentials, they must use FTP, HTTP, or Telnet. (HTTP is for the web and applies only to web browsers that can prompt for a username and password).
inbound	Authenticate inbound connections. Inbound means that the connection originates on the outside interface and is being directed to the inside interface.
outbound	Authenticate outbound connections. Outbound means that the connection originates on the inside and is being directed to the outside interface.
if_name	Interface name from which users require authentication. Use *if_name* in combination with the *local_ip* address and the *foreign_ip* address to determine where access is sought and from whom. The *local_ip* address is always on the highest security level interface and *foreign_ip* is always on the lowest.
local_ip	The IP address of the host or network of hosts to be authenticated. This address may be set to **0** to mean all hosts and to let the authentication server decide which hosts are authenticated.
local_mask	Network mask of *local_ip*. Always specify a specific mask value. Use **0** if the IP address is **0**. Use 255.255.255.255 for a host.
foreign_ip	The IP address of the hosts to be given the ability to access the *local_ip* address. Use **0** to mean all hosts.
foreign_mask	Network mask of *foreign_ip*. Always specify a specific mask value. Use **0** if the IP address is **0**. Use 255.255.255.255 for a host.
group_tag	The group tag set with the **aaa-server** command.

Example 8-2 shows how to configure the **aaa authentication** command and bind the statement to the **aaa server** command by way of the MYTACACS group name. Any IP address or network set to 0 and a corresponding mask set to 0 is the equivalent of **any** or **all hosts**.

Example 8-2 *Configuring AAA Authentication and Binding It to the AAA Server*

```
pixfirewall(config)# aaa-server MYTACACS protocol tacacs+
pixfirewall(config)# aaa-server MYTACACS (inside) host 10.0.0.2 secretkey timeout 10
pixfirewall(config)# aaa authentication include any inbound
  0.0.0.0 0.0.0.0 0.0.0.0 0.0.0.0 MYTACACS
pixfirewall(config)# aaa authentication include telnet outbound
  0.0.0.0 0.0.0.0 0.0.0.0 0.0.0.0 MYTACACS
pixfirewall(config)# aaa authentication include ftp dmz
  0.0.0.0 0.0.0.0 0.0.0.0 0.0.0.0 MYTACACS
pixfirewall(config)# aaa authentication exclude any outbound
  10.0.0.33 255.255.255.255 0.0.0.0 0.0.0.0 MYTACACS
```

NOTE   The **include** and **exclude** options are not backward compatible with PIX Firewall versions prior to 5.1. If you downgrade to an earlier version, the **aaa** command statements will be removed from your configuration.

Authentication of Other Services

The PIX Firewall authenticates users via Telnet, FTP, or HTTP. It is also possible to authenticate other services. For example, the PIX may be configured so that authentication is required to access a Microsoft file server on port 139. When users are required to authenticate to access services other than Telnet, FTP, or HTTP, they need to do one of the following:

- **Option 1**—Authenticate first by accessing a Telnet, FTP, or HTTP server before accessing other services.

- **Option 2**—Authenticate to the PIX Firewall *virtual Telnet* service before accessing other services.

When there are no Telnet, FTP, or HTTP servers to authenticate against, or just to simplify authentication for the user, the PIX Firewall allows a virtual Telnet or HTTP authentication option. This permits the user to authenticate directly with the PIX Firewall to the virtual Telnet or HTTP IP address.

Virtual Telnet

The virtual Telnet option provides a way to pre-authenticate users who require connections through the PIX Firewall using services or protocols that do not support authentication.

It is also for general user authentication when there is no convenient Telnet, FTP, or HTTP server to perform the authentication. The virtual Telnet IP address may be used to authenticate in and/or authenticate out of the PIX Firewall.

When an unauthenticated user Telnets to the virtual IP address, the user is challenged for a username and password. The user is authenticated by the TACACS+ or RADIUS server. Once authenticated, the user sees the message "Authentication Successful" and the authentication credentials are cached in the PIX Firewall for the duration of the **timeout uauth**. The Telnet session is then reset by the PIX firewall.

If a user wishes to log out to clear the entry in the PIX Firewall **uauth** cache, the user must again Telnet to the virtual address. The user is prompted for a username and password, the PIX Firewall removes the associated credentials from the **uauth** cache, and the user receives a "Logout Successful" message. Example 8-3 demonstrates a successful login and a successful logout.

Example 8-3 *Successful Login and Logout*

```
! Authenticating Login

>telnet 192.168.0.5
LOGIN Authentication
Username: aaauser
Password: *******
Authentication Successful

! Authenticating Logout

>telnet 192.168.0.5
LOGOUT Authentication
Username: aaauser
Password: *******
Logout Successful
```

The syntax for the **virtual telnet** command is as follows:

```
virtual telnet ip_address
```

For outbound virtual Telnet use, *ip_address* must be an address routed to the PIX Firewall. Use an address that is not in use on any interface. In the example shown in Figure 8-6, the PIX is configured to require authentication for outbound access of TCP port 49. The inside client at 10.0.0.10 has a default gateway set to the inside interface of the PIX Firewall at 10.0.0.1. The virtual Telnet address is 172.16.0.5. The inside client, 10.0.0.10, will Telnet to the virtual address of 172.16.0.5. The PIX will prompt the client for authentication. Once authenticated, the session from the client to the PIX will be dropped. The client can then get through the PIX using TCP port 49.

Figure 8-6 *Virtual Telnet*

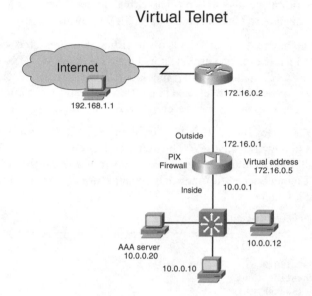

Example 8-4 demonstrates a partial configuration of the PIX.

Example 8-4 *Virtual Telnet Outbound*

```
pixfirewall(config)# ip address outside 172.16.0.1
pixfirewall(config)# ip address inside 10.0.0.1
pixfirewall(config)# global(outside) 1 172.16.0.30-172.16.0.50
  netmask 255.255.255.0
pixfirewall(config)# nat(inside) 1 0 0 0
pixfirewall(config)# aaa-server foxserver protocol TACACS+
pixfirewall(config)# aaa-server foxserver (inside) host 10.0.0.20
  secretkey timeout 10
pixfirewall(config)# aaa authentication include telnet outbound
  0.0.0.0 0.0.0.0 0.0.0.0 0.0.0.0 foxserver
pixfirewall(config)# aaa authentication include tcp/49 outbound
  0.0.0.0 0.0.0.0 0.0.0.0 0.0.0.0 foxserver
pixfirewall(config)# virtual telnet 172.16.0.5
```

Using the same figure, 8-6, an example of inbound virtual Telnet may be that a user on the outside (192.168.1.1) is required to access TCP port 49 on the inside host, 10.0.0.10. 10.0.0.10 is statically mapped to the address 172.16.0.25. The client, 192.168.1.1, first Telnets to the virtual address of 172.16.0.5. The PIX requires authentication. Once authenticated, the session is dropped. The client can then access TCP port 49 of host 172.16.0.25 (10.0.0.10).

Example 8-5 demonstrates a partial configuration of the PIX.

Example 8-5   *Virtual Telnet Inbound*

```
pixfirewall(config)# ip address outside 172.16.0.1
pixfirewall(config)# ip address inside 10.0.0.1
pixfirewall(config)# global(outside) 1 172.16.0.30-172.16.0.50
  netmask 255.255.255.0
pixfirewall(config)# nat(inside) 1 0 0 0
pixfirewall(config)# aaa-server foxserver protocol TACACS+
pixfirewall(config)# aaa-server foxserver (inside) host 10.0.0.20
  secretkey timeout 10
pixfirewall(config)# aaa authentication include telnet inbound
  0.0.0.0 0.0.0.0 0.0.0.0 0.0.0.0 foxserver
pixfirewall(config)# aaa authentication include tcp/49 inbound
  0.0.0.0 0.0.0.0 0.0.0.0 0.0.0.0 foxserver
pixfirewall(config)# virtual telnet 172.16.0.5
pixfirewall(config)# static(inside,outside) 172.16.0.25 10.0.0.10
  netmask 255.255.255.255 0 0
pixfirewall(config)# conduit permit tcp host 172.16.0.5 eq telnet any
pixfirewall(config)# conduit permit tcp host 172.16.0.25 eq 49 any
```

It is important to remember that to Telnet to the virtual Telnet address, you must log out of the authenticated virtual Telnet session.

Virtual HTTP

If authentication is required on sites outside the PIX as well as on the PIX itself, unusual browser behavior can sometimes be observed. Since browsers cache the username and password, it may appear that authentication is not occurring. To avoid this, an administrator may implement virtual HTTP. The browser is pointed toward the virtual address. After authentication to the virtual IP address, the message "Error: 501 Not Implemented" is received by the browser. At this point, with the browser, request to go to the destination web site beyond the PIX. There will be no additional reauthentication on the PIX for the length of time in the **timeout uauth**.

With the virtual HTTP option, web browsers work correctly with the PIX Firewall's HTTP authentication. The PIX Firewall assumes that the AAA server database is shared with a web server and automatically provides the AAA server and web server with the same information. The virtual HTTP option works with the PIX Firewall to authenticate the user, separate the AAA server information from the web client's URL request, and direct the web client to the web server. The virtual HTTP will redirect the web browser's initial connection to an IP address, which resides in the PIX Firewall, authenticating the user, then redirecting the browser back to the URL that the user originally requested. This option is so named because it accesses a virtual HTTP server on the PIX Firewall, which in reality does not exist.

This option is especially useful for PIX Firewall interoperability with Microsoft IIS, but is useful for other authentication servers. When using HTTP authentication to a site running

Microsoft IIS that has "Basic text authentication" or "NT Challenge" enabled, users may be denied access from the Microsoft IIS server. This occurs because the browser appends the string: "Authorization: Basic=Uuhjksdkfhk==" to the **HTTP GET** commands. This string contains the PIX Firewall authentication credentials. Windows NT Microsoft IIS servers respond to the credentials and assume that a Windows NT user is trying to access privileged pages on the server. Unless the PIX Firewall username and password combination is exactly the same as a valid Windows NT username and password combination on the Microsoft IIS server, the **HTTP GET** command is denied.

To solve this problem, the PIX Firewall redirects the browser's initial connection to its virtual HTTP IP address, authenticates the user, then redirects the browser back to the URL that the user originally requested.

CAUTION   Do not set the **timeout uauth** duration to 0 seconds when using the virtual HTTP option. This will prevent HTTP connections to the real web server.

The syntax for the **virtual http** command is as follows:

```
virtual http ip_address [warn]
```

For outbound use, *ip_address* must be an address routed to the PIX Firewall. Use an RFC 1918 address that is not in use on any interface.

For inbound use, *ip_address* must be an unused global address. An **access-list** or **conduit** and **static** command pair must provide access to *ip_address*, as well as an **aaa authentication** command statement.

For example for outbound use, if an inside client at 192.168.0.100 has a default gateway set to the inside interface of the PIX Firewall at 192.168.0.1, the IP address set with the **virtual http** command can be any IP address not in use on that segment, such as 192.168.0.120.

The **warn** option alerts **virtual http** command users that the command was redirected. This option is only applicable for text-based browsers where the redirect cannot happen automatically.

Authentication of Console Access

The **aaa authentication console** command can be used to require authentication verification to access the PIX Firewall's serial, enable, or Telnet consoles. The serial console options also log to a syslog server any changes made via the serial console.

Authenticated access to the PIX Firewall console has different types of prompts, depending on the option chosen. While the enable option allows three tries before stopping with an access denied message, both the serial and Telnet options cause the user to be prompted continually until a successful login.

Authentication of the serial console creates a potential deadlock situation if the authentication server requests are not answered and access to the console is necessary to attempt diagnosis. If the console login request times out, a user may gain access to the PIX Firewall from the serial console by entering the PIX Firewall username and the enable password. The PIX firewall username is "pix" if the TACACS+ or RADIUS server is not accessible.

The maximum password length for accessing the console is 16 characters

The syntax for the **aaa authentication console** command is as follows:

```
aaa authentication [serial | enable | telnet] console group_tag
```

Table 8-3 describes the parameters for this command.

Table 8-3   **aaa authentication** Command Description

Command Argument/Option	Description
serial	Requests a username and password before the first command-line prompt on the serial console connection.
enable	Requests a username and password before accessing privileged mode for serial or Telnet connections.
telnet	Forces the user to specify a username and password before the first command-line prompt of a Telnet console connection.
console	Specifies that access to the PIX Firewall console require authentication and, optionally, logs configuration changes to a syslog server.
group_tag	The group tag set with the **aaa-server** command.

Example 8-6 demonstrates how to configure the **aaa authentication** command with regard to the console.

Example 8-6   *Authentication of Console Access*

```
pixfirewall(config)# aaa authentication serial console MYTACACS
pixfirewall(config)# aaa authentication enable console MYTACACS
pixfirewall(config)# aaa authentication telnet console MYTACACS
```

The **telnet** command allows the administrator to specify which hosts can access the PIX Firewall console with Telnet. Prior to the version 5.0 operating system, Telnet to the PIX Firewall console was available only from an internal interface and not the outside interface. The capability to enable Telnet to the PIX Firewall on all interfaces now exists. However, the PIX Firewall enforces that all Telnet traffic to the outside interface be IPSec-protected. Therefore, to enable a Telnet session to the outside interface, configure IPSec on the outside interface to include IP traffic generated by the PIX Firewall and enable **telnet** on the outside interface. Only traffic back to the Telnet client is sent through the IPSec tunnel, not all traffic generated by the outside interface.

Changing Authentication Timeouts

Use the **timeout uauth** command to specify how long the cache should be kept after the user connections become idle. The **timeout** command value must be at least two minutes. Use the **clear uauth** command to delete all authorization caches for all users, which will cause them to reauthenticate the next time they create a connection. The **timeout uauth** command can be set to 0 (zero) to disable caching.

The syntax for the **timeout uauth** command is as follows:

```
timeout uauth [hh:mm:ss] [absolute | inactivity]
```

Table 8-4 describes the parameters for this command.

Table 8-4   **timeout uauth** *Command Description*

Command Argument/ Option	Description
uauth [*hh*:*mm*:*ss*]	Duration before authentication and authorization cache times out and user has to reauthenticate the next connection. This duration must be shorter than the **xlate** values. Set to **0** to disable caching. Do not set to **0** if passive FTP is used on the connections.
absolute	Run **uauth** timer continuously, but after timer elapses, wait to re-prompt the user until the user starts a new connection, such as clicking a link in a web browser. The default **uauth** timer is **absolute**. To disable **absolute**, set the **uauth** timer to **0** (zero).
inactivity	Start **uauth** timer after a connection becomes idle.

The **inactivity** and **absolute** qualifiers cause users to reauthenticate after either a period of inactivity or an absolute duration. The inactivity timer starts after a connection becomes idle. If a user establishes a new connection before the duration of the inactivity timer, the user is not required to reauthenticate. If a user establishes a new connection after the inactivity timer expires, the user must reauthenticate.

The absolute timer runs continuously, but waits to re-prompt the user when the user starts a new connection, such as clicking a link after the absolute timer has elapsed. If the timer expires and the user clicks on a new link, the user is prompted to reauthenticate. The absolute timer must be shorter than the xlate timer; otherwise, a user could be re-prompted after their session has already ended.

The inactivity timer gives users the best Internet access because they are not prompted to regularly reauthenticate. Absolute timers provide an increased level of security and manage the PIX Firewall connections better. By being prompted to reauthenticate regularly, users tend to manage the use of the resources more efficiently. Another benefit is that by being prompted again, the risk is minimized that someone will attempt to use another user's access after they leave their workstation, such as in a college computer lab. An absolute timer during peak hours and an inactivity timer during other times may be the best solution.

Both an inactivity timer and an absolute timer can operate at the same time. The absolute timer should be set for a longer time period than the inactivity timer. If the absolute timer is less than the inactivity timer is, the inactivity timer never occurs. For example, if the absolute timer is set to 10 minutes and the inactivity timer to an hour, the absolute timer re-prompts the user every 10 minutes, and the inactivity timer will never be started.

If the inactivity timer is set to a particular duration, but the absolute timer to zero, then users are only reauthenticated after the inactivity timer elapses. If both timers are set to zero, then users have to reauthenticate on every new connection.

NOTE	Do not set the **timeout uauth** duration to 0 seconds when using the virtual HTTP option, as this prevents HTTP connections to the real (destination) web server.

Example 8-7 demonstrates the configuration of the absolute and inactivity timeout periods.

Example 8-7   *Configureing Timeout Periods*

```
pixfirewall(config)# timeout uauth 3:00:00 absolute
pixfirewall(config)# timeout uauth 0:30:00 inactivity
```

Changing the Authentication Prompt

Use the **auth-prompt** command to create an AAA challenge text for HTTP, FTP, and Telnet access. This text displays above the username and password prompts displayed when logging in. The text for authentication rejection and acceptance may also be changed.

The syntax for the **auth-prompt** command is as follows:

```
auth-prompt [accept | reject | prompt] string
```

Table 8-5 describes the parameters for this command.

Table 8-5   **auth-prompt** *Command Description*

Command Argument/ Option	Description
accept	If a user authentication via Telnet is accepted, display the prompt *string*.
reject	If a user authentication via Telnet is rejected, display the prompt *string*.

continues

Table 8-5   **auth-prompt** *Command Description (Continued)*

Command Argument/ Option	Description
prompt	The AAA challenge prompt string follows this keyword. This keyword is optional for backward compatibility.
string	A string of up to 235 alphanumeric characters. Special characters should not be used; however, spaces and punctuation are permitted. Entering a question mark or pressing the **Enter** key ends the string. (The question mark appears in the string).

Example 8-8 demonstrates all three authentication prompts.

Example 8-8   *Changing the Authentication Prompt*

```
pixfirewall(config)# auth-prompt prompt Please Authenticate to the Firewall
pixfirewall(config)# auth-prompt reject Authentication Failed, Try Again
pixfirewall(config)# auth-prompt accept You've been Authenticated
```

NOTE   Microsoft Internet Explorer displays up to 37 characters in an authentication prompt, Netscape Navigator displays up to 120 characters, and Telnet and FTP display up to 235 characters in an authentication prompt.

Configuring Authorization

The PIX Firewall uses TACACS+ authorization services with an Access Control Server to determine what services an authenticated user may access. When authorizing for FTP, Telnet, and HTTP, the application name may be used in the **aaa authorization** command. It is important to remember that services not specified are authorized implicitly. If the intent is to create an exception to a previously stated rule, use the **exclude** parameter.

The syntax for the **aaa authorization** command is as follows:

```
aaa authorization include | exclude author_service inbound | outbound | if_name
local_ip local_mask foreign_ip foreign_mask
```

Table 8-5 describes the parameters for this command.

Table 8-6   **aaa authorization** Command Description

Command Argument/Option	Description
authorization	Enable or disable TACACS+ user authorization for services. The authentication server determines what services the user is authorized to access.
include	Create a new rule with the specified service to include.

Table 8-6   **aaa authorization** Command Description *(Continued)*

Command Argument/Option	Description
exclude	Create an exception to a previously stated rule by excluding the specified service from authentication, authorization, or accounting to the specified host. The **exclude** parameter improves the former **except** option by allowing the user to specify a port to exclude to a specific host or hosts.
author_service	The services which require authorization. Use **any**, **ftp**, **http**, **telnet**, or *protocol/port*. Services not specified are authorized implicitly. Services specified in the **aaa authentication** command do not affect the services which require authorization.
	For *protocol/port:*
	Protocol—the protocol (6 for TCP, 17 for UDP, 1 for ICMP, and so on).
	Port—the TCP or UDP destination port, or port range. The *port* can also be the ICMP type; that is, 8 for ICMP echo or ping. A port value of 0 (zero) means all ports. Port ranges only apply to the TCP and UDP protocols, not to ICMP. For protocols other than TCP, UDP, and ICMP, the *port* is not applicable and should not be used. A sample port specification follows:
	aaa authorization include udp/53-1024 inside 0 0 0 0
	This example enables authorization for DNS lookups to the inside interface for all clients, and authorizes access to any other services that have ports in the range of 53 to 1024.
	Specifying a port range may produce unexpected results at the authorization server. The PIX Firewall sends the port range to the server as a string with the expectation that the server will parse it out into specific ports. Not all servers do this. In addition, the intent may be to authorize users on specific services, which will not occur if a range is accepted.
inbound	Authenticate or authorize inbound connections. *Inbound* means the connection originates on the outside interface and is being directed to the inside interface.
outbound	Authenticate or authorize outbound connections. *Outbound* means the connection originates on the inside and is being directed to the outside interface.
if_name	Interface name from which users require authentication. Use *if_name* in combination with the *local_ip* address and the *foreign_ip* address to determine where access is sought and from whom. The *local_ip* address is always on the highest security level interface and *foreign_ip* is always on the lowest.
local_ip	The IP address of the host or network of hosts to be authenticated or authorized. This address may be set to **0** to mean all hosts and to let the authentication server decide which hosts are authenticated.

continues

Table 8-6   **aaa authorization** Command Description *(Continued)*

Command Argument/Option	Description
local_mask	Network mask of *local_ip*. Always specify a specific mask value. Use **0** if the IP address is **0**. Use 255.255.255.255 for a host.
foreign_ip	The IP address of the hosts to be given the ability to access the *local_ip* address. Use **0** to mean all hosts.
foreign_mask	Network mask of *foreign_ip*. Always specify a specific mask value. Use **0** if the IP address is **0**. Use 255.255.255.255 for a host.

Example 8-9 demonstrates a sample of the **include** and **exclude** parameters

Example 8-9   *Enable Authorization*

```
pixfirewall(config)# aaa authorization include ftp outbound
   0.0.0.0 0.0.0.0 0.0.0.0 0.0.0.0 MYTACACS
pixfirewall(config)# aaa authorization exclude ftp outbound
   10.0.0.33 255.255.255.255 0.0.0.0 0.0.0.0 MYTACACS
```

Adding an Authorization Rule to CSACS-NT

It is possible to authorize access to only one service for a particular group within CSACS. If the intent is for a user to be authorized for FTP only, for example, the following steps must be completed within CSACS (use Figure 8-7) and the user must be a part of the group being modified.

Step 1   In the navigation bar, select **Group Setup**. The Group Setup window opens.

Step 2   Select the Group to edit and select **Edit Settings**.

Step 3   Scroll down in **Group Setup** to **IOS Commands**.

Step 4   Select **IOS Commands** by putting a check mark in the box next to **IOS Commands**.

Step 5   Under **Unmatched Cisco IOS commands**, select **Deny**.

Step 6   Select **Command** by putting a check mark in the box next to **Command**.

Step 7   Enter the allowable service in the box below **Command: ftp**.

Step 8   Leave the **Arguments** field blank.

Step 9   Select **Permit (Unlisted arguments)**.

Step 10 Click **Submit** to add more rules, or click **Submit + Restart** when finished.

Figure 8-7   *Authorization Rules Allowing Specific Services*

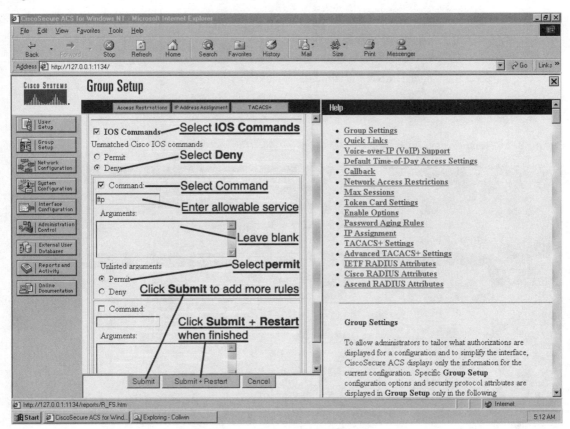

If the intent is for a user to be authorized for FTP to only two specific destination IP addresses (172.27.27.45 and 10.1.1.10) the following steps must be completed within CSACS (use Figure 8-8 for this example) and the user must be a part of the group being modified:

Step 1   In the navigation bar, select **Group Setup**. The Group Setup window opens.

Step 2   Select the Group to edit and select **Edit Settings**.

Step 3   Scroll down in **Group Setup** to **IOS Commands**.

Step 4   Select **IOS Commands** by putting a check mark in the box next to **IOS Commands**.

Step 5   Under **Unmatched Cisco IOS commands**, select **Deny**.

Step 6   Select **Command** by putting a check mark in the box next to **Command**.

Step 7   Enter the allowable service in the box below **Command**: **ftp**.

Step 8   In the **Arguments** field, enter the destination IP addresses permitted:

```
permit 172.27.27.45
permit 10.1.1.10
```

Step 9   Under **Unlisted** arguments, select **Deny**.

Step 10   Click **Submit** to add more rules, or click **Submit + Restart** when
finished.

Figure 8-8   *Authorization Rules Allowing Service to Specific Hosts*

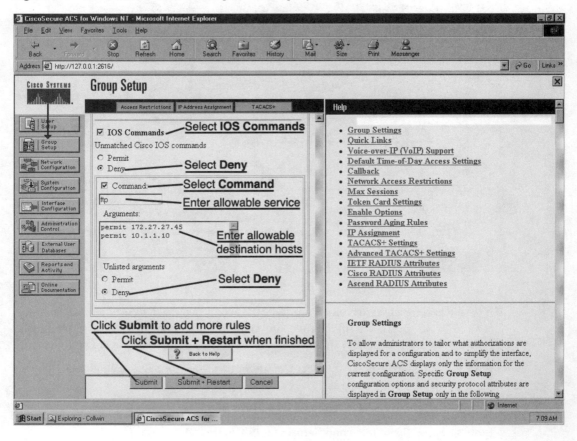

Authorization of Other Services

When authorizing services other than Telnet, FTP, or HTTP, the syntax of the **aaa
authorization** command is slightly different. When authorizing Telnet, FTP, or HTTP, the

application name may be used. When authorizing for other services, the protocol and port number must be specified. It is specified in the format protocol/port. When specifying the protocol, use the protocol number such as 6 for TCP and 17 for UDP and 1 for ICMP. When specifying the port, use the port number specified in RFC 1700, such as 23 for Telnet and 25 for SMTP. For the protocol ICMP use the message type instead of the port number. Port is not used for protocols other than TCP, UDP, and ICMP. Example 8-10 demonstrates use of the **aaa authorization** command.

Example 8-10 *Authorization of Non-Telnet, Non-FTP, or Non-HTTP Traffic*

```
pixfirewall(config)# aaa authorization include udp/0 inbound
   0.0.0.0 0.0.0.0 0.0.0.0 0.0.0.0 MYTACACS
pixfirewall(config)# aaa authorization include tcp/30-100 outbound
   0.0.0.0 0.0.0.0 0.0.0.0 0.0.0.0 MYTACACS
pixfirewall(config)# aaa authorization include icmp/8 outbound
   0.0.0.0 0.0.0.0 0.0.0.0 0.0.0.0 MYTACACS
```

The first line in Example 8-10 will authorize access to all UDP applications (designated by udp/0). The second line in Example 8-10 will authorize TCP ports 30 through 100 (designated by tcp/30-100). Port ranges may only be specified for TCP and UDP protocols. The third line in Example 8-10 will authorize ICMP echo-requests (designated by icmp/8, which is type 8—echo-request).

To configure authorization rules for specific non-Telnet, FTP, or HTTP services within CSACS for NT, complete the following steps:

Step 1   In the navigation bar, select **Group Setup**. The **Group Setup** window opens.

Step 2   Select the Group to edit and select **Edit Settings**.

Step 3   Scroll down in **Group Setup** to **IOS Commands**.

Step 4   Select **IOS Commands** by putting a check mark in the box next to **IOS Commands**.

Step 5   Under **Unmatched Cisco IOS commands**, select **Deny**.

Step 6   Select **Command** by putting a check mark in the box next to **Command**.

Step 7   Enter an allowable service using the following format: *protocol/port* (where *protocol* is the protocol number and *port* is the port number).

Step 8   Leave the **Arguments** field blank.

Step 9   Under **Unlisted arguments**, select **Permit**.

Step 10 Click **Submit** to add more rules, or click **Submit + Restart** when finished.

Figure 8-9 shows how the **Group Setup** window within CSACS should be configured. By selecting **Deny** within the **Unmatched Cisco IOS commands**, users will be able to access only those services listed (if **Permit** had been selected, users would be able to access all services not specifically listed). Notice that the service allowed is **1/8**. That would be protocol 1, which is ICMP, and message type 8, which is echo-request. Selecting **Permit** under **Unlisted arguments** will allow users to issue all arguments not specifically listed (If **Deny** had been selected, users would be allowed to issue only those arguments listed).

Figure 8-9   *Authorization of Non-Telnet, FTP, or HTTP Traffic on CSACS-NT*

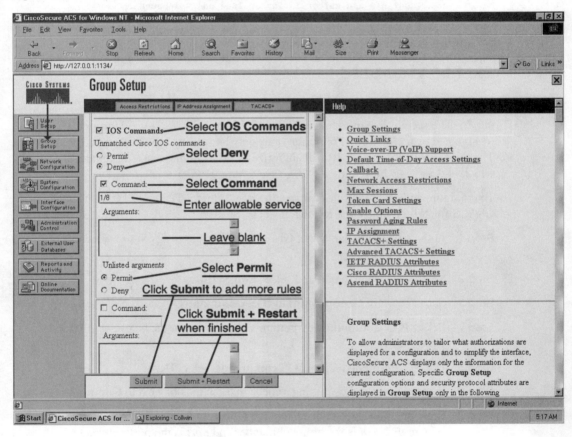

Configuring Accounting

After configuring authentication and authorization, it is often a requirement to also configure accounting. Accounting information can be used to keep track of who is accessing a specific host or application. Accounting records can show the amount of time a user is logged in. They can also show the amount of information transmitted and received. This information may be used for billing purposes.

The syntax for the **aaa accounting** command is as follows:

```
aaa accounting include | exclude acctg_service inbound | outbound |
   if_name local_ip local_mask foreign_ip foreign_mask group_tag
```

Table 8-6 describes the parameters for this command.

Table 8-7   **aaa accounting** *Command Description*

Command Argument/ Option	Description
accounting	Enable or disable accounting services with the authentication server. Use of this command requires that the **aaa-server** command was configured previously to designate an authentication server.
include	Create a new rule with the specified service to include.
exclude	Create an exception to a previously stated rule by excluding the specified service from authentication, authorization, or accounting to the specified host. The **exclude** parameter improves the former **except** option by allowing the user to specify a port to exclude to a specific host or hosts.
acctg_service	The accounting service. Accounting is provided for all services or the administrator can limit it to one or more services. Possible values are **any**, **ftp**, **http**, **telnet**, or *protocol/port*. Use **any** to provide accounting for all TCP services. To provide accounting for UDP services, use the *protocol/port* form.
	For *protocol/port*, the TCP *protocol* appears as 6, the UDP protocol appears as 17, and so on. *Port* is the TCP or UDP destination port. A port value of 0 (zero) means all ports. For protocols other than TCP and UDP, the *port* is not applicable and should not be used.
inbound	Authenticate or authorize inbound connections. *Inbound* means the connection originates on the outside interface and is being directed to the inside interface.
outbound	Authenticate or authorize outbound connections. *Outbound* means the connection originates on the inside and is being directed to the outside interface.
if_name	Interface name from which users require authentication. Use *if_name* in combination with the *local_ip* address and the *foreign_ip* address to determine where access is sought and from whom. The *local_ip* address is always on the highest security level interface and *foreign_ip* is always on the lowest.

continues

Table 8-7   **aaa accounting** *Command Description (Continued)*

Command Argument/ Option	Description
local_ip	The IP address of the host or network of hosts that are to be authenticated or authorized. This may be set to **0** to mean all hosts and to let the authentication server decide which hosts are authenticated.
local_mask	Network mask of *local_ip*. Always specify a specific mask value. Use **0** if the IP address is **0**. Use 255.255.255.255 for a host.
foreign_ip	The IP address of the hosts to be given the ability to access the *local_ip* address. Use **0** to mean all hosts.
foreign_mask	Network mask of *foreign_ip*. Always specify a specific mask value. Use **0** if the IP address is **0**. Use 255.255.255.255 for a host.
group_tag	The group tag set with the **aaa-server** command.

Example 8-11 demonstrates two uses of the **aaa accounting** command. The first example shows a requirement for accounting for any authenticated outbound traffic. The second statement sets up an exclusion of accounting for the specific IP address 10.0.0.33.

Example 8-11   *Configuring AAA Accounting*

```
pixfirewall(config)# aaa accounting include any outbound
   0.0.0.0 0.0.0.0 0.0.0.0 0.0.0.0 MYTACACS
pixfirewall(config)# aaa accounting exclude any outbound
   10.0.0.33255.255.255.255 0.0.0.0 0.0.0.0 MYTACACS
```

The first statement shows a requirement for accounting for any authenticated outbound traffic. The second statement sets up an exclusion of accounting for the specific IP address 10.0.0.33.

Viewing Accounting Records With CSACS-NT

Complete the following steps to view accounting records after accounting has been enabled on the PIX and the CSACS application has been installed:

Step 1   In the navigation bar select **Reports and Activity**. The **Reports and Activity** window opens.

Step 2   Under **Reports** first select **TACACS+ Accounting** and then select **TACACS+ Accounting active.csv** under **Select a TACACS+ Accounting file** to display the accounting records as demonstrated in Figure 8-10.

Figure 8-10 *Viewing Accounting Records*

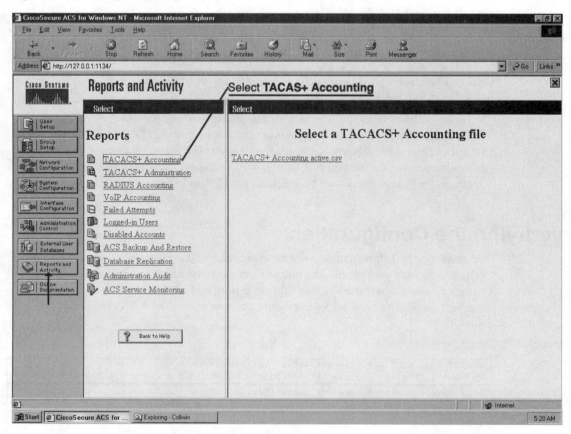

Accounting of Other Services

When configuring **aaa accounting** of non-Telnet, FTP, or HTTP traffic, the syntax of the command is slightly different from Telnet, FTP, or HTTP-specific traffic. As with **aaa authorization**, when setting up accounting for Telnet, FTP, or HTTP, the application name may be used. When configuring accounting services other than Telnet, FTP, or HTTP, the syntax for *acctg_service* is specified in the format *protocol/port*. When specifying the protocol, use the protocol number such as 6 for TCP and 17 for UDP. When specifying the port, use the port number specified in RFC 1700 such as 23 for Telnet and 25 for SMTP. Port is not used for protocols other than TCP and UDP.

Example 8-12 demonstrates an example of configuring AAA Accounting of non-Telnet, non-FTP, or non-HTTP traffic.

Example 8-12 *Configuring AAA Accounting of Non-Telnet, Non-FTP, or Non-HTTP Traffic*

```
pixfirewall(config)# aaa accounting include udp/53 inbound
   0.0.0.0 0.0.0.0 0.0.0.0 0.0.0.0 MYTACACS
pixfirewall(config)# aaa accounting include udp/54-100 outbound
   0.0.0.0 0.0.0.0 0.0.0.0 0.0.0.0 MYTACACS
```

The first statement will generate accounting records for port 53 (DNS) UDP applications (designated by udp/53), inbound for all IP addresses. The second statement will generate accounting records for the range of UDP ports 54 through 100, outbound for all IP addresses. Port ranges may only be specified for TCP and UDP protocols.

Verifying the Configuration

The **show aaa** and **show aaa-server** commands can be used to confirm the configuration of the various **aaa** commands. The output from the **show aaa** command reviews the configured **aaa authentication**, **aaa authorization,** and **aaa accounting** commands that have been input. Example 8-13 demonstrates how to review the AAA commands individually.

Example 8-13 *Reviewing AAA*

```
pixfirewall(config)# show aaa authentication
aaa authentication include http inbound 0.0.0.0 0.0.0.0 0.0.0.0 0.0.0.0 MYTACACS
```
```
pixfirewall(config)# show aaa authorization
aaa authorization include http inbound 0.0.0.0 0.0.0.0 0.0.0.0 0.0.0.0 MYTACACS
```
```
pixfirewall(config)# show aaa accounting
aaa accounting include http outbound 0.0.0.0 0.0.0.0 0.0.0.0 0.0.0.0 MYTACACS
```
```
pixfirewall(config)# show aaa
aaa authentication include http inbound 0.0.0.0 0.0.0.0 0.0.0.0 0.0.0.0 MYTACACS
aaa authentication telnet console MYTACACS
aaa authorization include http inbound 0.0.0.0 0.0.0.0 0.0.0.0 0.0.0.0 MYTACACS
aaa accounting include http outbound 0.0.0.0 0.0.0.0 0.0.0.0 0.0.0.0 MYTACACS
```

The **show aaa-server** command will detail the configured **aaa-server** commands as demonstrated in Example 8-14. The first two lines of output are the default parameters within the PIX configuration.

Example 8-14 *Reviewing AAA*

```
pixfirewall(config)# show aaa-server
aaa-server TACACS+ protocol tacacs+
aaa-server RADIUS protocol radius
aaa-server MYTACACS protocol tacacs+
aaa-server MYTACACS (inside) host 10.1.1.4 secretkey timeout 5
```

In order to remove the **aaa authentication, aaa authorization,** and **aaa accounting** commands, use the **no aaa authentication** and **no aaa accounting** commands. The **no aaa authentication** will remove the corresponding **aaa authorization** commands. The **clear aaa** command will also remove **aaa** command statements from the configuration.

To remove the **aaa-server MYTACACS (inside) host 10.1.1.4 secretkey timeout 5** command use the **no aaa-server MYTACACS (inside) host 10.1.1.4 secretkey timeout 5**.

To remove the **aaa-server MYTACACS protocol tacacs+** command, use the **clear aaa-server MYTACACS protocol tacacs+** command.

In order to verify the previously configured **auth-prompt** command, the **show auth-prompt** command may be issued as demonstrated in Example 8-15.

Example 8-15 *Verifying Authorization Prompts*

```
pixfirewall(config)# show auth-prompt
auth-prompt prompt prompt Authenticate to the Firewall
auth-prompt prompt accept You've been Authenticated
auth-prompt prompt reject Authentication Failed
```

Two additional **show** commands are the **show timeout uauth** and the **show virtual [http | telnet]** commands. The **show timeout** command displays the current uauth (user authentication) timer values for all authenticated users. The **show virtual http** command and **show virtual telnet** command display the virtual HTTP and virtual Telnet configuration.

Example 8-16 demonstrates sample output from each command.

Example 8-16 *Verifying Authorization Prompts*

```
pixfirewall(config)# show virtual
virtual http 192.168.0.2
virtual telnet 192.168.0.2
pixfirewall(config)# show timeout uauth
timeout uauth 3:00:00 absolute uauth 0:30:00 inactivity
```

Within the **show timeout** command, the **timeout uauth 3:00:00** shows the duration (in hours:minutes:seconds) before the authentication and authorization cache times out. In this example, it is three hours.

The **absolute uauth 0:30:00** causes the PIX to run the **uauth** timer continuously, but after the timer elapses (in this case 30 minutes), wait to re-prompt the user until the user starts a new connection, such as clicking a link in a web browser. The default **uauth** timer is **absolute**. To disable **absolute**, set the **uauth** timer to **0** (zero).

The parameter **inactivity** indicates that the PIX should start the **uauth** timer after a connection becomes idle.

Review Questions

To test what you have learned in this chapter, answer the following questions and then refer to Appendix F for the answers.

1   If AAA authentication is required for Telnet access through the PIX, how can the authentication challenge message be modified to read "User Authentication Required"?

2   True or False. A user may Telnet into the PIX from the inside interface only.

3   What are the three ways to authenticate for a service other than FTP, Telnet, or HTTP?

4   What is the command used on the PIX for identifying an AAA server with an IP address of 10.8.1.4, a *group_tag* of NYSERVERS, and a key of mysecret?

5   The following scenario exists:

The PIX is configured with AAA commands.

The PIX is using TACACS+.

The server *group_tag* is NYSERVERS.

How is the **aaa-server** command removed from the configuration of the PIX?

6   When configuring **aaa authorization,** what is the syntax for configuring the service to be authorized?

7   What is the correct syntax when configuring **aaa authentication** for the console?

Chapter 9 introduces the concepts and configuration elements of the Cisco Secure PIX Firewall features necessary to securely handle multichannel TCP applications. You will learn about

- Advanced Protocol Handling
- Multimedia Support
- Attack Guards

Cisco PIX Firewall Advanced Protocol Handling and Attack Guards

With only a few exceptions, advanced protocol handling is accomplished via a mechanism called a *fixup protocol*. The **fixup protocol** command operates not as a true proxy but as an *application aware agent*. In most cases, the fixup protocol acts by monitoring the control channel of an application to prevent protocol violations and enable the PIX to respond dynamically to a protocol's legitimate need to open an inbound connection securely by making a temporary exception in the ASA. When the exception is no longer needed, the fixup protocol closes it. Each new version of the PIX OS brings new and improved protocol handling. It is important to note that the PIX can only perform these operations on the fixups that are part of the PIX OS running on your PIX. Fixups are not user-definable or user-programmable. Fixups allow you to enable or disable processing for the supported protocols and determine what ports (standard or non-standard) to operate on.

The Need for Advanced Protocol Handling

Nearly every enterprise uses the Internet for business transactions. For these enterprises to keep their internal networks secure from potential threats from the Internet, they must implement firewalls to separate their trusted internal networks from the untrusted Internet. Even though firewalls help protect an enterprise's internal networks from external threats, implementation challenges have arisen as well.

- Some of the protocols and applications that enterprises used to communicate with outside resources prior to the installation of a firewall are now blocked by the firewall.

- Many popular protocols and applications negotiate connections to dynamically assign source or destination ports or IP addresses. To further complicate matters, some applications embed source or destination IP addressing information above the network layer (Layer 3).

A good firewall must inspect packets above the network layer and perform the following operations as required by the protocol or application:

- Securely open and close negotiated ports or IP addresses for legitimate client/server connections through the firewall.

- Use Network Address Translation (NAT)-relevant instances of IP addresses inside a packet.

- Use Port Address Translation (PAT)-relevant instances of ports inside a packet.
- Inspect packets for signs of malicious application misuse.

Through the use of the Cisco Secure PIX Firewall's **fixup protocol** *protocol* commands, you can provide secure passage for these applications.

The sections that follow explain how the specific **fixup protocol** *protocol* commands for Standard and Passive File Transfer Protocol (FTP), rsh (Remote Shell), and SQL*Net operate and how to configure them.

Standard Mode FTP

Standard mode FTP (also called *classic mode FTP*) uses two channels for communication. When a client behind a firewall initiates an FTP connection from their host, it opens a standard TCP channel from one of its high-order ports (TCP source port >1023) to destination TCP port 21 on the outside server. This connection is referred to as the *control channel*. When the client requests data from the server, it tells the server to send the data to a given high-order port. The server acknowledges the request and initiates an *inbound* connection from its own port 20 to the high-order port that the client requested. This connection is referred to as the *data channel* (port 20 FTP-DATA).

In the past, it was difficult to allow this inbound connection through the firewall to the requested port on the client without permanently opening port 20 connections from outside servers to inside clients for outbound FTP connections. This creates a huge potential vulnerability by allowing any inbound traffic from any host on the Internet with a TCP source port of 20, regardless of the intent!

Example 9-1 and Figure 9-1 demonstrate the TCP three-way handshake and the establishment of the FTP control channel (TCP port 21). Notice that in the second section of the trace, the FTP-DATA channel is initiated by the server 198.10.2.51 (ftp.cisco.com) with a source port of 20 and a random high port of 1066 (selected by the client).

Example 9-1   *Sniffer Trace Illustrating Classic Mode FTP*

```
#Setup connection to destination port 21 for control channel
[10.10.2.51]      [198.133.219.27] TCP: D=21 S=1065 SYN SEQ=1763920874 LEN=0
[198.133.219.27] [10.10.2.51] TCP: D=1065 S=21 SYN ACK=1763920875 SEQ=2208726475 LEN=0
[10.10.2.51]      [198.133.219.27] TCP: D=21 S=1065 ACK=2208726476


#FTP server negotiates FTP-DATA channel with TCP source port 20

[10.10.2.51]      [198.133.219.27] FTP: C PORT=1065 LIST
[198.133.219.27] [10.10.2.51]      TCP: D=1066 S=20 SYN SEQ=2209373687 LEN=0
[10.10.2.51] [198.133.219.27] TCP: D=20 S=1066 SYN ACK=2209373688 SEQ=1765279364 LEN=0
[198.133.219.27]  [10.10.2.51]      TCP: D=1065 S=21 ACK=1763920967
[198.133.219.27]  [10.10.2.51]      TCP: D=1066 S=20 ACK=1765279365
[198.133.219.27]  [10.10.2.51] FTP: R PORT=1065 150 ASCII mode data connection for
/bin/ls.
[198.133.219.27]  [10.10.2.51]      FTP: R PORT=1066 Text Data
```

Figure 9-1   *Standard Mode FTP Client/Server Transactions*

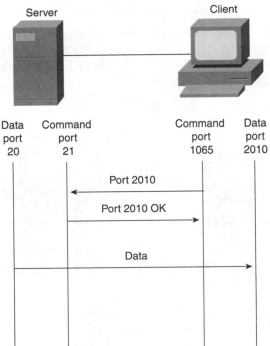

The Cisco Secure PIX Firewall uses the **fixup protocol ftp** command to securely enable the exception required by the FTP-DATA connection. The Cisco Secure PIX Firewall handles FTP in the following manner for outbound and inbound connections:

- **Outbound Connections**—When the client requests data, the PIX Firewall opens a temporary inbound conduit to allow the data channel from the server. This conduit is torn down immediately after the data is sent.

- **Inbound Connections**—If a conduit exists allowing inbound connections to an FTP server, and if all outbound TCP traffic is implicitly allowed, no special handling is required because the server initiates the data channel from the inside.

  If a conduit exists allowing inbound FTP control connections to an FTP server, and if all outbound TCP traffic is not implicitly allowed, the PIX Firewall opens a temporary conduit for the data channel from the server. This conduit is torn down after the data is sent.

Passive Mode FTP

Passive mode FTP also uses two channels for communications. The control channel works the same as in a standard FTP connection, but the data channel setup works differently. When requesting data from the server, the client asks the server if it accepts PASV connections. If the server accepts PASV connections, it sends the client a high-order port number to use for the data channel. The client then initiates the data connection from its own high-order port to the port that the server sent.

Because the client initiates both the command and data connections, early firewalls could easily support this without exposing inside clients to attack. Figure 9-2 shows transactions between the client and server with passive mode FTP. Most web browsers use passive mode FTP by default.

Figure 9-2 *Passive Mode FTP Client/Server Transactions*

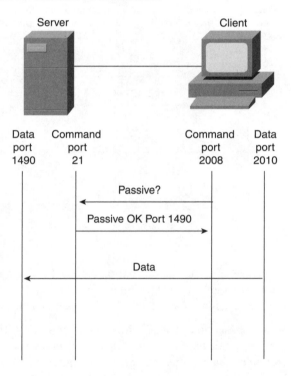

For passive mode FTP traffic, the PIX Firewall behaves in the following manner for outbound and inbound PASV connections:

- **Outbound PASV Connections**—If all outbound TCP traffic is implicitly allowed, no special handling is required because the client initiates both the command and data channels from the inside.

  If all outbound TCP traffic is not implicitly allowed, the PIX Firewall opens a temporary conduit for the data channel from the client. This conduit is torn down after the data is sent.

- **Inbound PASV Connections**—If a conduit exists allowing inbound FTP control connections to a PFTP server, the PIX Firewall opens a temporary inbound conduit for the data channel initiated by the client. This conduit is torn down after the data is sent.

fixup protocol FTP Command

The syntax of the **fixup protocol ftp** command is as follows:

```
fixup protocol ftp port[-port] [strict]
no fixup protocol ftp port[-port]
clear fixup protocol ftp
```

where *port[-port]* is the single port or port range that the PIX Firewall will inspect for FTP connections.

By default, the **fixup protocol ftp 21** command is enabled and the PIX Firewall inspects port 21 connections for FTP control traffic. If you have FTP servers using ports other than port 21, you need to use the **fixup protocol ftp** *port-number* command to have the PIX Firewall inspect these non-standard ports for FTP traffic. The **strict** option causes **fixup protocol ftp** to require that every FTP request be acknowledged before a new command is allowed and prevents web browsers from embedding commands in FTP requests. Any FTP packets containing embedded commands are dropped. Example 9-2 demonstrates the use of the **fixup protocol ftp** command and its **no** form to both configure and remove standard and non-standard ports for FTP.

Example 9-2   *Configuring and Removing Standard and Non-standard Ports for FTP*

```
pixfirewall#(config) fixup protocol ftp 2121
pixfirewall#(config) fixup protocol ftp 2001
pixfirewall#(config) no fixup protocol ftp 2121
pixfirewall#(config) no fixup protocol ftp 2001
```

The **fixup protocol ftp** command enables the PIX Firewall to perform the following operations for FTP traffic on the indicated port:

- Perform NAT or PAT in packet payload.
- Dynamically create conduits for FTP data connections.
- Log FTP commands (when syslog is enabled and the logging level is debug).

Use the **no** form of the command as indicated in Example 9-2 to disable the inspection of traffic on the indicated port for FTP connections. If the **fixup protocol ftp** command is not enabled for a given port, then

- Outbound standard FTP will not work properly on that port.
- Outbound passive FTP will work properly on that port as long as outbound traffic is not explicitly disallowed.

- Inbound standard FTP will work properly on that port if a conduit to the inside server exists.
- Inbound passive FTP will not work properly on that port.

Using the **clear fixup protocol ftp** command without any arguments causes the PIX Firewall to clear all previous **fixup protocol ftp** assignments and set port 21 back as the default.

Remote Shell (rsh)

The rsh daemon running on a UNIX or Windows host provides remote execution facilities with authentication based on privileged port numbers from trusted hosts. Typically, the daemon checks the requesting client's source IP address and source port. The source port should be in the range of 512–1023; otherwise the service should abort the connection.

A second connection is then created from the rsh daemon to the specified port on the client's machine for *standard error output*.

The rsh daemon then validates the host/client name by checking the /etc/hosts.equiv and ~/.rhosts files. If the check fails, the connection is aborted and a diagnostic message is returned.

CAUTION   Many reconnaissance tools look for misconfigured rsh services as a first step to gain unauthorized access to your hosts. Because there are Windows ports of rsh available, this should no longer be considered a *UNIX-only* vulnerability. The safest approach to rsh is to prohibit inbound rsh connections from outside your network.

Figure 9-3 shows transactions between the client and server for rsh.

The **fixup protocol rsh** command enables the PIX Firewall to secure rsh requests in the following manner:

- **Outbound connections**—When standard error messages are sent from the server, the PIX Firewall opens a temporary inbound conduit for this channel. This conduit is torn down once it is no longer needed.
- **Inbound connections**—If a conduit exists allowing inbound connections to an rsh server, and if all outbound TCP traffic is implicitly allowed, no special handling is required because the server initiates the standard error channel from the inside.

If a conduit exists allowing inbound connections to an rsh server, and if all outbound TCP traffic is not implicitly allowed, the PIX Firewall opens a temporary conduit for the standard error channel from the server. This conduit is torn down after the messages are sent.

Figure 9-3   *rsh Client/Server Transactions*

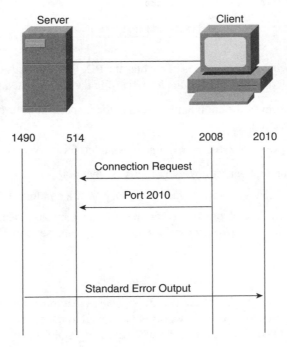

fixup protocol rsh Command

The syntax of the **fixup protocol rsh** command is as follows:

```
fixup protocol rsh port[-port]
no fixup protocol rsh port[-port]
clear fixup protocol rsh
```

where *port[-port]* is the single port or port range that the PIX Firewall will inspect for rsh connections.

By default, the PIX Firewall inspects port 514 connections for rsh traffic. If you have rsh servers using ports other than port 514, use the **fixup protocol rsh** command as shown in Example 9-3 to instruct the PIX Firewall to inspect these other ports for rsh traffic.

Example 9-3 *Configuring and Removing Standard and Non-Standard Ports for RSH*

```
pixfirewall#(config) fixup protocol rsh 514
pixfirewall#(config) fixup protocol rsh 5141
pixfirewall#(config) no fixup protocol rsh 514
pixfirewall#(config) no fixup protocol rsh 5141
```

The **fixup protocol rsh** command enables the PIX Firewall to dynamically create conduits for rsh standard error connections for rsh traffic on the indicated port.

Use the **no** form of the command to disable the inspection of traffic on the indicated port for rsh connections.

If the **fixup protocol rsh** command is not enabled for a given port, then

- Outbound rsh will not work properly on that port.
- Inbound rsh will work properly on that port if a conduit to the inside server exists.

Using the **clear fixup protocol rsh** command without any arguments causes the PIX Firewall to clear all previous **fixup protocol rsh** assignments and set port 514 back as the default.

SQL*Net

SQL*Net is used to query remote SQL databases. Although the protocol was written by Oracle for Oracle databases, it works equally well to query the SQL databases of other vendors. The main issue to consider when securing SQL*Net is that while it only uses one TCP port for communications, that port can be redirected to a different port and, even more commonly, to a different secondary server altogether. When a client starts an SQL*Net connection, it opens a standard TCP channel from one of its high-order ports to port 1521 on the server. The server then proceeds to redirect the client to a different port or IP address. The client tears down the initial TCP connection and establishes the second connection using the redirected port.

NOTE   While the default port inspected by the **fixup protocol sqlnet** command is 1521, Oracle registered TCP and UDP port 66 with IANA (Internet Assigned Numbers Authority). You may be required to add **fixup protocol 66** to your configuration to support your particular implementation. Please see the following web page for details: www.iana.org/cgi-bin/usr-port-number.pl

---

Figure 9-4 illustrates transactions between the client and the server for SQL*Net connections.

Figure 9-4   *SQL*Net Client/Server Transactions*

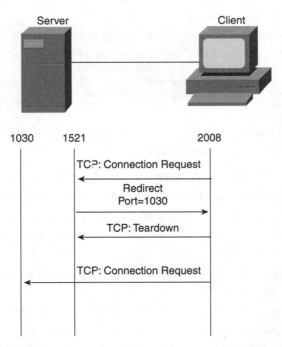

For SQL*Net traffic, the PIX Firewall behaves in the following manner:

- **Outbound connections**—If all outbound TCP traffic is implicitly allowed, no special handling is required because the client initiates all TCP connections from the inside.

  If all outbound TCP traffic is not implicitly allowed, the PIX Firewall opens a conduit for the redirected channel between the server and the client.

- **Inbound connections**—If a conduit exists allowing inbound SQL*Net connections to an SQL*Net server, the PIX Firewall opens an inbound conduit for the redirected channel.

fixup protocol sqlnet Command

The syntax of the **fixup protocol sqlnet** command is as follows:

```
fixup protocol sqlnet port[-port]
no fixup protocol sqlnet port[-port]
clear fixup protocol sqlnet
```

where *port*[*-port*] is a single port or port range that the PIX Firewall will inspect for SQL*Net connections.

By default, the PIX Firewall inspects port 1521 connections for SQL*Net traffic. If you have SQL*Net servers using ports other than port 1521, use the **fixup protocol sqlnet** command as illustrated in Example 9-4 to instruct the PIX Firewall to inspect these other ports for SQL*Net traffic.

Example 9-4 *Adding and Removing Standard and Non-standard Ports for SQL*NET*

```
pixfirewall#(config) fixup protocol sqlnet 1521
pixfirewall#(config) fixup protocol sqlnet 66
pixfirewall#(config) no fixup protocol sqlnet 1521
pixfirewall#(config) no fixup protocol sqlnet 66
```

The **fixup protocol sqlnet** command causes the PIX Firewall to do the following for SQL*Net traffic on the indicated port:

- Perform NAT in packet payload.

- Dynamically create conduits for SQL*Net redirected connections.

Use the **no** form of the command to disable the inspection of traffic on the indicated port for SQL*Net connections. If the **fixup protocol sqlnet** command is not enabled for a given port, then the following will occur:

- Outbound SQL*Net will work properly on that port as long as outbound traffic is not explicitly disallowed.

- Inbound passive SQL*Net will not work properly on that port.

Using the **clear fixup protocol sqlnet** command without any arguments causes the PIX Firewall to clear all previous **fixup protocol sqlnet** assignments and set port 1521 back as the default.

Multimedia Support

This section discusses multimedia: advantages and supported applications, H.323 support, and important multimedia configuration considerations.

Multimedia applications present a particularly daunting challenge to a firewall, as clients may transmit requests on TCP, get responses on UDP or TCP, use dynamic ports, may use the same port for source and destination, and so on. Every application behaves in a different way. Implementing support for all multimedia applications using a single secure method is very difficult.

Two examples of multimedia client applications are as follows:

- RealAudio clients send the originating connection request to TCP port 7070. The RealAudio server replies with multiple UDP streams anywhere from UDP port 6970 through 7170 on the client machine.

- The CUseeMe client sends the originating request from TCP port 7649 to TCP port 7648. The CUseeMe datagram is unique in that it includes the legitimate IP address in the header as well as in the payload and sends responses from UDP port 7648 to UDP port 7648.

The Cisco Secure PIX Firewall dynamically opens and closes UDP ports for secure multimedia connections. This significantly reduces the security risk posed by opening a large range of ports and mitigates the need to reconfigure application clients.

Also, the PIX Firewall supports multimedia with or without NAT. Firewalls that cannot support multimedia with NAT limit multimedia usage to registered users only or require exposing inside IP addresses to the Internet. Lack of NAT support for multimedia often forces multimedia vendors to join proprietary alliances with firewall vendors to accomplish compatibility for their applications.

Real Time Streaming Protocol (RTSP)

The Real Time Streaming Protocol (RTSP), described in RFC 2326, is a real-time audio and video delivery protocol used by many popular multimedia applications. It uses one TCP channel and sometimes two additional UDP channels. RTSP applications use the well-known port 554, usually TCP and rarely UDP. RFC 2326 requires only TCP so the PIX Firewall only supports TCP. This TCP channel is the control channel and is used to negotiate the other two UDP channels depending on the transport mode that is configured on the client.

The first UDP channel is the data connection and may use one of the following transport modes:

- Real-Time Transport Protocol (RTP)
- Real Data Transport Protocol (RDT) (developed by RealNetworks, Inc.)

The second UDP channel is another control channel, and it may use one of the following modes:

- RTP Control Protocol (RTCP)
- UDP Resend

RTSP also supports a TCP-only mode. This mode contains only one TCP connection, which is used as the control and data channels. Because this mode contains only one constant standard TCP connection, no special handling by the PIX Firewall is required.

The following RTSP applications are supported by the PIX Firewall:

- Cisco IP/TV
- Apple QuickTime 4
- RealNetworks

- RealAudio
- RealPlayer
- RealServer

Note that RDT Multicast mode is not supported.

RTP Mode

In standard RTP mode, the following three channels are used by RTSP:

- **TCP control channel**—Standard TCP connection initiated from the client to the server.

- **RTP data channel**—Simplex (unidirectional) UDP session used for media delivery using the RTP packet format from the server to the client. The client's port is always an even-numbered port.

- **RTCP reports**—Duplex (bi-directional) UDP session used to provide synchronization information to the client and packet-loss information to the server. The RTCP port is always the next consecutive port from the RTP data port.

Figure 9-5 illustrates the communication between client and server in standard RTP mode for RTSP.

Figure 9-5 *Standard RTP Mode Client/Server Transactions*

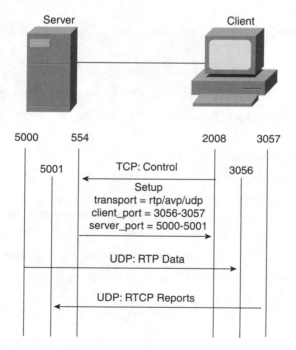

For standard RTP mode RTSP traffic, the PIX Firewall behaves in the following manner:

- **Outbound connections**—After the client and the server negotiate the transport mode and the ports to use for the sessions, the PIX Firewall opens temporary inbound conduits for the RTP data channel and RTCP report channel from the server.

- **Inbound connections**—If a conduit exists allowing inbound RTSP connections to an RTSP server, and if all outbound UDP traffic is implicitly allowed, no special handling is required, since the server initiates the data and report channel from the inside.

  If a conduit exists allowing inbound RTSP connections to an RTSP server, and if all outbound TCP traffic is not implicitly allowed, the PIX Firewall opens temporary conduits for the data and report channels from the server.

RealNetworks' RDT Mode

In RealNetworks' RDT mode, the following three channels are used by RTSP:

- **A TCP control channel**—Standard TCP connection initiated from the client to the server.

- **A UDP data channel**—Simplex (unidirectional) UDP session used for media delivery using the standard UDP packet format from the server to the client.

- **A UDP resend**—Simplex (unidirectional) UDP session used for the client to request that the server resend lost data packets.

Figure 9-6 illustrates the communication between client and server in RealNetworks' RDT mode for RTSP.

For RealNetworks' RDT mode RTSP traffic, the PIX Firewall will behave in the following manner:

- **Outbound connections**—If outbound UDP traffic is implicitly allowed, and after the client and the server negotiate the transport mode and the ports to use for the session, the PIX Firewall opens a temporary inbound conduit for the UDP data channel from the server.

  If outbound UDP traffic is not implicitly allowed, and after the client and the server negotiate the transport mode and the ports to use for the session, the PIX Firewall opens a temporary inbound conduit for the UDP data channel from the server and a temporary outbound conduit for the UDP resend channel from the client.

- **Inbound connections**—If a conduit exists allowing inbound RTSP connections to an RTSP server, and if all outbound UDP traffic is implicitly allowed, the PIX Firewall opens a temporary outbound conduit for the UDP data channel from the server.

If a conduit exists allowing inbound connections to an RTSP server, and if all outbound TCP traffic is not implicitly allowed, the PIX Firewall opens temporary conduits for the UDP data and UDP resend channels from the server and client, respectively.

Figure 9-6 *RealNetworks' RDT Mode Client/Server Transactions*

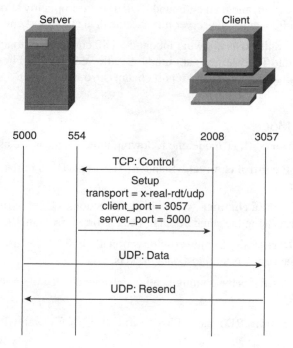

By default, the PIX Firewall does not inspect any ports for RTSP connections. To enable the PIX Firewall to inspect specific ports for RTSP traffic, such as the standard port 554, use the **fixup protocol rtsp** command.

The **fixup protocol rtsp** command enables the PIX Firewall to dynamically create conduits for RTSP UDP channels for RTSP traffic on the indicated port. The syntax of the **fixup protocol rtsp** command is as follows:

```
fixup protocol rtsp port[-port]
no fixup protocol rtsp port[-port]
clear fixup protocol rtsp
```

where *port*[*-port*] is the single port or port range that the PIX Firewall will inspect for RTSP connections.

Use the **no** form of the command as shown in Example 9-5 to disable inspection of traffic on the indicated port for RTSP connections. If the **fixup protocol rtsp** command is not enabled for a given port, then neither inbound nor outbound RTSP will work properly on that port.

Example 9-5   *Adding and Deleting Standard and Non-standard Ports for RTSP*

```
pixfirewall#(config) fixup protocol rtsp 554
pixfirewall#(config) fixup protocol rtsp 8554-8574
pixfirewall#(config) no fixup protocol rtsp 554
pixfirewall#(config) no fixup protocol rtsp 8554-8574
```

NOTE   To allow support for Cisco IP/TV the RTSP fixup protocol needs to be configured for TCP port 8554 as well as the default of TCP port 554 using **fixup protocol rtsp 8554**.

Using the **clear fixup protocol rtsp** command without any arguments causes the PIX Firewall to clear all previous **fixup protocol rtsp** assignments.

H.323

H.323 is more complicated than other protocols because it uses two TCP connections and several UDP sessions for a single "call." (Only one of the TCP connections goes to a well-known port; all the other ports are negotiated and thus temporary.) Furthermore, the content of the streams is far more difficult for firewalls to understand than existing protocols, because H.323 encodes packets using Abstract Syntax Notation (ASN.1).

Other protocols and standards supported within H.323 are

- H.225-Registration, Admission, and Status (RAS)
- H.225-Call Signaling
- H.245-Control Signaling
- TPKT Header
- Q.931 Messages
- Abstract Syntax Notation (ASN.1) (PIX Firewall 5.2)

Supported H.323 versions are as follows:

- H.323 v1
- H.323 v2 (PIX Firewall 5.2)

PIX Firewall supported H.323 applications include

- Cisco Multimedia Conference Manager
- Microsoft NetMeeting

- Intel Video Phone
- CUseeMe Networks
  - — MeetingPoint
  - — CUseeMe Pro
- VocalTec
  - — Internet Phone
  - — Gatekeeper

fixup protocol h323 Command

By default, the PIX Firewall inspects port 1720 connections for H.323 traffic. If you have H.323 servers operating on ports other than port 1720, use the **fixup protocol h323** command to have the PIX Firewall inspect those non-standard ports for H.323 traffic. The syntax of the **fixup protocol h323** command is as follows:

```
fixup protocol h323 port[-port]
no fixup protocol h323 port[-port]
clear fixup protocol h323
```

where *port*[*-port*] is a single port or port range that the PIX Firewall will inspect for H.323 connections.

Example 9-6 demonstrates the typical use of the **fixup protocol h323** command and its **no** form to add and delete standard and non-standard ports for H.323 traffic.

Example 9-6   *Adding and Deleting Standard and Non-standard Ports for H.323*

```
pixfirewall(config)# fixup protocol h323 1720
pixfirewall(config)# fixup protocol h323 7720-7740
pixfirewall(config)# no fixup protocol h323 1720
pixfirewall(config)# no fixup protocol h323 7720-7740
```

The **fixup protocol h323** command causes the PIX Firewall to do the following for H.323 traffic on the indicated port:

- Perform NAT in packet payload.
- Dynamically create conduits for TCP or UDP channels.

Use the **no** form of the command to disable the inspection of traffic on the indicated port for H.323 connections. If the **fixup protocol h323** command is not enabled for a given port, then neither outbound nor inbound H.323 will work properly on that port.

Using the **clear fixup protocol h323** command without any arguments causes the PIX Firewall to clear all previous **fixup protocol h323** assignments and set port 1720 back as the default.

Attack Guards

This section discusses the Attack Guards features put in place to mitigate attacks via e-mail; Domain Name System (DNS); fragmentation; authentication, authorization, and accounting (AAA); and SYN flooding.

MailGuard

MailGuard provides a mechanism to safeguard Simple Mail Transfer Protocol (SMTP) connections from the outside to an e-mail server. MailGuard allows a mail server to be deployed on a network protected by the PIX without it being exposed to known security problems with certain mail server implementations. Bearing this in mind, Cisco recommends placing mail servers on a DMZ interface and *not* on the inside network.

Only the SMTP commands specified in RFC 821 section 4.5.1 are allowed on a mail server. These are: **HELO**, **MAIL**, **RCPT**, **DATA**, **RSET**, **NOOP**, and **QUIT**. When the PIX Firewall observes an SMTP command not in the preceding list, the PIX Firewall proxies a response of "500 command unrecognized" to the remote device and drops the packet before it reaches the protected mail server.

MailGuard isn't a panacea. While it proxies connections, limits the types of SMTP messages that reach your mail server, and hides the SMTP banner that indicates the type and version of the protected mail server, MailGuard can't protect your mail server from all known attacks. Even protected by MailGuard, your mail server needs to be properly configured and patched against known threats.

Also, certain configurations of Microsoft Exchange Server require the use of commands not allowed by MailGuard. In this scenario, MailGuard must be disabled using the **no fixup protocol smtp 25** command.

By default, the PIX Firewall inspects port 25 connections for SMTP traffic. If you have SMTP servers using ports other than port 25, you must use the **fixup protocol smtp** *port-number* command to have the PIX Firewall inspect these other ports for SMTP traffic. The syntax of the **fixup protocol smtp** command is as follows:

```
fixup protocol smtp port[-port]
no fixup protocol smtp port[-port]
clear fixup protocol smtp
```

where *port*[-*port*] is a single port or port range that the PIX Firewall will inspect for SMTP connections.

Use the **no** form of the command to disable the inspection of traffic on the indicated port for SMTP connections. If the **fixup protocol smtp** command is not enabled for a given port, then potential mail server vulnerabilities are exposed. Example 9-7 illustrates configuration and removal of the MailGuard feature with standard and non-standard ports.

Using the **clear fixup protocol smtp** command without any arguments causes the PIX Firewall to clear all previous **fixup protocol smtp** assignments and set port 25 back as the default.

Example 9-7 *Adding and Deleting Standard and Non-standard Ports for Mail Guard*

```
pixfirewall(config)# fixup protocol smtp 25
pixfirewall(config)# fixup protocol smtp 2525
pixfirewall(config)# no fixup protocol smtp 25
pixfirewall(config)# no fixup protocol smtp 2525
```

DNS Guard

DNS Guard identifies an outbound DNS query request and allows only a single DNS response back to the sender. A host may query several servers for a response in case the first server is slow in responding; however, only the first answer to the specific question will be allowed back in. All the additional answers from other servers are dropped. After the client issues a DNS request, a dynamic conduit allows UDP packets to return from the DNS server. The default UDP timer expires in two minutes. Because DNS is frequently attacked, leaving the conduit open for two minutes creates an unnecessary risk. DNS Guard is enabled by default and cannot be configured or disabled. DNS Guard performs the following actions:

* Automatically tears down the UDP conduit on the PIX Firewall as soon as the DNS response is received. It doesn't wait for the default UDP timer to close the session.

* Prevents against UDP session hijacking and denial of service (DoS) attacks.

Figure 9-7 illustrates the PIX's involvement in DNS queries.

Fragmentation Guard

Use the **sysopt security fragguard** command to enable the Fragmentation Guard (FragGuard) feature. This feature enforces two additional security checks on IP packets in addition to the security checks recommended by RFC 1858 against the many IP fragment-style attacks: teardrop, land, and so on. The first security check requires that each non-initial IP fragment be associated with an already-seen valid initial IP fragment. As of PIX OS version 5.1, an initial fragment is not required. This is because fragments may arrive out of order. For the second security check, IP fragments are rated 100 full IP fragmented packets per second to each internal host. This means the PIX can process 1200 packet fragments a second. The FragGuard feature operates on all interfaces in the PIX Firewall and cannot be selectively enabled or disabled by interface.

Figure 9-7   *DNS Guard*

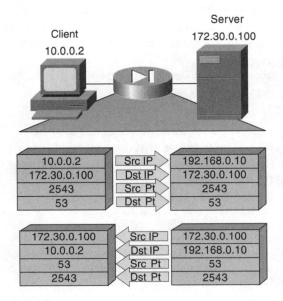

FragGuard and Virtual Reassembly

The following virtual reassembly features are new in version 5.1:

- Version 5.1 enhances IP fragment protection and performs full reassembly of all ICMP error messages and virtual reassembly of the remaining IP fragments that are routed through the PIX Firewall. The previous restriction with the FragGuard feature that the initial fragment must arrive first has been lifted.

- A new teardrop syslog message has been added to notify of any fragment overlapping and small fragment offset anomalies.

- Syslog message, **%PIX-2-106020: Deny IP teardrop fragment (size = *num*, offset = *num*) from *IP_addr* to *IP_addr*** was added in this release to log teardrop.c attacks. This message occurs when the PIX Firewall discards an IP packet with a teardrop signature with either a small offset or fragment overlapping. You should treat this event as a hostile attempt to circumvent the PIX Firewall or the Cisco Secure Intrusion Detection System.

- IP packets fragmented into more than 12 elements cannot pass through the PIX Firewall. Twelve is the maximum number of 1500 byte fragments required to assemble a 16 KB payload. 16,384 bytes is the maximum IP MTU for Token Ring.

The PIX Firewall uses the **sysopt security fragguard** command to enforce the security policy determined by an **access-list permit** or **access-list deny** command to permit or deny packets through the PIX Firewall. The **sysopt security fragguard** command is disabled by default. The syntax for the **sysopt security fragguard** command is as follows:

```
sysopt security fragguard
no sysopt security fragguard
```

This command has no arguments.

CAUTION   Use of the **sysopt security fragguard** command breaks normal IP fragmentation conventions. However, not using this command exposes PIX Firewall-protected hosts to the possibility of IP fragmentation attacks. Cisco recommends that packet fragmentation not be permitted on the network if at all possible.

TIP   If the PIX Firewall is used as a tunnel for FDDI packets between routers, the FragGuard feature should be disabled.

TIP   Because many Linux and UNIX implementations send IP fragments in reverse order, fragmented Linux packets will not pass through the PIX Firewall with the **sysopt security fragguard** enabled. By sending the final fragment first, the Linux/UNIX host knows the final offset of the payload and can pre-allocate an interface buffer.

AAA Floodguard

While using AAA with the PIX to identify, authorize, and monitor your users helps mitigate the problem of unauthorized access to information resources, it also provides a hacker with an opportunity for mischief. If all connections *must* be authenticated, what would happen if someone forged so many authentication requests that the PIX's AAA resources were overwhelmed? Denial of service!

The **floodguard** command allows you to automatically reclaim PIX Firewall resources if the user authentication (uauth) subsystem runs out of resources. If an inbound or outbound uauth connection is being attacked or overused, the PIX actively reclaims TCP user resources. When resources are depleted, the PIX Firewall lists messages indicating that it is out of resources or out of TCP users. If the PIX Firewall uauth subsystem is depleted,

TCP user resources in different states are reclaimed depending on urgency in the following order:

1 Timewait

2 FinWait

3 Embryonic

4 Idle

The **floodguard** command is enabled by default.

The syntax of the **floodguard** command is as follows:

```
floodguard enable | disable
```

where **enable** enables the AAA Floodguard and **disable** disables the AAA Floodguard.

SYN Floodguard

SYN flood attacks, also known as *TCP flood* or *half-open connections* attacks, are common DoS attacks perpetrated against IP servers. SYN flood attacks are perpetrated as follows:

1 The attacker spoofs a nonexistent source IP address or IP addresses and floods the target with SYN packets pretending to come from the spoofed host(s).

2 SYN packets to a host are the first step in the three-way handshake of a TCP-type connection; therefore, the target responds as expected with SYN-ACK packets destined to the spoofed host or hosts.

3 Because these SYN-ACK packets are sent to hosts that do not exist, the target waits for the corresponding ACK packets that never show up. This causes the target to overflow its port buffer with embryonic or half-open connections and stop responding to legitimate requests.

Figure 9-8 illustrates this type of attack.

To protect internal hosts against DoS attacks, use the **static** command to limit the number of embryonic connections allowed to the server. Use the *em_limit* argument to limit the number of embryonic or half-open connections that the server or servers you are trying to protect can handle without being attacked by a DoS.

In version 5.2 of the PIX OS the TCP Intercept feature was added to the SYN Floodguard. The TCP Intercept feature improves the embryonic connection response of the PIX Firewall. When the number of embryonic connections exceeds the configured threshold, the PIX Firewall intercepts and proxies new connections.

Figure 9-8 *SYN Flood Attack*

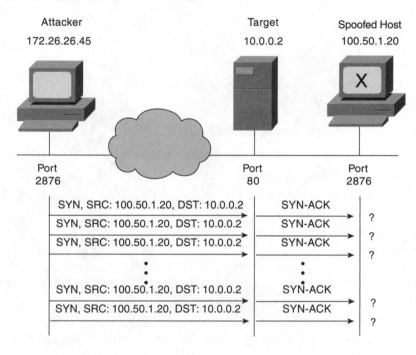

Prior to version 5.2, the PIX did not allow new connections after the embryonic connection threshold was exceeded. While it protected the internal host from having all of its TCP connection slots filled, it still resulted in DoS.

This feature requires no change to the PIX Firewall command set, only that the embryonic connection limit on the **static** command has a new behavior.

The syntax used in the **static** command for enabling the SYN Floodguard is as follows:

```
static [(internal_if_name, external_if_name)] global_ip local_ip [netmask network_mask]
  [max_conns [em_limit]]
```

Table 9-1 provides descriptions for the **static** command arguments.

Table 9-1   **static** *Command Arguments*

Argument	Description
internal_if_name	The internal network interface name.
external_if_name	The external network interface name.
global_ip	The global IP address for an outside interface. This address cannot be a PAT IP address.

Table 9-1 **static** *Command Arguments (Continued)*

local_ip	The local IP address on an inside network.
network_mask	The network mask for the *global_ip* and *local_ip*.
max_conns	The maximum connections permitted to the *local_ip*. The default = 0 (unlimited).
em_limit	The maximum embryonic connection permitted to the *local_ip*. The default = 0 (unlimited).

Setting the *max_conns* and *em_limit* arguments should not be taken lightly. If you set the limit too high, you risk overloading the IP stack of your statically translated host and falling victim to a DoS attack. If the limits are set too low, there is the risk of denying service to legitimate users. Example 9-9 demonstrates setting the maximum connection and embryonic connection limits on two hosts. The command shown in Example 9-9 is for illustration purposes only and should not be arbitrarily used. While no firm guidelines exist for setting these limits, the general rule is to set the *em-limit* and *max_conn* parameters to a value that won't have a negative impact on the host. Contact the company that wrote the IP stack of your hosts for information on the maximum number of TCP connection slots available and set the *em_limit* lower than the maximum.

The **show local-host** command assists you in characterizing your "normal" load on a statically translated host, both before and after setting limits.

The **show local-host** command shows you the current number of connections and embryonic connections against any limit you have set using the **static** command.

Example 9-8 shows sample output from the **show local-host** command, indicating that this host has no embryonic connection limit set.

Example 9-8 **show local-hosts** *Command Output*

```
show local-host 10.1.1.15
local host: <10.1.1.15>, conn(s)/limit = 2/0, embryonic(s)/limit = 0/0
   Xlate(s):
        PAT Global 172.16.3.200(1024) Local 10.1.1.15(55812)
        PAT Global 172.16.3.200(1025) Local 10.1.1.15(56836)
        PAT Global 172.16.3.200(1026) Local 10.1.1.15(57092)
        PAT Global 172.16.3.200(1027) Local 10.1.1.15(56324)
        PAT Global 172.16.3.200(1028) Local 10.1.1.15(7104)
   Conn(s):
        TCP out 192.150.49.10:23 in 10.1.1.15:1246 idle 0:00:20 Bytes 449 flags UIO
        TCP out 192.150.49.10:21 in 10.1.1.15:1247 idle 0:00:10 Bytes 359 flags UIO
```

The Xlate(s) field describes the translation slot information and the Conn(s) field provides connection state information.

Example 9-9 demonstrates how you would configure maximum connections and embryonic connection limits to statically translated hosts.

Example 9-9 *Configuring Maximum Connections and Embryonic Connection Limits to Statically Translated Hosts*

```
pixfirewall(config)# static (inside, outside) 200.100.1.10 10.100.1.10
   netmask 255.255.255.255 1000 1500
pixfirewall(config)# static (inside, outside) 200.100.1.15 10.100.1.10
   netmask 255.255.255.255 2000 2500
```

In order to protect external hosts against DoS attacks and to limit the number of embryonic connections allowed to the server, use the **nat** command. Use the *em_limit* argument to limit the number of embryonic or half-open connections that the server or servers you are trying to protect can handle without being attacked by a DoS.

The syntax used in the **nat** command for enabling the SYN Floodguard is as follows:

> **nat** [(*if_name*)] *nat_id local_ip* [*netmask* [*max_conns* [*em_limit*]]]

Table 9-2 provides descriptions for the **nat** command arguments.

Table 9-2 **nat** *Command Arguments*

Argument	Description
if_name	The internal network interface name.
nat_id	A number used for matching with a corresponding global pool of IP addressees. The matching global pool must use the same *nat_id*.
local_ip	The internal IP address or networks that will be translated to a global pool of IP addresses.
netmask	The network mask for the *local_ip*.
max_conns	The maximum connections permitted to hosts accessed from *local_ip*. The default = 0 (unlimited).
em_limit	The maximum embryonic connection permitted to hosts accessed from *local_ip*. The default = 0 (unlimited).

Setting the maximum connection and embryonic connection limits on outbound traffic must be considered carefully. If you set the limit too high, you risk giving individuals in your organization the ability to *perpetrate* a DoS attack. If the limits are set too low, there is the risk of denying service to legitimate internal users. Example 9-10 demonstrates how to set the maximum connection and embryonic connection limits for the Inside and DMZ interfaces. The DMZ interface uses much lower limits due to the low number of connections initiated from that interface

Example 9-10 *Configuring Maximum Connections and Embryonic Connection Limits to Protect Against Initiating DoS Attacks*

```
pixfirewall(config)# nat (inside) 1 0.0.0.0 0.0.0.0 5000 5000
pixfirewall(config)# nat (dmz) 1 0.0.0.0 0.0.0.0 500 500
```

Summary

This section summarizes the key points in this chapter.

- The PIX offers an application-aware feature called a *fixup protocol* to enable the PIX to respond to the needs of complex mutlichannel applications by monitoring their control channels and dynamically opening and closing ports as needed by the protocol being monitored.

- The PIX is able to securely handle the popular RTSP and H.323 multimedia protocols.

- The PIX also features attack guards to mitigate threats to e-mail servers, DNS responses, fragmentation attacks, and certain types of DoS attacks.

Review Questions

To test what you have learned in this chapter, answer the following questions and then refer to Appendix F for the answers.

1 How does a **fixup protocol** command know when to open a conduit for an inbound connection?

2 My UNIX administrator has asked me to allow rsh access through the PIX Firewall to administer servers from home. Is this a good idea?

3 If the **fixup protocol rtsp 554** is disabled by default, why are my users able to view content?

4 I'm planning to install a PIX Firewall, but I've heard that the MailGuard feature is incompatible with Microsoft Exchange Server. What can be done to overcome this?

This chapter introduces you to the knowledge necessary to configure failover and stateful failover on the PIX Firewall. Specifically, this chapter covers the following topics:

- Failover Operation
- Configuration Replication
- Failover Monitoring
- Fail Back Rules
- Interface Testing
- Failover Considerations in Switched Environments
- Stateful Failover
- Failover Commands and Configuration

CHAPTER 10

Cisco PIX Firewall Failover

The failover function for the Cisco Secure PIX Firewall provides a safeguard in case a PIX Firewall fails. Specifically, when one PIX Firewall fails, another immediately takes its place.

In the failover process, there are two PIX Firewalls: the primary PIX Firewall and the secondary PIX Firewall. Under normal operation, the primary PIX Firewall functions as the active PIX Firewall, performing normal network functions. The secondary PIX Firewall functions as the standby PIX Firewall, ready to take control should the active PIX Firewall fail to perform. When the primary PIX Firewall fails, the secondary PIX Firewall becomes active while the primary PIX Firewall goes on standby. This entire process is called *failover*.

The primary PIX Firewall is connected to the secondary PIX Firewall through a failover connection: a failover cable. The failover cable has one end labeled *primary*, which plugs into the primary PIX Firewall, and the other end labeled *secondary*, which plugs into the secondary PIX Firewall. The role of primary or secondary is established by the failover cable. Even though a PIX Firewall may switch between active or standby, once primary and secondary roles are established by the placement of the failover cable, they never change.

A failover occurs when one of the following situations occurs:

- The **standby active** command is issued on the standby PIX.
- Block memory exhaustion occurs for 15 consecutive seconds or more on the active PIX Firewall.
- Network interface card (NIC) status. If the link status of an NIC is *down*, the unit will fail. Down means that the NIC is not plugged into an operational port. If an NIC has been configured as administratively down, it does not fail this test.
- Failover Network communications. The two units send hello packets to each other over all network interfaces. If no hello messages are received for two failover poll intervals, the non-responding interface is put in testing mode to determine the problem.
- Failover cable communication. The two units send hello messages to each other over the failover cable. If the standby doesn't hear from the active within two failover poll intervals, and the cable status is OK, the standby takes over as active.

- Cable errors. The failover cable is wired so that each unit can distinguish between the following:
    — A power failure in the other unit
    — A cable unplugged from this unit
    — A cable unplugged from the other unit
- If the standby detects that the active is powered off (or set to reload/reset), it takes active control. If the failover cable is unplugged, a syslog is generated but no switching will occur.

CAUTION At bootup, if both units are powered up without the failover cable installed, they both become active, creating a duplicate IP address with different MAC addresses, causing conflict on your network. The failover cable must be installed for failover to work correctly.

When actively functioning, the primary PIX Firewall uses system IP addresses and MAC addresses. The secondary PIX Firewall, when on standby, uses failover IP addresses and MAC addresses.

When the primary PIX Firewall fails and the secondary PIX Firewall becomes active, the secondary PIX Firewall assumes the system IP addresses and MAC addresses of the primary PIX Firewall. Then the primary PIX Firewall, functioning in standby, assumes the failover IP addresses and MAC addresses of the secondary PIX Firewall.

Failover Operation

In the "Failover Operation" section, you will learn the functional components of failover and the commands necessary to enable Hot Standby and stateful failover.

Failover Cable

The failover cable is the only additional hardware required to support failover. The failover cable is a modified RS-232 serial link cable with a speed setting of 9600 baud. A failover cable is shipped with every PIX Firewall.

NOTE In PIX Software Release 5.2, the speed was increased to 115.2K baud.

Basic failover communication is performed though the failover cable. Communication through failover cable is message-based and reliable. Every message sent requires acknowledgment (an *ACK*). If a message is not ACK'd by the other PIX within 3 seconds, the message is retransmitted. After 5 retransmissions without an ACK (for a total of 15 seconds), a failover condition is triggered and the standby PIX fails the primary and becomes the active PIX.

The orientation of the failover cable is crucial to correct failover operation. The end of the failover cable labeled primary must be connected to the failover port of the Primary-Active PIX.

CAUTION   If you install the primary end of the cable in the secondary PIX, the secondary PIX will (by virtue of the orientation of the failover cable) synchronize its potentially blank configuration to the primary PIX.

TIP   If you have made the mistake of incorrectly orienting the failover cable, and have, in fact, overwritten the configuration of the primary PIX, remove the failover cable from both PIXs and power cycle the primary PIX. Unless you issue a **write memory** on the secondary, the change does not overwrite the startup configuration.

Failover communicates the following messages through the failover cable:

- MAC addresses exchange
- Hello (keepalive)
- State (Active/Standby)
- Network Link Status
- Configuration Replication

Configuration Replication

Configuration replication is the function of synchronizing the configuration of the primary PIX Firewall to the secondary PIX Firewall. For configuration replication to succeed, both the primary and secondary PIX Firewalls must be *exact* matches of each other in both hardware and software. Each PIX Firewall must be the same model, run the same OS version, and have the same number of interfaces. Also, if the primary PIX has a DES or 3DES license for use with IPSec, the secondary PIX also requires this license. Configuration replication occurs over the failover cable from the active PIX Firewall to the standby PIX Firewall when any of the three following events occurs:

- When the standby PIX Firewall completes its initial bootup, the active PIX Firewall replicates its entire configuration to the standby PIX Firewall.

- As commands are entered on the active PIX Firewall, they are sent across the failover cable to the standby PIX Firewall.

- By entering the **write standby** command on the active PIX Firewall, which forces the entire configuration in memory to be sent to the standby PIX Firewall.

Configuration replication only occurs from the *running config* of the primary to the *running config* of the secondary. Because this is not a permanent place to store configurations, you must use the **write memory** command to write the configuration into flash memory on both units. If failover occurs during replication, the new active PIX Firewall will have only a partial configuration. To recover from a configuration synchronization failure, you will need to force the primary back to active and use the **write standby** command to update the secondary.

When replication starts, the PIX Firewall console displays the message *Sync Started*, and when complete, displays the message *Sync Completed*. During replication, information cannot be entered on the PIX Firewall console. Replication can take a long time to complete for a large configuration because the failover cable is used. This is especially true on PIXs running PIX OS 5.1 or earlier, when the baud rate of the failover connection was only 9600.

Failover Monitoring

There is a failover poll interval of 15 seconds to monitor network activity, failover communications, and power status. A failure of any of these parameters on the active unit will cause the standby unit to take active control. Whenever a unit is determined to have failed, it shuts down its network interfaces.

NOTE   As of PIX OS version 5.2, the failover poll interval is user configurable with the **failover poll** command. The syntax of the **failover poll** command follows:

    failover poll seconds
where *seconds* is a value between 3 and 15 seconds.

The two units send special failover hello packets to each other over the failover cable and all interfaces every 15 seconds (excluding those interfaces that are shut down by the administrator). If either unit does not hear the hello on an interface for two consecutive poll checks, the PIX puts that LAN interface into testing mode to determine where the fault lies.

If a standby PIX does not receive a hello from the failover cable for three consecutive poll checks, the standby PIX initiates a switchover and declares the other PIX failed. If the active PIX does not hear the hello messages, it stays active and sets the other PIX as failed. A network interface is placed in testing mode if a hello packet is not received. Testing of a network interface is non-intrusive, meaning that, while it is in testing mode, it still attempts to pass normal traffic. The testing process consists of four individual tests geared toward stimulating network traffic:

- **NIC status test**—The PIX performs link up/link down tests for up to five seconds.

- **Network activity test**—If all interfaces on both PIXs pass the link test, the PIX will listen for up to five seconds for network activity on all interfaces. If no activity is received on an interface, the offending PIX is failed.

- **Address Resolution Protocol (ARP) test**—If the preceding two tests pass, the PIX reads the 10 most recent ARP entries and attempts to ping each of them.

- **PING test**—As a final arbiter, should the previous three tests all pass, the PIX will send directed broadcasts out on each interface and listen for responses.

If an interface that is in testing mode is capable of receiving traffic, it is considered operational. If it can hear other network traffic, it is assumed the error must be with the other unit not being able to send the hello packet. This results in failing the other unit. If it is determined that the testing unit cannot receive network traffic while the other can, the testing unit fails itself.

In addition to monitoring all network interfaces, failover also monitors the power status of the other unit, as well as the status of the failover cable itself. The failover cable provides the ability to detect if the other unit is plugged in and powered on. If the cable is unplugged from either unit, switching is disabled. If an active unit loses power, the standby unit takes over within 15 seconds. A unit in the failed state waits 15 seconds, and then tries to transition to the standby state. If the transition triggers a failure, the unit fails again. You can use the **failover reset** command to manually reset the PIX from the failed to standby state. If the transition triggers a failure, the unit will fail again. A PIX in the failed state cannot switch into active state.

If the failure is due to a link down condition on an interface, a link up condition clears the failed state (for example, if an interface is unplugged and then later plugged in).

Failover Monitoring Using the **show failover** Command

The following examples assume the failover cable is installed and operational. They also assume that the units have been configured with a system IP address of 192.168.10.1 and a failover IP address of 192.168.10.2 for the outside interface and a system IP address of 10.10.10.1 and failover IP address of 10.10.10.2 for the inside interface.

CAUTION	Configuring a firewall for failover and not setting the failover IP address can lead to the two PIXs flip-flopping between active and standby.

Example 10-1 shows the normal output of the **show failover** command. Note that the IP address of each unit is displayed. If no failover IP address has been entered, it displays 0.0.0.0 and monitoring of the interfaces remains in the *waiting* state. See Example 10-2 for an explanation of the waiting state.

Example 10-1 *Normal Failover*

```
pixfirewall# (config) show failover
  Failover On
    Cable status: Normal
    Reconnect timeout 0:00:00
      This host: Primary - Active
          Active time: 6885 (sec)
          Interface Outside (192.168.10.1): Normal
          Interface Inside (10.10.10.1): Normal
      Other host: Secondary - Standby
          Active time: 0 (sec)
          Interface Outside (192.168.10.2): Normal
          Interface Inside (10.10.10.2): Normal
```

Failover does not start monitoring the network interfaces until it has heard the second hello packet from the other unit on that interface. Using the default **failover poll 15** setting, this should take 30 seconds. If the PIXs are attached to a Layer 2 switch running Spanning Tree Protocol (STP), this takes twice the *forward delay* time configured in the switch (typically configured as 15 seconds), plus this 30-second delay, or one minute. At PIX bootup and immediately following a failover event, the Layer 2 switch detects a temporary bridge loop. Upon detection of the loop, it stops forwarding packets on these interfaces for the forward delay time. It then enters the *listen* mode for an additional forward delay time, during which time the switch is listening for bridge loops but not forwarding traffic (and thus not forwarding failover hello packets). After twice the forward delay time (30 seconds), traffic should resume flowing. Each PIX remains in waiting mode until it hears 30 seconds worth of hello packets from the other unit. During the time the PIX is passing traffic, it does not fail the other unit based on not hearing the hello packets. All other failover monitoring is still occurring (that is, Power, Interface Loss of Link, and Failover Cable hello). Example 10-2 shows the failover interfaces in the waiting state, indicating that two failover hellos have yet to be exchanged.

TIP   To mitigate the effects of the spanning tree forwarding delay on Cisco Layer 2 switches, use the **spantree portfast** command. Additionally, trunking and EtherChannel should be disabled on any switch port the PIX connects to. As this is configured differently on different Cisco Catalyst switches, please refer to your product documentation for syntax assistance.

Example 10-2   *Failover in the Waiting State (Uninitialized)*

```
pixfirewall# (config) show failover
    Failover On
    Cable status: Normal
    Reconnect timeout 0:00:00
        This host: Primary - Active
            Active time: 6930 (sec)
            Interface Outside (192.168.10.1): Normal (Waiting)
            Interface Inside (10.10.10.1): Normal (Waiting)
        Other host: Secondary - Standby
            Active time: 15 (sec)
            Interface Outside (192.168.10.2): Normal (Waiting)
            Interface Inside (10.10.10.2): Normal (Waiting)
```

In Example 10-3, the failover process has detected an interface failure. Note that interface inside on the primary unit is the source of the failure. The units are back in waiting mode because of the failure. During this process, the primary PIX Firewall swaps its system IP addresses with the secondary PIX Firewall's failover IP addresses.

The failed unit has removed itself from the network (interfaces are down) and is no longer sending hello packets on the network. The active unit remains in a waiting state until the failed unit is replaced and failover communications starts again.

Example 10-3   *The Failover Process Detects an Interface Failure*

```
pixfirewall# (config) show failover
    Failover On
    Cable status: Normal
    Reconnect timeout 0:00:00
        This host: Primary - Standby (Failed)
            Active time: 7140 (sec)
            Interface Outside (192.168.10.2): Normal (Waiting)
            Interface Inside (10.10.10.2): Failed (Waiting)
        Other host: Secondary - Active
            Active time: 30 (sec)
            Interface Outside (192.168.10.1): Normal (Waiting)
            Interface Inside (10.10.10.1): Normal (Waiting)
```

Fail Back

Fail back is the term used to describe the action of restoring PIX operation from the secondary-active back to the primary-failed PIX. Fail back to the primary unit is not automatically forced, as there is no reason to switch active and standby roles. When a failed primary unit is repaired and brought back on line, it does not automatically resume as the active unit. To force a unit to be the active unit, use the **failover active** command on the primary-standby unit or the **no failover active** command on the secondary-active unit.

The results of issuing **failover active** vary depending on whether failover or stateful failover are configured, as follows:

- If stateful failover is used, connection state information is passed from the active unit to the standby unit.

- In failover mode, state information is not tracked and sessions must be re-established by applications. This means all active connections are dropped after a switchover.

Configuring Failover

This section discusses what failover and stateful failover modes are, and how to configure both.

As stated earlier in the chapter, failover enables the standby PIX Firewall to take over the duties of the active PIX Firewall when the active PIX Firewall fails. There are two types of failover:

- **Failover**—When the active PIX Firewall fails and the standby PIX Firewall becomes active, all connections are lost and client applications must initiate a new connection to restart communication through the PIX Firewall. The disconnection occurs because the standby PIX Firewall has no facility to receive connection information from the active PIX Firewall. The channel provided by the failover cable lacks the bandwidth necessary to maintain state synchronization between the two PIX Firewalls.

- **Stateful failover**—When the active PIX Firewall fails and the standby PIX Firewall becomes active, the same connection information is available at the new active PIX Firewall, and end-user applications are not required to do a reconnect to keep the same communication session. The connections remain because the stateful failover feature passes per-connection state information to the standby PIX Firewall. The TCP connection table (except HTTP) is synchronized with the secondary PIX over the interface chosen for stateful failover.

Stateful failover requires a 100-Mbps Ethernet interface on each PIX to be used exclusively for passing state information between the two PIX Firewalls. These interfaces can be connected by any of the following:

- Category 5 crossover cable directly connecting the primary PIX Firewall to the secondary PIX Firewall (100-Mbps half- or full-duplex)
- 100BaseTX half-duplex hub using straight Category 5 cables

- 100BaseTX full duplex on a dedicated switch or dedicated virtual LAN (VLAN) of a switch using straight Category 5 cables

---

NOTE   The PIX Firewall does not support the use of either Token Ring or FDDI for the stateful failover dedicated interface. Data is passed over the dedicated interface using IP protocol 105. No hosts or routers should be on this interface.

TIP   On a PIX 535, it is possible to use Gigabit interfaces for inside and outside. In this configuration, it is recommended to dedicate a Gigabit interface on the primary and secondary PIX to transfer state information. A 100-Mbps full-duplex interface would easily be swamped, trying to maintain session state at Gigabit speeds.

Example 10-4 shows the output of the **show failover** command with stateful failover enabled.

NOTE   Because interface VPN is administratively shut down, it does not participate in the failover interface poll.

Example 10-4   *Interface Rescue Configured as the Stateful Failover Link with Stateful Statistics*

```
pixfirewall# (config) show failover
Failover On
Cable status: Normal
Reconnect timeout 0:00:00
Poll frequency 4 seconds
        This host: Secondary - Active
                Active time: 167464 (sec)
                Interface VPN (200.16.1.1): Link Down (Shutdown)
                Interface Rescue (172.30.255.1): Normal
                Interface DMZ (100.2.1.1): Normal
                Interface Outside (192.168.10.1): Normal
                Interface Inside (10.1.10.1): Normal
        Other host: Primary - Standby
                Active time: 0 (sec)
                Interface VPN (200.16.1.2): Link Down (Shutdown)
                Interface Rescue (172.30.255.2): Normal
                Interface DMZ (100.2.1.2): Normal
                Interface Outside (192.168.10.2): Normal
                Interface Inside (10.10.10.2): Normal
```

continues

Example 10-4 *Interface Rescue Configured as the Stateful Failover Link with Stateful Statistics (Continued)*

```
Stateful Failover Logical Update Statistics
    Link : Rescue
    Stateful Obj    xmit         xerr         rcv          rerr
    General         22501          0         34259           0
    sys cmd         16007          0         33961          13
    up time             4          0             2           0
    xlate            5094          0             6           0
    tcp conn          514          0           290           0
    udp conn            0          0             0           0
    ARP tbl           882          0             0           0
    RIP Tbl             0          0             0           0
    Logical Update Queue Information
                Cur     Max    Total
    Recv Q:       0       3     34259
    Xmit Q:       0       7     22504
```

The syntax for the **failover** command is as follows:

```
failover [active]
no failover
failover ip address if_name ip_address
failover link [stateful_if_name]
no failover link
failover poll seconds
failover reset
no failover active
show failover
```

Table 10-1 provides a syntax description for the failover command arguments and options.

Table 10-1 **failover** *Command Arguments/Options*

Argument/Option	Description
active	Make a PIX Firewall the active unit. Use this command when you need to force control of the connection back to the unit you are accessing, such as when you want to switch control back from a unit after you have fixed a problem and want to restore service to the primary unit. Either enter **no failover active** on the secondary unit to switch service to the primary, or **failover active** on the primary unit.
if_name	Interface on which the standby unit resides.
ip_address	The IP address used by the standby unit to communicate with the active unit. Use this IP address with the ping command to check the status of the standby unit. This address must be on the same network as the system IP address. For example, if the system IP address is 192.159.1.3, set the failover IP address to 192.159.1.4.
link	Specify the interface where a fast LAN link is available for stateful failover.
stateful_if_name	In addition to the failover cable, a dedicated fast LAN link is required to support stateful failover. Do not use FDDI because of its block size or Token Ring because Token Ring requires additional time during initialization to insert into the ring. The default interface is the highest LAN port with failover configured.

Table 10-1   **failover** *Command Arguments/Options (Continued)*

Argument/Option	Description
poll seconds	Specify how long failover waits before sending special failover hello packets between the primary and standby units over all network interfaces and the failover cable. The default is 15 seconds. The minimum value is 3 seconds and the maximum is 15 seconds. Set to a lower value for stateful failover. With a faster poll time, the PIX Firewall can detect failure and trigger failover faster. However, faster detection may cause unnecessary switchovers when the network is temporarily congested or a network card starts slowly.
reset	Force both units back to an unfailed state. Use this command once the fault has been corrected. The failover reset command can be entered from either unit, but it is best to always enter commands from the active unit. Entering the failover reset command at the active unit will unfail the standby unit.

Use the **failover** command without an argument after you connect the optional failover cable between your primary firewall and a secondary firewall. The default configuration has failover enabled. Enter **no failover** in the configuration file for the PIX Firewall if you will not be using the failover feature. Use the **show failover** command as demonstrated in Examples 10-1 through 10-4 to verify the status of the connection and to determine which unit is active.

Lab Exercise

Complete the following lab exercise to practice the skills you learned in this chapter.

Complete the following tasks:

- Configure the primary PIX Firewall for failover to the secondary PIX Firewall.
- Make the primary PIX Firewall active.
- Configure the primary PIX Firewall for stateful failover.

Figure 10-1 illustrates the configuration you will complete in this lab exercise.

Equipment required to perform the lab includes the following:

- Two PIX-515-UR with at least three interfaces
- Category 5 patch cables
- 100BaseT Hubs or Catalyst switch with 100 Mb ports
- PC running a web server and FTP server
- PC for the Inside subnet with a web browser and FTP client

Figure 10-1 *Failover Lab Topology*

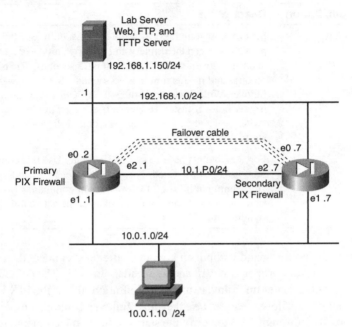

Task 1: Configure the Primary PIX Firewall for Failover to the Secondary PIX Firewall

Step 1 Cable the PIX Firewalls as shown in Figure 10-1. Use one hub for each subnet (interface). Begin with the secondary PIX cabled up but powered off. Enter the initial configuration on the primary PIX to get started, as shown here:

```
hostname Lab-PIX
nameif ethernet0 outside sec0
nameif ethernet1 inside sec100
interface ethernet0 100full
interface ethernet1  100full
ip address inside 10.0.1.1 255.255.255.0
ip address outside 192.168.1.1 255.255.255.0
nat (inside) 1 0.0.0.0 0.0.0.0
global (outside) 1 192.168.1.10-192.168.1.20
conduit permit icmp any any
```

Step 2 Configure the interface for stateful failover. Assign the PIX Firewall with a name of *rescue* to the failover interface and security level 55:

```
Lab-PIX (config)# nameif ethernet2 RESCUE security55
```

Step 3 Enable the interface and configure it for 10BaseT operation.

```
Lab-PIX (config)# interface ethernet2 100full
```

Step 4 Assign an IP address to the interface.

```
Lab-PIX (config)# ip address RESCUE 10.1.1.1
```

Step 5 Save all changes to Flash memory.

```
Lab-PIX (config)# write memory
```

Step 6 Test access to the PC (192.168.1.150) using FTP and HTTP.

Step 7 Be certain that your console cable is connected to the primary PIX Firewall. Enter the **failover** command to enable failover.

```
Lab-PIX (config)# failover
```

Step 8 Verify that the primary PIX Firewall is enabled by using the **show failover** command:

```
Lab-PIX (config)# show failover
```

Step 9 Enter the **failover ip address** command to configure the primary PIX Firewall with the secondary PIX Firewall IP addresses for each interface that is being used, as shown here:

```
Lab-PIX (config)# failover ip address outside 192.168.1.7
Lab-PIX (config)# failover ip address inside 10.0.1.7
Lab-PIX (config)# failover ip address RESCUE 10.1.1.7
```

NOTE   The most common configuration error seen in failover labs is forgetting the keyword failover when applying the commands in Step 9. Leaving failover off causes the primary PIX Firewall's interfaces to be re-addressed.

Step 10 Save your configuration to Flash memory.

```
Lab-PIX(config) write memory
```

Step 11 Connect the failover cable to the primary PIX. It's critical to connect the end of the cable marked Primary.

Step 12 Connect the end of the failover cable marked Secondary to the secondary PIX Firewall.

Step 13 Power up the secondary PIX Firewall so the primary PIX will replicate its configuration to the secondary PIX.

Step 14 After the secondary PIX Firewall is operational, enter the **show failover** command on the primary PIX Firewall to make sure that the replication is complete and that communication between the PIX Firewalls is working, as shown here:

```
Lab-PIX(config)# show failover
Failover On
Cable status: Normal
Reconnect timeout 0:00:00
        This host: Primary - Active
                Active time: 7350 (sec)
                Interface RESCUE (10.1.1.1): Normal
                Interface outside (192.168.1.2): Normal
                Interface inside (10.0.1.1): Normal
        Other host: Secondary - Standby
                Active time: 0 (sec)
                Interface RESCUE (10.1.1.7): Normal
                Interface outside (192.168.1.7): Normal
                Interface inside (10.0.1.7): Normal
```

Step 15 Test connections to 192.168.1.150 by using FTP.

Log back in to your FTP server.

Step 16 Momentarily power down the primary PIX Firewall to test failover. This ensures that the secondary PIX Firewall will take over as active.

Step 17 After the primary reboots, enter the following command to verify that the secondary PIX Firewall is now active, as shown here:

```
Lab-PIX (config)# show failover
Failover On
Cable status: Normal
Reconnect timeout 0:00:00
        This host: Primary - Standby
                Active time: 0 (sec)
                Interface RESCUE (10.1.1.7): Normal
                Interface outside (192.168.1.7): Normal
                Interface inside (10.0.1.7): Normal
        Other host: Secondary - Active
                Active time: 7350 (sec)
                Interface RESCUE (10.1.1.1): Normal
                Interface outside (192.168.1.2): Normal
                Interface inside (10.0.1.1): Normal
```

NOTE	Because your PIX Firewalls aren't yet configured for stateful failover, your previous FTP session is lost. This is normal operation in standard failover mode.

Step 18 Test connections to 192.168.1.150 by using FTP. Log back in to your FTP server.

Task 2: Force the Primary PIX Firewall to Become Active Again

Perform the following lab steps to make the primary PIX Firewall the active PIX Firewall:

Step 1 Make the primary PIX Firewall the active PIX Firewall by using the **failover active** command. Verify you are connected to the primary PIX Firewall's console port:

```
Lab-PIX (config)# failover active
```

Step 2 Verify that the **failover active** command worked by using the **show failover** command. The Primary PIX should show that it's in active mode and the secondary PIX Firewall is in standby mode.

```
Lab-PIX (config)# show failover
Failover On
Cable status: Normal
Reconnect timeout 0:00:00
        This host: Primary - Active
                Active time: 525 (sec)
                Interface RESCUE (10.1.1.1): Normal
                Interface outside (192.168.1.2): Normal
                Interface inside (10.0.1.1): Normal
        Other host: Secondary - Standby
                Active time: 2300 (sec)
                Interface RESCUE (10.1.1.7): Normal
                Interface outside (192.168.1.7): Normal
                Interface inside (10.0.1.7): Normal
```

Task 3: Configure the Primary PIX Firewall for Stateful Failover

Perform the following steps to configure the primary PIX Firewall for stateful failover:

Step 1 Activate stateful failover to the secondary PIX Firewall by using the **failover link** command:

```
Lab-PIX (config)# failover link RESCUE
```

Step 2   Ensure that the secondary PIX Firewall has the latest changes to the configuration by using the **write memory** command. This will sync up the configuration on both firewalls:

```
Lab-PIX (config)# write memory
```

Step 3   Verify that stateful failover is operational by using the **show failover** command:

```
Lab-PIX (config)# show failover
Failover On
Cable status: Normal
Reconnect timeout 0:00:00
        This host: Primary - Active
              Active time: 525 (sec)
              Interface RESCUE (10.1.1.1): Normal
              Interface outside (192.168.1.2): Normal
              Interface inside (10.0.1.1): Normal
        Other host: Secondary - Standby
              Active time: 0 (sec)
              Interface RESCUE (10.1.1.7): Normal
              Interface outside (192.168.1.7): Normal
              Interface inside (10.0.1.7): Normal

Stateful Failover Logical Update Statistics
        Link : RESCUE
        Stateful Obj    xmit        xerr        rcv         rerr
        General         84          0           82          0
        sys cmd         84          0           80          0
        up time         0           0           2           0
        xlate           0           0           0           0
        tcp conn        0           0           0           0
        udp conn        0           0           0           0
        ARP tbl         0           0           0           0
        RIP Tbl         0           0           0           0

        Logical Update Queue Information
                        Cur     Max     Total
        Recv Q:         0       1       84
        Xmit Q:         0       1       86
```

Step 4   Test stateful failover to 192.168.1.150 by opening an FTP session from the PC on the inside subnet. Once you're logged in to the FTP server, enable hash mark printing and tell the FTP server you'll be downloading a binary file:

```
C:\> ftp 192.168.1.150
Connected to 192.168.1.150.
```

```
220 3Com 3CDaemon FTP Server Version 2.0
User (192.168.1.150:(none)): anonymous
331 User name ok, need password
Password: user
230 User logged in
ftp> bin
200 Type set to I.
ftp> hash
Hash mark printing On  ftp: (2048 bytes/hash mark) .
```

NOTE   If you use an FTP server other than 3Com's 3CDaemon, your actual display will differ from the examples that follow of the FTP session.

Step 5   Download a large file from the FTP server you just logged into. Enter the following command at the FTP prompt:

```
ftp> get largefile.zip
```

NOTE   You will be required to create this file. It's important for the file to be large enough to require more than a minute to download, as you'll need a few seconds to perform Steps 6 and Step 7.

   The easiest approach to create the large file is to use WinZip to combine a large number of files into one file. A 30-day evaluation copy of WinZip is available on the web at www.winzip.com.

Step 6   Start a continuous ping to 192.168.1.150 by using the following command in a DOS window:

```
C:\ ping 192.168.1.150 -t
```

Step 7   Reload the primary PIX Firewall:

```
Lab-PIX(config)# reload
```

Step 8   When asked to confirm the reload, press **Enter**. The FTP session should look similar to the display below. You should observe a few pings timeout and the FTP session will "hang" for about one second before resuming.

```
ftp> get largefile.zip
200 PORT command successful.
```

```
150 File status OK ; about to open data connection
################################################################
#####################.....######################################
################################################################
################################################################
################################################################
################################################################
################################################################
################################################################
################################################################
################################################################
226 Closing data connection; File transfer successful.
ftp: 11727970 bytes received in 12.88Seconds 910.63Kbytes/sec.
```

Review Questions

To test what you have learned in this chapter, answer the following questions and then refer to Appendix F for the answers.

1   What verion of PIX OS do I need to run to use stateful failover?

2   Does the PIX stop forwarding packets when it begins testing to see why it hasn't received two keepalives?

3   Can I upgrade the Standby PIX while it's connected to the primary?

4   Can I run different versions of the PIX OS when they're configured for failover?

5   We run IPSec between our HQ PIX and several of our field offices. Does stateful failover preserve IPSec tunnels?

6   Can I run stateful failover on my PIX 515-R?

7   What happens if the primary PIX is powered off?

8   What is the range of time that can be set for the **failover poll** interval?

9   What is the most common misconfiguration?

This chapter includes the following topics:

- The PIX Firewall Enables a Secure VPN
- IPSec Configuration Tasks
- Scale PIX Firewall VPNs
- PIX Firewall with CA Enrollment
- Example Topologies and Configurations

CHAPTER 11

Configuring IPSec for Cisco PIX Firewalls

The Cisco Secure PIX Firewall Enables a Secure VPN

A virtual private network (VPN) is a service offering secure, reliable connectivity over a shared public network infrastructure such as the Internet. Because the infrastructure is shared, connectivity can often be provided at a lower cost than on existing dedicated private networks.

The PIX Firewall is a powerful enabler of VPN services. The PIX Firewall's high performance, conformance to open standards, and ease of configuration make it a versatile VPN gateway. An optional VPN Accelerator Card is available for the PIX 515, 520, 525, and 535. The VAC offers 100-Mbps 3DES performance without the need for additional software and without modification to the PIX configuration.

The PIX Firewall enables VPNs in several topologies, as illustrated in Figure 11-1 and discussed in the list that follows.

- **PIX to PIX secure VPN gateway**—Two or more PIX Firewalls can enable a VPN, which secures traffic from devices behind the PIX Firewalls. The secure VPN gateway topology prevents the user from having to implement VPN devices or software inside the network, making the secure gateway transparent to users.

- **PIX to Cisco IOS router secure VPN gateway**—The PIX Firewall and Cisco router, running Cisco Secure VPN software, can interoperate to create a secure VPN gateway between networks.

- **Cisco VPN Client to PIX via dialup**—The PIX Firewall can become a VPN endpoint for the Cisco VPN Client over a dialup network. The dialup network can consist of ISDN, Public Switched Telephone Network (PSTN), (analog modem), or digital subscriber line (DSL) communication channels.

- **Cisco VPN Client to PIX via network**—The PIX Firewall can become a VPN endpoint for the Cisco Secure VPN 3000 Client over an IP network.

- **Other vendor products to PIX**—Products from other vendors can connect to the PIX Firewall if they conform to open VPN standards.

Figure 11-1 *Diverse VPN Topologies*

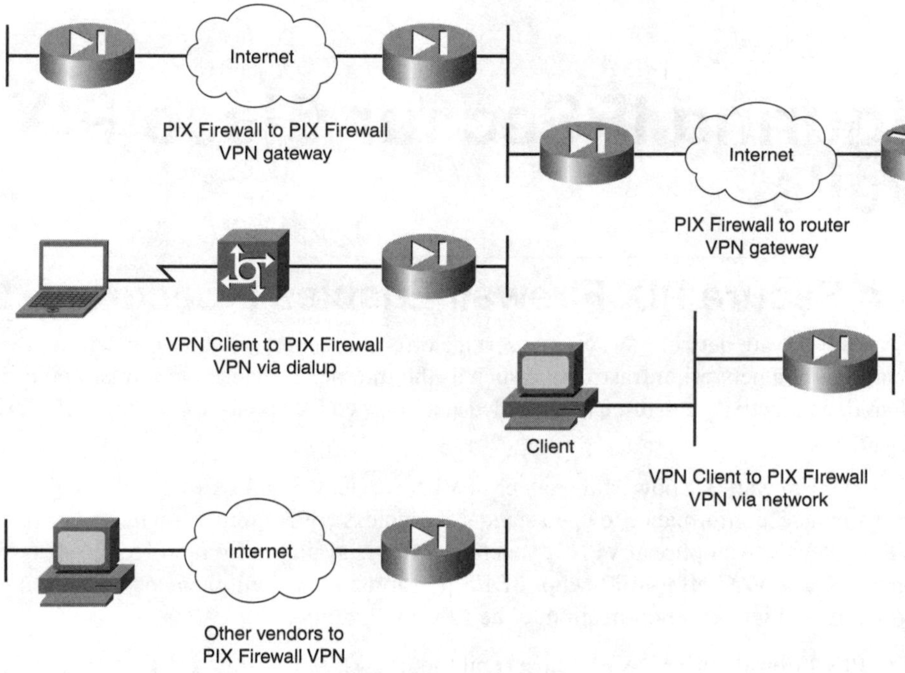

CAUTION IPSec compatibility with non-Cisco products should be tested carefully, as "IPSec compatible" doesn't guarantee interoperability.

A VPN itself can be constructed in a number of scenarios. The most common are as follows:

- **Internet VPN**—A private communications channel over the public access Internet. This type of VPN can be divided into the following:
  - Connecting remote offices across the Internet
  - Connecting remote dial users to their home gateway via an Internet service provider (ISP)
- **Intranet VPN**—A private communications channel within an enterprise or organization that may or may not involve traffic traversing a WAN.
- **Extranet VPN**—A private communications channel between two or more separate entities that may involve data traversing the Internet or some other WAN.

In all cases, the VPN or tunnel consists of two endpoints that may be represented by PIX Firewalls, Cisco routers, individual client workstations running the Cisco VPN Client, or other vendors' VPN products that conform to open standards.

PIX, VPNs, and IPSec

The PIX Firewall running PIX OS 5.0 and higher uses the industry-standard IP Security (IPSec) protocol suite to enable advanced VPN features. The PIX IPSec implementation is based on Cisco IOS IPSec that runs on Cisco routers.

IPSec provides a mechanism for secure data transmission over IP networks, ensuring confidentiality, integrity, and authenticity of data communications over unprotected networks, such as the Internet.

IPSec enables the following PIX Firewall VPN features:

- **Data confidentiality**—The IPSec sender can encrypt packets before transmitting them across a network.

- **Data integrity**—The IPSec receiver can authenticate IPSec peers and packets sent by the IPSec sender to ensure that the data has not been altered during transmission.

- **Data origin authentication**—The IPSec receiver can authenticate the source of the IPSec packets sent. This service is dependent upon the data integrity service.

- **Anti-replay**—The IPSec receiver can detect and reject replayed packets, helping prevent spoofing and man-in-the-middle attacks.

IPSec is a set of security protocols and algorithms used to secure data at the network layer. IPSec and related security protocols conform to open standards promulgated by the Internet Engineering Task Force (IETF) and documented RFCs and IETF-draft papers.

IPSec can be used to scale from small to very large networks.

The PIX Firewall supports the following IPSec and related standards:

- IPSec (IP Security Protocol)
- Internet Key Exchange (IKE)
- Data Encryption Standard (DES)
- Triple DES (3DES)
- Diffie-Hellman (D-H)
- Message Digest 5 (MD5)
- Secure Hash Algorithm-1 (SHA-1)
- Ravist-Shamir-Adelman signatures (RSA)
- Certificate Authorities (CA)
- Security Association (SA)

Now that you have some of the IPSec vocabulary, the following sections define the terms and give them context.

IPSec

IPSec is a framework of open standards that provides data confidentiality, data integrity, and data authentication between participating peers at the IP layer. IPSec can be used to protect one or more data flows between IPSec peers. IPSec is documented in a series of Internet RFCs, all available for viewing at the following web site:

http://www.ietf.org/html.charters/ipsec-charter.html

The overall IPSec implementation is guided by RFC 2401, "Security Architecture for the Internet Protocol." IPSec consists of the following two main protocols:

- **Authentication Header (AH)**—A security protocol that provides authentication and optional replay-detection services. AH acts as a digital signature to ensure that tampering has not occurred to the complete IP packet. With the exception of fields that change in transit, such as checksum and time to live, AH provides authentication for the entire packet, not just for the data payload. AH was assigned IP Protocol number 51 by IANA (Internet Assigned Numbers Authority). AH does not provide data encryption and decryption services. AH can be used either by itself or with Encapsulating Security Payload (ESP).

- **Encapsulating Security Payload (ESP)**—A security protocol that provides data confidentiality and protection with optional authentication and replay-detection services. The PIX Firewall uses ESP to encrypt the data payload of IP packets. ESP can be used either by itself or in conjunction with AH. ESP was assigned IP protocol number 50.

IKE

IKE is a hybrid protocol composed of the ISAKMP and Oakley standards that provides utility services for IPSec: authentication of the IPSec peers, negotiation of IKE and IPSec security associations, and establishment of keys for encryption algorithms used by IPSec. IKE operates over assigned UDP port 500.

SA

The concept of a security association (SA) is fundamental to IPSec. An SA is a connection between IPSec peers that determines the IPSec services available between the peers, similar to a TCP or UDP port. Each IPSec peer maintains an SA database in memory containing SA parameters. SAs are uniquely identified by IPSec peer address, security protocol, and security parameter index (SPI). You will need to configure SA parameters and monitor SAs on the PIX Firewall.

DES

DES refers to the Data Encryption Standard, which was published in 1977. DES encrypts and decrypts packet data. DES is used by both IPSec and IKE. DES uses a 56-bit key, ensuring high-performance encryption.

CAUTION   With the advent of fast desktop computers, DES is no longer considered strong encryption. In 1998, the Electronic Frontier Foundation, using a specially developed computer called the DES Cracker, managed to break DES in less than three days—this was done for under $250,000. The encryption chip that powered the DES Cracker was capable of processing 88 billion keys per second. To protect your production data, Cisco recommends using 3DES.

3DES

3DES is a variant of DES, which iterates three times with three separate keys, effectively doubling the strength of DES. IPSec uses 3DES to encrypt and decrypt data traffic. 3DES uses a 168-bit key, ensuring strong encryption.

D-H

Diffie-Hellman is a public-key cryptography protocol that allows two parties to establish a shared secret key over an insecure communications channel. D-H is used within IKE to establish session keys. 768-bit (Group 1) and 1024-bit (Group 2) D-H groups are supported in the PIX Firewall. The 1024-bit group is more secure. IKE on the PIX Firewall uses a D-H exchange to derive symmetrical secret keys on each IPSec peer used by encryption algorithms. The D-H exchange can be authenticated with RSA (or pre-shared keys).

MD5

Message Digest version 5 (MD5) is a hash algorithm that authenticates packet data. A hash is a one-way encryption algorithm that takes an input message of arbitrary length and produces a fixed-length output message digest. IKE, AH, and ESP can use MD5 for authentication. MD5 processes its input in 512-bit blocks and produces a 128-bit message digest.

SHA-1

Secure Hash Algorithm (SHA) is a hash algorithm that signs and authenticates packet data. The PIX Firewall uses the SHA-1 HMAC variant, which provides an additional level of hashing. IKE, AH, and ESP can use SHA-1 for authentication.

RSA Signatures

RSA is a public-key cryptographic system for authentication. In public-key cryptography, each user has a *public key* and a *private key*. The public key is made public while the private key remains secret. Encryption is performed with the public key and decryption is performed using the private key. The *RSA public-key cryptosystem* is the most popular form of public-key cryptography. RSA stands for Rivest, Shamir, and Adleman, the inventors of the RSA cryptosystem.

CA

Certificate Authority (CA) support of the PIX Firewall allows the IPSec-protected network to scale by providing the equivalent of a digital identification card for each device. These digital ID cards are called digital certificates. When two IPSec peers want to communicate, they exchange digital certificates to prove their identities (thus, removing the need to manually exchange public keys with each peer or to manually specify a shared key at each peer). The digital certificates are obtained from a CA. CA support on the PIX Firewall uses RSA signatures to authenticate the CA exchange.

Configuring PIX Firewall IPSec Support

This section shows you how to configure basic IPSec in the PIX Firewall using pre-shared keys for authentication. It presents an overview of the tasks and steps you must perform to configure IPSec, provides details about IPSec-related commands in the PIX Firewall, and shows command examples. This chapter finishes with a case study based on an IPSec tunnel between two hosts.

The intent of this section is to configure PIX Firewalls to become secure IPSec gateways that will encrypt and protect traffic flows of networks behind the PIX Firewalls, using pre-shared keys for authentication. The use of IKE pre-shared keys for authentication of IPSec sessions is relatively easy to configure yet does not scale well for a large number of IPSec peers; in which case, digital certificates should be employed.

Figure 11-2 shows the simplified topology for the XYZ Company used in examples in this section.

Figure 11-2 *XYZ Company Topology for PIX Firewall IPSec*

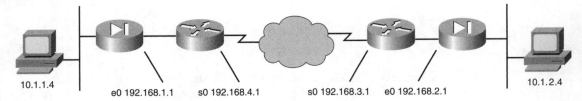

10.1.1.4   e0 192.168.1.1   s0 192.168.4.1   s0 192.168.3.1   e0 192.168.2.1   10.1.2.4

Four key tasks are involved in configuring IPSec encryption using pre-shared keys on the PIX Firewall:

- **Task 1: Prepare for IPSec**—Preparing for IPSec involves determining the detailed encryption policy, including identifying the hosts and networks you want to protect, choosing an authentication method, determining details about the IPSec peers, identifying the IPSec features you need, and ensuring that existing access lists permit IPSec traffic. If you have a filtering perimeter router in front of your PIX Firewall, it must allow IP Protocols 50 and 51 and UDP port 500.

- **Task 2: Configure Internet Key Exchange (IKE) for pre-shared keys**— Configuring IKE involves enabling IKE, creating the IKE policies, setting the identity mode, and validating the configuration.

- **Task 3: Configure IPSec**—IPSec configuration includes creating crypto access lists, defining transform sets, creating crypto map entries, and applying crypto map sets to interfaces.

- **Task 4: Test and verify the overall IPSec configuration**—This task involves using **show**, **debug**, and related commands to test and verify that IPSec encryption works and to troubleshoot problems.

The following sections discuss each of these configuration tasks in more detail.

Task 1: Prepare for IPSec

Successful implementation of an IPSec network requires careful planning before you begin to configure individual PIX Firewalls and other IPSec peers. Configuring IPSec encryption can be complicated. You should begin by defining the detailed IPSec security policy based on the overall company security policy. The following are some planning steps for preparing for IPSec:

Step 1   Determine the IKE (IKE Phase 1, or main mode) policy between IPSec peers based on the number and location of the peers.

Step 2   Determine the IPSec (IKE Phase 2, or quick mode) policy, including IPSec peer details such as IP addresses and IPSec transform sets and modes.

Step 3   Check the current configuration by using **write terminal**, **show isakmp**, **show isakmp policy**, **show crypto map**, and other **show** commands.

Step 4   Ensure that the network works without encryption to eliminate basic routing problems by using the **ping** command and by running test traffic before testing encryption.

Step 5   Ensure that existing access lists in the perimeter router and PIX Firewall permit IPSec traffic, or the desired traffic will be filtered out.

Task 2: Configure IKE for Pre-Shared Keys

The next major task in configuring PIX Firewall IPSec is to configure IKE parameters gathered earlier. Note that in PIX configuration commands, ISAKMP is synonymous with IKE. Configuring IPSec encryption can be complicated. You must plan in advance if you want to configure IPSec encryption correctly the first time and minimize misconfiguration. You should begin this task by defining the overall security needs and strategy based on the overall company security policy. Some planning steps include the following:

Step 1   Enable or disable IKE with the **isakmp enable** command.

Step 2   Create IKE policies with the **isakmp policy** commands.

Step 3   Configure pre-shared keys with the **isakmp key** and associated commands.

Step 4   Verify what method IKE will use to verify its crypto peer. When two peers use IKE to establish IPSec security associations, each peer sends its ISAKMP identity to the remote peer. It will send either its IP address or host name depending on how each has its ISAKMP identity set. By default, the PIX Firewall unit's ISAKMP identity is set to the IP address. As a general rule, set the PIX Firewall and its peer's identities in the same way to avoid an IKE negotiation failure. This failure could be due to either the PIX Firewall or its peer not recognizing its peer's identity. To determine what method the PIX will use to verify the identity of the peer, use the **show isakmp identity** command. The default identity is the IP address.

Step 5   Verify the IKE configuration with the **show isakmp** [**policy**] command.

The following sections describe these steps in detail.

Step 1: Enable or Disable IKE

The first step in configuring IKE is to enable or disable IKE on interfaces used to terminate IPSec tunnels. You enable and disable IKE on individual interfaces by using the **isakmp enable** command. IKE is enabled by default, and you use the **no** form of the command to disable IKE. The command syntax is as follows:

```
isakmp enable interface-name
pixfirewall#(config) isakmp enable outside
```

The *interface-name* argument specifies the name of the interface on which to enable IKE negotiation.

Step 2: Create IKE Policies

The next major step in configuring PIX Firewall IKE support is to define a suite of IKE policies. The goal of defining a suite of IKE policies is to establish IKE peering between two IPSec endpoints. Use the IKE policy details gathered during the planning task.

Table 11-1 summarizes IKE policy details that are configured in examples in this chapter.

Table 11-1   *IKE Policy Example for Peer PIX Firewalls*

Parameter	Peer A Value	Peer B Value
Message encryption algorithm	DES (default)	DES (default)
Message integrity (hash) algorithm	MD5	MD5
Peer authentication method	Pre-shared key	Pre-shared key
Key exchange parameters (Diffie-Hellman group identifier)	768-bit Diffie-Hellman group 1 (default)	768-bit Diffie-Hellman group 1 (default)
IKE-established security association's lifetime	86,400 (default)	86,400 (default)
IP address of IPSec peer	192.168.2.2	192.168.1.2

Use the **isakmp policy** command to define an IKE policy. IKE policies define a set of parameters to be used during the IKE negotiation. Use the **no** form of this command to delete an IKE policy. The command syntax is as follows:

```
pixfirewall#(config) isakmp policy 10 authentication pre-share
isakmp policy priority encryption {des | 3des}
pixfirewall#(config) isakmp policy 10 encryption 3des
isakmp policy priority {group1 | group2}
pixfirewall#(config) isakmp policy 10 group2
isakmp policy priority hash {md5 | sha}
pixfirewall#(config) isakmp policy 10  hash sha
isakmp policy priority lifetime seconds
pixfirewall#(config) isakmp policy 10 lifetime 86400
```

Table 11-2 describes the command parameters.

Table 11-2   **isakmp policy** *Command Parameters*

Command Parameter	Description
policy *priority*	Uniquely identifies the IKE policy and assigns it a priority. Use an integer from **1** to **65,534**, with **1** being the highest priority and **65,534** the lowest.
authentication pre-share	Specifies pre-shared keys as the authentication method.
authentication rsa-sig	Specifies RSA signatures as the authentication method.
encryption des	Specifies 56-bit DES-CBC as the encryption algorithm to be used in the IKE policy. This is the default value.
encryption 3des	Specifies that the Triple DES encryption algorithm is to be used in the IKE policy.
group 1	Specifies that the 768-bit Diffie-Hellman group is to be used in the IKE policy. This is the default value.

continues

Table 11-2   **isakmp policy** *Command Parameters (Continued)*

Command Parameter	Description
group 2	Specifies that the 1024-bit Diffie-Hellman group is to be used in the IKE policy.
hash md5	Specifies MD5 (HMAC variant) as the hash algorithm to be used in the IKE policy.
hash sha	Specifies SHA-1 (HMAC variant) as the hash algorithm to be used in the IKE policy. This is the default hash algorithm.
lifetime *seconds*	Specifies how many seconds each security association should exist before expiring. Use an integer from **60** to **86,400** seconds (one day). You can usually leave this value at the default of **86,400**.

If you do not specify one of these commands for a policy, the default value is used for that parameter. You can reset a value to its default by using the **no** form of the command. For example, to reset to DES as the encryption method previously set to 3DES, use the **no isakmp policy 100 encryption** command.

For more details on how IKE policies work, see the section "Internet Key Exchange" in Chapter 15, "Understanding Cisco IPSec Support" in the Cisco Press book *Managing Cisco Network Security.*

Examples 11-1 and 11-2 show sample IKE policies for PIX 1 and PIX 2. Note that policy 10 on PIX 1 matches policy 20 on PIX 2. Default values are not shown.

Example 11-1   *Sample IKE Policies for PIX 1*

```
isakmp policy 10 authentication pre-share
isakmp policy 10 encryption 3des
isakmp policy 10 hash sha
isakmp policy 10 group 2
isakmp policy 10 lifetime 86400
```

Example 11-2   *Sample IKE Policies for PIX 2*

```
isakmp policy 20 authentication pre-share
isakmp policy 20 encryption 3des
isakmp policy 20 hash sha
isakmp policy 20 group 2
isakmp policy 20 lifetime 86400
```

Step 3: Configure Pre-Shared Keys

The next step in configuring PIX Firewall IKE support is to optionally set the identity mode and to configure the pre-shared keys, as discussed in the following sections.

Setting the Identity Mode

IPSec peers authenticate each other during IKE negotiations using the pre-shared key and the IKE identity. The identity can be either the peer's IP address or its host name. The PIX Firewall uses the IP address identity method by default. If you choose to use the address identity method, you must specify the method with the **isakmp identity** command. Use the **no** form of this command to reset the IKE identity to the default value (host name). The command syntax is as follows:

```
isakmp identity {address | hostname}
```

The **address** keyword sets the IKE identity to the IP address of the interface that communicates with the remote peer during IKE negotiations for pre-shared keys. This keyword is typically used when only one interface will be used by the peer for IKE negotiations and the IP address is known.

The **hostname** keyword sets the IKE identity to the host name concatenated with the domain name (for example, myhost.domain.com). This keyword should be used if more than one interface on the peer might be used for IKE negotiations or if the interface's IP address is unknown (such as with dynamically assigned IP addresses).

Configuring Pre-Shared Keys

You configure a pre-shared authentication key with the **isakmp key** configuration command. You must configure this key whenever you specify pre-shared keys in an IKE policy. Use the **no** form of this command to delete a pre-shared authentication key. The command syntax is as follows:

```
isakmp key keystring address peer-address [netmask mask]
```

Table 11-3 describes the command arguments and options for this command sequence.

Table 11-3   **isakmp key** *Command Arguments/Options*

Command Parameter	Description
keystring	Specifies the pre-shared key. Use any combination of alphanumeric characters up to 128 bytes. This pre-shared key must be identical at both peers.
address	Specifies that the remote peer IKE identity was set with its IP address.
peer-address	Specifies the IP address of the remote peer. The address of 0.0.0.0 can be entered as a wildcard, indicating that the key could be used by any IPSec peer with a matching key.
peer-hostname	Specifies the host name of the remote peer. This is the peer's host name concatenated with its domain name (for example, myhost.domain.com).
netmask *mask*	(Optional) Specifies the netmask. The netmask 0.0.0.0 can be entered as a wildcard along with an address of 0.0.0.0, indicating that the key could be used for any peer that does not have a key associated with its specific IP address.

A wildcard peer address and netmask of 0.0.0.0 0.0.0.0 may be configured to share the pre-shared key among many peers. However, Cisco strongly recommends using a unique key for each peer.

NOTE   As with any IPSec peer using pre-shared keys, the same pre-shared key must be configured on each pair of IPSec peers when using pre-shared keys for IKE authentication. It is highly recommended that a different pre-shared key be configured on each pair of IPSec peers. Using the same pre-shared key for more than one pair of IPSec peers presents a security risk.

Step 4: Verify the IKE Configuration

You can use the **show isakmp** [**policy**] command to display configured and default policies. Example 11-3 shows the resultant IKE policy for PIX 1 (PIX 2's configuration is identical).

Example 11-3   *IKE Policy for PIX 1*

```
Pix1# show isakmp policy
Protection suite of priority 100
        encryption algorithm:   DES - Data Encryption Standard (56-bit keys)
        hash algorithm:         Message Digest 5
        authentication method:  Pre-Shared Key
        Diffie-Hellman group:   #1 (768 bit)
        lifetime:               86400 seconds, no volume limit
Default protection suite
        encryption algorithm:   DES - Data Encryption Standard (56-bit keys)
        hash algorithm:         Secure Hash Standard
        authentication method:  Rivest-Shamir-Adleman Signature
        Diffie-Hellman group:   #1 (768 bit)
        lifetime:               86400 seconds, no volume limit
```

The **show isakmp** command displays configured policies much as they would appear with the **write terminal** command, as shown in Example 11-4.

Example 11-4   *Display Configured Policies with* **show isakmp**

```
Pix1# show isakmp
isakmp enable outside
isakmp policy 100 authentication rsa-sig
isakmp policy 100 encryption 3des
isakmp policy 100 hash sha
isakmp policy 100 group 1
isakmp policy 10 lifetime 86400
```

The **write terminal** command displays configured policies. Example 11-5 shows the isakmp relevant portions of the configuration. Here the pre-shared key is cisco1234, and the peer is PIX 2 at 192.168.2.2.

Example 11-5 *Policies Configured with* **write terminal**

```
Pix1# write terminal
isakmp enable outside
isakmp key cisco1234 address 192.168.2.2 netmask 255.255.255.255
isakmp policy 100 authentication pre-share
isakmp policy 100 encryption des
isakmp policy 100 hash sha
isakmp policy 100 group 1
isakmp policy 100 lifetime 86400
```

Task 3: Configure IPSec

The next major task in configuring PIX Firewall IPSec is to configure the IPSec parameters previously gathered. This section presents the steps used to configure IPSec. The general tasks and commands used to configure IPSec encryption on PIX Firewalls are summarized here. Subsequent sections discuss each configuration step in detail.

Step 1 Configure crypto access lists with the **access-list** command.

Step 2 Configure transform set suites with the **crypto ipsec transform-set** command.

Step 3 (Optional) Configure global IPSec security association lifetimes with the **crypto ipsec security-association lifetime** command.

Step 4 Configure crypto maps with the **crypto map** command.

Step 5 Apply crypto maps to the terminating/originating interface with the **crypto map map-name interface** command.

Step 6 Verify IPSec configuration with the variety of available **show** commands.

Table 11-4 summarizes IPSec encryption policy details that will be configured in examples in this chapter.

Table 11-4 *IPSec Policies for Two Peers*

Parameter	Peer A Value	Peer B Value
Transform set	Authentication Header (AH)-MD5, Encapsulating Security Payload (ESP)-DES	AH-MD5, ESP-DES
IPSec mode	Tunnel	Tunnel
Hash algorithm	MD5	MD5

continues

Table 11-4 *IPSec Policies for Two Peers (Continued)*

Parameter	Peer A Value	Peer B Value
Peer host name	PIX 2	PIX 1
Peer interface	Ethernet 0 (outside)	Ethernet 0 (outside)
Peer IP address	192.168.2.2	192.168.1.2
IP address of hosts to be protected	10.1.1.0 /24	10.2.1.0 /24
Traffic (packet) type to be encrypted	TCP	TCP
SA establishment	**ipsec-isakmp**	**ipsec-isakmp**

Step 1: Create Crypto Access Lists

Crypto access lists define which IP traffic is or is not protected by IPSec. Crypto access lists perform the following functions for IPSec:

- Select outbound traffic to be protected by IPSec.

- Process inbound traffic in order to filter out and discard traffic that should have been protected by IPSec.

- Determine whether to accept requests for IPSec security associations for the requested data flows when processing IKE negotiations.

The crypto access lists identify the traffic flows to be protected. Although the crypto access list syntax is the same as that for regular access lists, the meanings are slightly different for crypto access lists: **permit** specifies that matching packets must be encrypted, and **deny** specifies that matching packets will not be encrypted. Crypto access lists behave similar to an access list applied to outbound traffic on a PIX Firewall interface.

To configure a crypto access list, use the **access-list** configuration command. To delete a single line of an access list, use the **no** form of the command. To delete the entire **access-list** and its associated **access-group** command, use the **clear access-list** command. The command syntax is as follows:

```
access-list acl_name [deny | permit] protocol src_addr src_mask
[operator port [port]] dest_addr dest_mask [operator port [port]]
```

Table 11-5 describes the arguments and options for this command sequence.

Table 11-5 **access-list** *Command Arguments/Options*

Command Parameter	Description
acl_name	Specifies the name or number of an access list.
deny	Does not select a packet for IPSec protection. Prevents traffic from being protected by IPSec in the context of that particular crypto map entry.

Table 11-5   **access-list** *Command Arguments/Options (Continued)*

Command Parameter	Description
permit	Selects a packet for IPSec protection. Causes all IP traffic that matches the specified conditions to be protected by IPSec, using the policy described by the corresponding crypto map entry.
protocol	Specifies the name or number of an IP protocol. It can be one of the keywords **icmp**, **ip**, **tcp**, or **udp**, or an integer in the range 1 to 254 representing an IP protocol number. To match any Internet protocol, use the keyword **ip**.
src_addr dest_addr	Specifies the address of the network or host from which the packet is being sent or from where the packet was received. There are three other ways to specify the source or destination: Use a 32-bit quantity in four-part, dotted-decimal format. Use the keyword **any** as an abbreviation for a source and source-netmask or destination and destination netmask of 0.0.0.0 0.0.0.0. This keyword is normally not recommended for use with IPSec. Use host source or host destination as an abbreviation for a source and source-netmask of 255.255.255.255 or a destination and destination-netmask of destination 255.255.255.255.
src_mask dest_mask	Specifies the netmask bits (mask) to be applied to source or destination. There are three other ways to specify the source or destination netmask: Use a 32-bit quantity in four-part dotted-decimal format. Place zeroes in the bit positions you want to ignore. Use the keyword **any** as an abbreviation for a source and source-netmask or destination and destination-netmask of 0.0.0.0 0.0.0.0. This keyword is not recommended. Use host source or host destination as an abbreviation for a source and source-netmask of source 255.255.255.255 or a destination and destination-netmask of destination 255.255.255.255.
operator	(Optional) Specifies a port or a port range to compare source or destination ports. Possible operands include **lt** (less than), **gt** (greater than), **eq** (equal), **neq** (not equal), and **range** (inclusive range). The **range** operator requires two port numbers. Each of the other operators requires one port number.
port	IP service(s) you permit based on TCP or UDP protocol. Specify ports by either a literal name or a number in the range of 0 to 65,535. You can specify all ports by not specifying a port value.

Here are some additional details for access lists:

- PIX Firewall version 5.0 supports the IP protocol only with granularity to the network, subnet, and host level.

- PIX Firewall version 5.1 and higher supports granularity to either the TCP or UDP protocol and corresponding port.

- The use of port ranges can dramatically increase the number of IPSec tunnels that the PIX can originate or terminate. A new tunnel is created for each port.

Any unprotected inbound traffic that matches a permit entry in the crypto access list for a crypto map entry flagged as IPSec will be dropped.

CAUTION   Cisco recommends that you avoid using the **any** keyword to specify source or destination addresses. The **permit any** statement is strongly discouraged because it causes all outbound traffic to be encrypted to all destinations (as well as all traffic sent to the peer specified in the corresponding crypto map entry) and requires all inbound traffic be encrypted. Then, all inbound packets that lack IPSec protection are silently dropped. Also, you might experience increased CPU utilization and accompanying network throughput degradation.

Try to be as precise as possible when defining which packets to protect in a crypto access list. If you must use the **any** keyword in a **permit** statement, you must preface that statement with a series of **deny** statements to filter out any traffic (that would otherwise fall within that permit statement) that you do not want to be protected.

NOTE   See the "Step 3: Create Crypto Access Lists" section of Chapter 16 of the Cisco Press book *Managing Cisco Network Security* for more details on how to configure crypto access lists. Keep in mind that Cisco IOS Software uses wildcard masks and the PIX uses standard masks; 255.255.255.0 on the PIX becomes 0.0.0.255 on Cisco IOS Software.

It's imperative that you configure mirror-image crypto access lists for use by IPSec. The crypto access lists on each peer should be symmetrical.

NOTE   Failure to create symmetrical access lists on both crypto peers will result in the inability to form an SA.

For example, the source criteria of PIX 1 should be exactly the same as the destination criteria of PIX 2, and the destination criteria of PIX 1 should be exactly the same as the source criteria of PIX 2. On each PIX Firewall, both inbound and outbound traffic is evaluated against the same outbound IPSec access list. The access list's criteria are applied in the forward direction to traffic exiting the PIX Firewall and are applied in the reverse direction to traffic entering the PIX Firewall. When a PIX Firewall receives encrypted packets from an IPSec peer, it uses the same access list to determine which inbound packets to decrypt by viewing the source and destination addresses in the access list in reverse order.

Example 11-6 shows a crypto access list pair and illustrates why symmetrical access lists are recommended (refer to Figure 11-1 for a network diagram).

Example 11-6 *A Crypto Access List Pair*

```
Pix1(config)# show static
static (inside,outside) 192.168.1.10 10.1.1.4 netmask 255.255.255.255 0 0
pix1(config)# show access-list
access-list 110 permit ip host 192.168.1.10 host 192.168.2.10
Pix2(config)# show static
static (inside,outside) 192.168.2.10 10.2.1.4 netmask 255.255.255.255 0 0
Pix2(config)# show access-list
access-list 101 permit ip host 192.168.2.10 host 192.168.1.10
```

In the example for Site 1, IPSec protection is applied to traffic between the hosts at Site 1 and Site 2. Network address translation is configured on the PIX Firewalls. The host at Site 1 of 10.1.1.4 is statically mapped to global address 192.168.1.10 on PIX 1. The host at Site 2 of 10.2.1.4 is statically mapped to global address 192.168.2.10 on PIX 2. The access lists use the global address in the **static** command to specify interesting traffic. For traffic from the Site 1 host to the Site 2 host, the access list entry on PIX 1 is evaluated as follows:

- The source is host 192.168.1.10 (statically mapped to 10.1.1.4).
- The destination is host 192.168.2.10 (statically mapped to 10.2.1.4).

For incoming traffic from the Site 2 host to the Site 1 host, the same access list entry on PIX 1 is evaluated as follows:

- The source is host 192.168.2.10 (statically mapped to 10.2.1.4).
- The destination is host 192.168.1.10 (statically mapped to 10.1.1.4).

Step 2: Configure Transform Set Suites

The next major step in configuring the PIX Firewall IPSec is to use the IPSec security policy to define a transform set. A *transform set* is a combination of individual IPSec transforms that enact a security policy for traffic. Transform sets combine the following IPSec factors:

- A mechanism for packet authentication—the AH transform
- A mechanism for payload encryption and optional authentication—the ESP transform
- The IPSec mode, either transport or tunnel

You define a transform set with the **crypto ipsec transform-set** command. To delete a transform set, you use the **no** form of the command. The command syntax is as follows:

```
crypto ipsec transform-set transform-set-name transform1 [transform2 [transform3]]
```

Table 11-6 describes the command arguments for the **crypto ipsec transform-set** command.

Table 11-6   *crypto ipsec transform-set Command Arguments*

Command Parameter	Description
transform-set-name	Specifies the name of the transform set to create (or modify).
transform1 *transform2* *transform3*	Specifies up to three transforms. Transforms define the IPSec security protocol(s) and algorithm(s). Each transform represents an IPSec security protocol (ESP, AH, or AH plus ESP, or AH plus ESP and the ESP-HMAC) plus the algorithm you want to use.

Up to three transforms can be in a set. The default mode for each transform is *tunnel*. Sets are limited to up to one AH and up to two ESP transforms. Make sure you configure matching transform sets between IPSec peers.

When IKE is not used to establish security associations, a single transform set must be used. The transform set is not negotiated. If you specify an ESP protocol in a transform set, you can specify just an ESP encryption transform or both an ESP encryption transform and an ESP authentication transform.

Table 11-7 shows the IPSec transforms supported by the PIX Firewall.

Table 11-7   *PIX-Supported IPSec Transforms*

Transform	Description
ah-md5-hmac	AH-md5-hmac transform used for authentication
ah-sha-hmac	AH-sha-hmac transform used for authentication
esp-des	ESP transform using DES cipher (56 bits)
esp-3des	ESP transform using 3DES cipher (168 bits)
esp-md5-hmac	ESP transform with HMAC-MD5 authentication used with an **esp-des** or **esp-3des** transform to provide additional integrity of ESP packets
esp-sha-hmac	ESP transform with HMAC-SHA authentication used with an **esp-des** or **esp-3des** transform to provide additional integrity for ESP packets

Choosing Transforms

Choosing IPSec transform combinations can be complex. The following tips might help you select transforms that are appropriate for your situation:

- If you want to provide data confidentiality, include an ESP encryption transform.

- Consider including an ESP authentication transform or an AH transform to provide authentication services for the transform set.
- To ensure data authentication for the outer IP header as well as the data, include an AH transform.
- To ensure data authentication (using either ESP or AH), you can choose from the MD5 or SHA (HMAC keyed hash variants) authentication algorithms.
- The SHA algorithm is generally considered stronger than MD5, but it is slower.

Transform Set Examples

Transform sets are limited to one AH transform and one or two ESP transforms. Some suggested combinations are shown in Examples 11-7 and 11-8.

Example 11-7   *ESP Encryption with 56-Bit DES and ESP with SHA-1 for Authentication in Tunnel Mode (the Default) to Give Strong Security and Higher Performance*

```
esp-des esp-sha-hmac
```

Example 11-8   *ESP Encryption with 3DES and ESP with SHA-1 for Authentication in Tunnel Mode (the Default) to Give Stronger Security*

```
esp-3des esp-sha-hmac
```

NOTE   As with Cisco routers, AH is seldom used with ESP because authentication is available with the esp-sha-hmac and esp-md5-hmac transforms. AH is also incompatible with network address translation (NAT) and port address translation (PAT) because they change the IP address in the TCP/IP packet header, breaking the authentication established by AH. You can use AH for data authentication alone, but it does not protect the confidentiality of the packet contents because it does not provide encryption.

Transform Set Negotiation

Transform sets are negotiated during quick mode in IKE Phase 2 using previously configured transform sets. You can configure multiple transform sets and then specify one or more of the transform sets in a crypto map entry. You should configure the transforms from most secure to least secure as per your policy. The transform set defined in the crypto map entry is used in the IPSec security association negotiation to protect the data flows specified by that crypto map entry's access list.

During the negotiation, the peers search for a transform set that is the same at both peers. When such a transform set is found, it is selected and applied to the protected traffic as part of both peers' IPSec security associations. IPSec peers agree on one transform proposal per SA (unidirectional).

Step 3: Configure Global IPSec Security Association Lifetimes

The IPSec security association lifetime determines how long IPSec SAs remain valid before they are renegotiated. The PIX Firewall supports a global lifetime value that applies to all crypto maps. The global lifetime value can be overridden within a crypto map entry. The lifetimes apply only to security associations established via IKE. Manually established security associations do not expire. When a security association expires, a new one is negotiated without interrupting the data flow.

A Transform Set Negotiated Between IPSec Peers

You can change global IPSec security association lifetime values by using the **crypto ipsec security-association lifetime** configuration command. To reset a lifetime to the default value, use the **no** form of the command. The command syntax is as follows:

```
crypto ipsec security-association lifetime {seconds seconds | kilobytes kilobytes}
```

where the **seconds** *seconds* parameter specifies the number of seconds a security association will live before it expires. The default is 28,800 seconds (8 hours). The **kilobytes** *kilobytes* parameter specifies the volume of traffic (in kilobytes) that can pass between IPSec peers using a given security association before that security association expires. The default is 4,608,000 KB (10 MBps for 1 hour).

Cisco recommends that you use the default lifetime values. The SAs are configured using crypto maps, which are covered in the section "Configuring Crypto Maps" later in this chapter.

NOTE   The lifetime you set for ISAKMP is separate from the IPSec lifetime just discussed. They can be set to different values.

Global IPSec SA Lifetime Examples

A general principle in cryptanalysis is that, given enough time or enough traffic protected under a single key, an attacker can break that key. Over time, a key's effective lifetime is reduced by advances made in cryptanalysis. The PIX Firewall allows you to fine-tune the key lifetime with the **crypto ipsec security-association lifetime** command. Consider the sample global IPSec security association lifetime shown in Example 11-9.

Example 11-9   *Sample Global IPSec Security Association Lifetime*

```
crypto ipsec security-association lifetime kilobytes 1382400
```

This lifetime is about 3 Mbps for one hour, adequate for a PIX Firewall behind a perimeter router with an E1 wide-area network (WAN) interface to an ISP at 2.048 MBps. Example

11-10 shows a lifetime of 15 minutes, which is rather short but provides less time for breaking a key.

Example 11-10 *Sample Lifetime of 15 Minutes*

```
crypto ipsec security-association lifetime seconds 900
```

Before a key expires, IKE negotiates another one based on the IPSec SA lifetime value to allow for a smooth transition from key to key without the need to tear down connections.

Step 4: Create Crypto Maps

Crypto map entries must be created for IPSec to set up SAs for traffic flows that must be encrypted. Crypto map entries created for IPSec set up security association parameters, tying together the various parts configured for IPSec, including the following:

- Which traffic should be protected by IPSec (crypto access-list)
- The granularity of the traffic to be protected by a set of security associations
- Where IPSec-protected traffic should be sent (who the remote IPSec peer is)
- The local interface to be used for the IPSec traffic
- What IPSec security protocol should be applied to this traffic (transform sets)
- Whether security associations are established manually or via IKE
- IPSec security association lifetime
- Other parameters that might be necessary to define an IPSec security association

The following sections consider crypto map parameters, examine the **crypto map** command, show how to configure crypto maps, and consider examples of crypto maps.

Crypto Map Parameters

You can apply only one crypto map set to a single interface. The crypto map set can include a combination of IPSec using IKE and IPSec with manually configured SA entries. Multiple interfaces can share the same crypto map set if you want to apply the same policy to multiple interfaces.

If you create more than one crypto map entry for a given interface, use the sequence number (seq-num) of each map entry to rank the map entries: the lower the seq-num, the higher the priority. At the interface that has the crypto map set, traffic is evaluated against higher-priority map entries first. You must create multiple crypto map entries for a given interface if you have any of the following conditions:

- Different data flows are to be handled by separate IPSec peers.
- You want to apply different IPSec security to different types of traffic (to the same or separate IPSec peers), for example, if you want traffic between one set of subnets to

be authenticated and traffic between another set of subnets to be both authenticated and encrypted. In this case, the different types of traffic should have been defined in two separate access lists, and you must create a separate crypto map entry for each crypto access list.

- You are not using IKE to establish a particular set of security associations, and you want to specify multiple access list entries. You must create separate access lists (one per permit entry) and specify a separate crypto map entry for each access list.

Backup Gateways

You can define multiple remote peers by using crypto maps to allow for gateway redundancy. If one peer fails, there will still be a protected path. The peer that packets are actually sent to is determined by the last peer that the PIX Firewall heard from (received either traffic or a negotiation request from) for a given data flow. If the attempt fails with the first peer, IKE tries the next peer on the crypto map list.

Configuring Crypto Maps

You use the **crypto map** configuration command to create or modify a crypto map entry. You set the crypto map entries referencing dynamic maps to be the lowest-priority entries in a crypto map set (that is, to have the highest sequence numbers). Use the **no** form of this command to delete a crypto map entry or set. The command syntax is as follows:

```
crypto map map-name seq-num {ipsec-isakmp | ipsec-manual} [dynamic dynamic-map-name]
crypto map map-name seq-num match address acl_name
crypto map map-name seq-num set peer {hostname | ip-address}
crypto map map-name seq-num set pfs [group1 | group2]
crypto map map-name seq-num set security-association lifetime {seconds seconds |
  kilobytes kilobytes}
crypto map map-name seq-num set transform-set transform-set-name1
  [transform-set-name6]
crypto map map-name client authentication aaa-server-name
crypto map map-name client configuration address {initiate | respond}
```

Table 11-8 shows the arguments and options for the **crypto map** command sequence.

Table 11-8   **crypto map** *Command Arguments/Options*

Command Parameter	Description
map-name	Assigns a name to the crypto map set.
seq-num	Assigns a number to the crypto map entry.
ipsec-manual	Indicates that IKE will not be used to establish the IPSec security associations for protecting the traffic specified by this crypto map entry.
ipsec-isakmp	Indicates that IKE will be used to establish the IPSec security associations for protecting the traffic specified by this crypto map entry.

Table 11-8   **crypto map** *Command Arguments/Options (Continued)*

Command Parameter	Description
acl_name	Identifies the named encryption access list. This name should match the name argument of the named encryption access list being matched.
match address	Specifies an access list for a crypto map entry.
set peer	Specifies an IPSec peer in a crypto map entry. Specify multiple peers by repeating this command. The peer is the terminating interface of the IPSec peer.
hostname	Specifies a peer by its host name. This is the peer's host name concatenated with its domain name, such as myhost.example.com.
ip-address	Specifies a peer by its IP address.
set pfs	Specifies that IPSec should ask for perfect forward secrecy (PFS). With PFS, every time a new security association is negotiated, a new Diffie-Hellman exchange occurs. PFS provides additional security for secret key generation at a cost of additional processing.
group 1	Specifies that IPSec should use the 768-bit Diffie-Hellman prime modulus group when performing the new Diffie-Hellman exchange. Used with the **esp-des** or **esp-3des** transform.
group 2	Specifies that IPSec should use the 1024-bit Diffie-Hellman prime modulus group when performing the new Diffie-Hellman exchange. Used with the **esp-des** or **esp-3des** transform.
set transform-set	Specifies which transform sets can be used with the crypto map entry. List multiple transform sets in order of priority, with the highest-priority (most secure) transform set first.
transform-set-name	Specifies the name of the transform set. For an ipsec-manual crypto map entry, you can specify only one transform set. For an ipsec-isakmp or dynamic crypto map entry, you can specify up to six transform sets.
kilobytes *kilobytes*	Specifies the volume of traffic (in kilobytes) that can pass between peers using a given security association before that SA expires. The default is 4,608,000 KB. The security association lifetime in a crypto map entry overrides the global security association lifetime value.
seconds *seconds*	Specifies the number of seconds a security association will live before it expires. The default is 3600 seconds (one hour).
dynamic	(Optional) Specifies that this crypto map entry references a pre-existing static crypto map. If you use this keyword, none of the crypto map configuration commands will be available.
dynamic-map-name	(Optional) Specifies the name of the dynamic crypto map set that should be used as the policy template.

continues

Table 11-8 **crypto map** *Command Arguments/Options (Continued)*

Command Parameter	Description
aaa-server-name	Specifies the name of the AAA server that will authenticate the user during IKE authentication. The two available AAA server options are TACACS+ and RADIUS.
initiate	Indicates that the PIX Firewall attempts to set IP addresses for each peer.
respond	Indicates that the PIX Firewall accepts requests for IP addresses from any requesting peer.

Here are some additional guidelines for configuring crypto maps:

- Identify the crypto map with a unique crypto map name and sequence number.
- Use **ipsec-isakmp** for CA server support.
- After you define crypto map entries, you can assign the crypto map set to interfaces using the **crypto map** *map-name* **interface** *interface-name* command.

NOTE   Access lists for crypto map entries tagged as ipsec-manual are restricted to a single permit entry, and subsequent entries are ignored. The security associations established by that particular crypto map entry are only for a single data flow. To support multiple manually established security associations for different kinds of traffic, define multiple crypto access lists and then apply each one to a separate ipsec-manual crypto map entry. Each access list should include one permit statement defining what traffic to protect.

Example 11-11 illustrates a crypto map with two peers specified for redundancy purposes.

Example 11-11 *A Crypto Map with Two Peers Specified for Redundancy*

```
Pix1(config)# access-list 151 permit ip host 192.168.1.10 host 192.168.2.10
Pix1(config)# access-list 151 permit ip host 192.168.1.10 host 192.168.3.10
Pix1(config)# crypto map mymap 10 ipsec-isakmp
Pix1(config)# crypto map mymap 10 match address 151
Pix1(config)# crypto map mymap 10 set peer 192.168.2.2
Pix1(config)# crypto map mymap 10 set peer 192.168.3.2
Pix1(config)# crypto map mymap 10 set pfs group 1
Pix1(config)# crypto map mymap 10 set transform-set mytransform
Pix1(config)# crypto map mymap 10 set security-association lifetime 2700
```

If the first peer cannot be contacted, the second peer will be used. There is no limit to the number of redundant peers that can be configured.

Setting Manual Keys

You can configure IPSec SAs manually and not use IKE to set up the SA. Cisco recommends that you use IKE to set up the SAs because it is very difficult to ensure that the SA values match between peers, and D-H is a more secure method to generate secret keys between peers. If you must, you can use **crypto map** commands to manually specify the IPSec session keys and other SA parameters within a crypto map entry.

Security associations established via the **crypto map** command do not expire (unlike security associations established via IKE). Session keys at one peer must match the session keys at the remote peer. If you change a session key, the security association using the key will be deleted and reinitialized.

NOTE	See the "Configuring Manual IPSec" section of the "Configuring IPSec" chapter in *Configuration Guide for the Cisco Secure PIX Firewall* for more details on manual IPSec: www.cisco.com/univercd/cc/td/doc/product/iaabu/pix/pix_v53/ipsec/conipsec.htm#71524

Step 5: Apply Crypto Maps to Interfaces

The last step in the actual IPSec configuration process is to apply the crypto map set to an interface. Apply the crypto map to the PIX Firewall's interface connected to the Internet with the **crypto map** command in configuration mode. Use the **no** form of the command to remove the crypto map set from the interface. The command syntax is as follows:

```
crypto map map-name interface interface-name
```

where *map-name* specifies the name of the crypto map set and the **interface** *interface-name* parameter specifies the identifying interface to be used by the PIX Firewall to identify itself to peers. If IKE is enabled and you are using a CA to obtain certificates, this should be the interface with the address specified in the CA certificates.

IPSec tunnels can be terminated on any PIX Firewall interface. This does not mean you terminate traffic coming from the outside on the inside interface. Traffic terminated on the inside interface is traffic from the inside network. Traffic terminated on the outside is traffic from the outside. Traffic terminated on a DMZ is traffic from the DMZ.

As soon as you apply the crypto map, the security association database should initialize in system memory. The SAs are available for setup when traffic defined by the crypto access list is transmitted or received.

Only one crypto map set can be assigned to an interface. If multiple crypto map entries have the same map name but a different seq-num, they are considered part of the same set and are all applied to the interface. The crypto map entry with the lowest seq-num is considered the highest priority and is evaluated first.

Example 11-12 is an example of applying a crypto map to an outside interface.

Example 11-12 *Applying a Crypto Map to an Outside Interface*

```
crypto map mymap interface outside
```

Step 6: Verify IPSec Configuration

The last step in configuring IPSec on the PIX Firewall is to verify the IPSec configuration using available **show** commands.

You can view all configured access lists with the **show access-list** command. In Example 11-13, the hitcnt=0 value shows that no traffic has been evaluated against this access list.

Example 11-13 *Showing Configured Access Lists with the* **show access-list** *Command*

```
Pix2# show access-list
access-list 101 permit ip host 192.168.2.9 host 192.168.1.9 (hitcnt=0)
```

You can view the currently defined transform sets with the **show crypto ipsec transform-set** command. This command has the following syntax:

```
show crypto ipsec transform-set [tag transform-set-name]
```

where the optional **tag** *transform-set-name* parameter shows only the transform sets with the specified *transform-set-name*.

If no keyword is used, all transform sets configured at the PIX Firewall are displayed. Example 11-14 shows the transform sets with the names **CSPF** and **verysecure**.

Example 11-14 *Transform Sets with the Names* **CSPF** *and* **verysecure**

```
Pixfirewall# show crypto ipsec transform-set
Transform set CSPF: { esp-des  }
will negotiate = { Tunnel,  },
Transform set verysecure: { esp-3des ah-sha-hmac
esp-sha-hmac }
will negotiate = { Tunnel,  },
```

You can use the **show crypto ipsec security-association lifetime** command to view the current global IPSec SA lifetime. In Example 11-15, the global IPsec security-association lifetime is 2,305,000 KB and 3600 seconds.

Example 11-15 *A Global* **ipsec security-association lifetime** *of 2305000 KB and 3600 Seconds*

```
Pix1# show crypto ipsec security-association lifetime
Security-association lifetime: 2305000 kilobytes/3600 seconds
```

You can use the **show crypto map** command to view the crypto map configuration. If no keywords are used, all crypto maps configured at the PIX Firewall are displayed. The command syntax is as follows:

```
show crypto map [interface interface | tag map-name]
```

where the **interface** *interface* parameter shows only the crypto map set applied to the specified interface.

Example 11-16 shows an example of crypto maps for PIX 1 and PIX 2. Note how the crypto map pulls together the six IPSec-related values.

Example 11-16 *Crypto Maps for PIX 1 and PIX 2*

```
Pix1(config)# show crypto map
Crypto Map "peer2" 10 ipsec-isakmp
   Peer = 192.168.2.2
   access-list 101 permit ip host 192.168.1.10 host 192.168.2.10 (hitcnt=0)
   Current peer: 192.168.2.2
   Security association lifetime: 4608000 kilobytes/28800 seconds
   PFS (Y/N): N
   Transform sets={ pix2, }
```

```
Pix2(config)# show crypto map
Crypto Map "peer1" 10 ipsec-isakmp
   Peer = 192.168.1.2
   access-list 101 permit ip host 192.168.2.10 host 192.168.1.10 (hitcnt=0)
   Current peer: 192.168.1.2
   Security association lifetime: 4608000 kilobytes/28800 seconds
   PFS (Y/N): N
   Transform sets={ pix1, }
```

Task 4: Test and Verify the Overall IPSec Configuration

The final step in configuring IPSec for pre-shared keys is to verify that all the IKE and IPSec values were configured correctly and to test it to ensure that it works properly. The PIX Firewall contains a number of **show**, **clear**, and **debug** commands that are useful for testing and verifying IKE and IPSec, which are summarized in this section.

Test and Verify IKE Configuration

You can use the commands summarized in Table 11-9 to observe IKE configuration and operation.

Table 11-9 *Commands Used to Observe IKE*

Command	Description
show isakmp	Displays configured IKE policies in a format similar to a **write terminal** command
show isakmp policy	Displays default and any configured IKE policies

Test and Verify IPSec Configuration

You can test and verify IPSec configuration on the PIX Firewall with the commands listed in Table 11-10.

Table 11-10 *Commands for Observing IKE*

Command	Description
show access-list	Lists the **access-list** command statements in the configuration. Used to verify that crypto access lists select interesting traffic. Displays the number of packets that match the access list.
show crypto map	Displays crypto access lists assigned to a crypto map. Displays configured crypto map parameters.
show crypto ipsec transform-set	Displays configured IPSec transform sets.
show crypto ipsec security-association lifetime	Displays correct global IPSec SA lifetime values.

Monitor and Manage IKE and IPSec Communications

You can observe the IKE and IPSec setup and monitor and manage IKE and IPSec communications between the PIX Firewall and IPSec peers with the commands listed in Table 11-11.

NOTE   You must be in configuration mode to execute **debug** commands.

Table 11-11 *Commands for Observing IKE*

Command	Description
show isakmp sa	Displays the current status of IKE security associations.
show crypto ipsec sa	Displays the current status of IPSec security associations. Useful for ensuring that traffic is being encrypted. Also displays the number of packets encrypted and decrypted over that SA.
clear crypto isakmp sa	Clears IKE security associations.
clear crypto ipsec sa	Clears IPSec security associations.
debug crypto isakmp	Displays IKE communications between the PIX Firewall and IPSec peers.
debug crypto ipsec	Displays IPSec communications between the PIX Firewall and IPSec peers.

The **show isakmp sa** command is useful for viewing all current IKE SAs at a peer, as shown in Example 11-17.

Example 11-17 *The* **show isakmp sa** *Command for Viewing All Current IKE SAs at a Peer*

```
Pix1# show isakmp sa
    dst            src          state       conn-id   slot
192.168.1.2    192.168.2.2    QM_IDLE          93       0
```

The **clear isakmp** command clears active IKE connections, as shown in Example 11-18.

Example 11-18 *The* **clear isakmp** *Command for Clearing Active IKE Connections*

```
Pix1# show crypto isakmp sa
    dst            src          state       conn-id   slot
192.168.1.2    192.168.2.2    QM_IDLE          93       0
Pix1# clear crypto isakmp 93
2w4d: ISADB: reaper checking SA,
Pix1# show crypto isakmp sa
    dst            src          state       conn-id   slot
```

Scaling PIX Firewall VPNs

The use of pre-shared keys for IKE authentication works only when you have a few IPSec peers. CAs enable scaling to a large number of IPSec peers.

Other IKE authentication methods require manual intervention to generate and distribute the keys on a per-peer basis. The CA server enrollment process can be largely automated so that it scales well to large deployments. Each IPSec peer individually enrolls with the CA server and obtains a digital certificate compatible with other peers enrolled with the server.

PIX Firewall with CA Enrollment

Peers enroll with a CA server in a series of steps in which specific keys are generated and then exchanged by the PIX Firewall and the CA server to ultimately form a signed certificate. The enrollment steps can be summarized as follows:

Step 1   The PIX Firewall generates an RSA key pair.

Step 2   The PIX Firewall obtains the CA's certificate, which contains the CA's public key.

Step 3   The PIX Firewall requests a signed certificate from the CA using the generated RSA (public) keys and the public key/certificate from the CA server.

Step 4   The CA administrator verifies the request and sends a signed certificate.

NOTE See the "About CA" and "Configuring CA" sections in the "Configuring IPSec" chapter of the *Configuration Guide for the Cisco Secure PIX Firewall Version 5.3* for more details on how CA servers work and how to configure the PIX Firewall for CA support:

www.cisco.com/univercd/cc/td/doc/product/iaabu/pix/pix_v53/ipsec/index.htm

Case Study 1: Configuring PIX Firewall IPSec for Point-to-Point Hosts Using Pre-Shared Keys

This case study illustrates how to configure IPSec as taught in this chapter in the hypothetical XYZ Company. Read the case study scenario, examine the topology diagram, and read the security policy. Then analyze the sample configuration to see how the security policy statements are enacted for the PIX Firewalls.

XYZ Company wants to use PIX Firewalls to create a secure VPN over the Internet between sites. The company wants you to configure a secure VPN gateway using IPSec between two PIX Firewalls to use pre-shared keys and allow access to the web server.

Figure 11-3 illustrates the portion of the XYZ network that is configured in this case study. Note that the focus here is on the PIX Firewall at each site.

Figure 11-3 *XYZ Company Configures a Secure VPN Gateway Between PIX Firewalls*

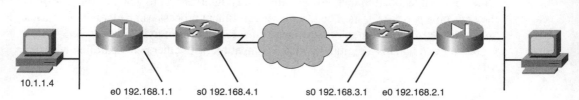

10.1.1.4
e0 192.168.1.1   s0 192.168.4.1   s0 192.168.3.1   e0 192.168.2.1

Network Security Policy

The network security policy that XYZ Company wants to implement is as follows:

- Use the Internet to connect a branch office to the corporate network for casual traffic.

- Authenticate data traffic between the corporate network and branch offices over the Internet to ensure that no one is inserting or changing packets in transit.

- Use IKE pre-shared keys and SHA for authentication.

- Ensure the data integrity of traffic between the corporate network and branch offices over the Internet using 56-bit DES encryption.

- Encrypt web traffic between internal NT servers at each site.

Sample Configuration for the PIX 1 Firewall

Examine the configuration shown in Example 11-19 for the PIX 1 Firewall of the XYZ Company. The example implements the network security policy statements related to IPSec network security. One possible configuration of the PIX Firewall for the specified security policy might look like the one shown in Example 11-19. You might choose to configure the PIX Firewall differently to enact the same security policy requirements. Unused interfaces and other unrelated commands have been deleted for brevity.

Example 11-19 *Configuration File for PIX 1 Firewall*

```
! Configures the IP addresses for each PIX Firewall interface.
ip address outside 192.168.1.1  255.255.255.0
ip address inside 10.1.1.3 255.255.255.0
ip address dmz 192.168.11.1 255.255.255.0
! Creates a global pool on the outside interface, enables NAT.
global (outside) 1 192.168.1.20-192.168.1.254 netmask 255.255.255.0
nat (inside) 1 10.0.0.0 255.0.0.0 0 0
! Creates a static translation between the global and the inside
! Windows NT server.
static (inside,outside) 192.168.1.10 10.1.1.4 netmask 255.255.255.255 0 0
! Crypto access list specifies that traffic between the internal Windows NT
! servers behind PIX Firewalls is encrypted. The source
! and destination IP addresses are the global IP addresses of the statics.
! The access lists for PIX 1 and PIX 2 are mirror images of each other.
access-list 101 permit ip host 192.168.1.10 host 192.168.2.10
! The conduits permit ICMP and Web access for testing.
conduit permit icmp any any
route outside 0.0.0.0 0.0.0.0 192.168.1.2 1
! Enables IPSec to bypass access list, access, and conduit restrictions.
sysopt connection permit-ipsec
! Defines a crypto map transform set to use esp-des.
crypto ipsec transform-set pix2 esp-des
crypto map peer2 10 ipsec-isakmp
! Defines the crypto map.
crypto map peer2 10 match address 101
! Defines the crypto map to point to the peer by specifying the peer PIX's
! outside interface IP address.
crypto map peer2 10 set peer 192.168.2.1
! Defines the crypto map to use the transform set.
crypto map peer2 10 set transform-set pix2
! Assigns the crypto map set to the outside PIX interface.
! As soon as the crypto map is assigned to the interface, the IKE and IPSec
! policy is active.
crypto map peer2 interface outside
! Enables IKE on the outside interface.
isakmp enable outside
! Defines the preshared IKE key.
isakmp key cisco123 address 192.168.2.1 netmask 255.255.255.255
! Defines the IKE policy to use preshared keys for authentication.
isakmp policy 10 authentication pre-share
isakmp policy 10 encryption des
isakmp policy 10 hash sha
! Specifies use of D-H group 1. Could have used D-H group 2 for stronger security
```

continues

Example 11-19 *Configuration File for PIX 1 Firewall (Continued)*

```
! along with translation esp-3des, but would require more CPU time to execute.
isakmp policy 10 group 1
! Specifies the IKE lifetime.
isakmp policy 10 lifetime 86400
```

Sample Configuration for the PIX 2 Firewall

Example 11-20 provides a summary of the configuration for PIX 2.

Example 11-20 *PIX 2 Configuration Example*

```
! Configures the IP addresses for each PIX Firewall interface.
ip address outside 192.168.2.1  255.255.255.0
ip address inside 10.2.1.3 255.255.255.0
ip address dmz 192.168.12.1 255.255.255.0
! Creates a global pool on the outside interface, enables NAT.
global (outside) 1 192.168.2.20-192.168.2.254 netmask 255.255.255.0
nat (inside) 1 10.0.0.0 255.0.0.0 0 0
! Creates a static translation between the global and inside Windows NT server.
static (inside,outside) 192.168.2.10 10.2.1.4 netmask 255.255.255.255 0 0
! Crypto access list specifies that traffic between the internal Windows NT
! servers behind PIX Firewalls is encrypted.
! The source and destination IP addresses are the global IP addresses of the
! statics. The access lists for PIX 2 and PIX 1 are mirror images of each other.
access-list 101 permit ip host 192.168.2.10 host 192.168.1.10
! The conduits permit ICMP and Web access for testing.
conduit permit icmp any any
route outside 0.0.0.0 0.0.0.0 192.168.2.2 1
! Enables IPSec to bypass access list, access, and conduit restrictions.
sysopt connection permit-ipsec
! Defines a crypto map transform set to use esp-des.
crypto ipsec transform-set pix1 esp-des
crypto map peer1 10 ipsec-isakmp
! Defines the crypto map.
crypto map peer1 10 match address 101
! Defines the crypto map to point to the peer by specifying the peer PIX's
! outside interface IP address.
crypto map peer1 10 set peer 192.168.1.1
! Defines the crypto map to use the transform set.
crypto map peer1 10 set transform-set pix1
! Assigns the crypto map set to the outside PIX interface. As soon as the
! crypto map is assigned to the interface, the IKE and IPSec policy is active.
crypto map peer1 interface outside
! Enables IKE on the outside interface.
isakmp enable outside
! Defines the preshared IKE key.
isakmp key cisco123 address 192.168.2.2 netmask 255.255.255.255
! Defines the IKE policy to use preshared keys for authentication.
isakmp policy 10 authentication pre-share
isakmp policy 10 encryption des
isakmp policy 10 hash sha
! Specifies use of D-H group 1. Could have used D-H group 2 for stronger security
! along with translation esp-3des, but would require more CPU time to execute.
```

Example 11-20 *PIX 2 Configuration Example (Continued)*

```
isakmp policy 10 group 1
! Specifies the IKE lifetime.
isakmp policy 10 lifetime 86400
```

Case Study 2: Three-Site Full-Mesh IPSec Tunnels Using Pre-Shared Keys

In this case study, the ABC Company has three sites connected to the Internet. Their goal is to save money for site-to-site communication by using the Internet for secure communications between offices. This will allow them to eliminate the costly point-to-point T1s that they currently have in place. In this case study, all traffic from internal users bound for the Internet is sent unencrypted. Traffic bound for another office's internal network will be protected by IPSec.

Figure 11-4 shows the proposed topology that's now possible using IPSec.

Figure 11-4 *IPSec Topology for ABC Company*

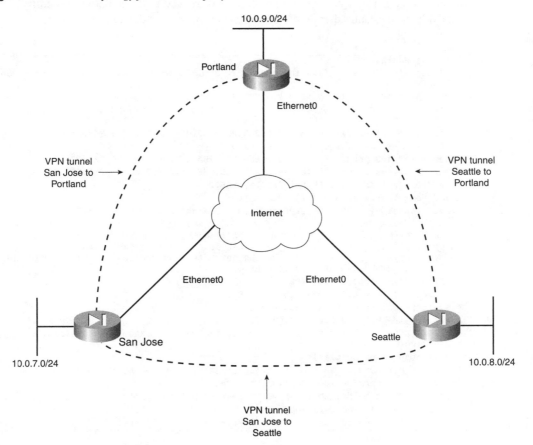

Network Security Policy

The network security policy that ABC Company wants to implement is as follows:

- Use the Internet to securely connect its two branch offices to the corporate network in Portland.

- Authenticate data traffic between the corporate network and branch offices over the Internet to ensure that no one is inserting or changing packets in transit.

- Use IKE pre-shared keys and SHA for authentication.

- Ensure data integrity of traffic between the corporate network and branch offices over the Internet using 168-bit 3DES encryption.

Sample Configuration for Portland, Seattle, and San Jose PIX Firewalls

Examine the configuration examples shown in Examples 11-21, 11-22, and 11-23 for the Portland, Seattle, and San Jose PIX Firewalls of the ABC Company. These examples implement the network security policy statements related to IPSec network security. Unused interfaces and other unrelated commands have been deleted for brevity.

Example 11-21 *PIX Configuration for Portland*

```
hostname Portland
! access-list 101 specifies that any ip traffic from Portland to Seattle will be
encrypted
access-list 101 permit ip 10.0.9.0 255.255.255.0 10.0.8.0 255.255.255.0
! access-list 102 specifies that any ip traffic from Portland to San Jose will be
encrypted
access-list 102 permit ip 10.0.9.0 255.255.255.0 10.0.7.0 255.255.255.0
! access-list 103 is used by nat 0 below
access-list 103 permit ip 10.0.9.0 255.255.255.0 10.0.8.0 255.255.255.0
access-list 103 permit ip 10.0.9.0 255.255.255.0 10.0.7.0 255.255.255.0
ip address outside 192.168.9.2 255.255.255.0
ip address inside 10.0.9.1 255.255.255.0
global (outside) 1 192.168.9.20-192.168.9.254 netmask 255.255.255.0
! nat 0 is used here with access-list 103.  The effect of the access-list bound to
nat 0 is that traffic going to and coming from the Inside networks specified in the
access-list will not be translated.  This is necessary because translation occurs
before encryption.  Failure to add the nat 0 and the access-list will result in
failure to communicate to crypto peers.
nat (inside) 0 access-list 103
nat (inside) 1 10.0.9.0 255.255.255.0 0 0
conduit permit icmp any any echo-reply
route outside 0.0.0.0 0.0.0.0 192.168.9.1 1
! Allow IPSec protected traffic to bypass the regular conduit/access-list
processing.
sysopt connection permit-ipsec
! Use 168-bit 3DES to encrypt traffic between the protected networks.
crypto ipsec transform-set Portland esp-3des
! Use ISAKMP to establish the phase 1 SA to the first peer.
crypto map VPN 10 ipsec-isakmp
! Apply protection to any traffic specified in this access-list
```

Example 11-21 *PIX Configuration for Portland (Continued)*

```
crypto map VPN 10 match address 101
! Define the first crypto peer.
crypto map VPN 10 set peer 192.168.8.2
! Use transform-set Portland for the first peer.
crypto map VPN 10 set transform-set Portland
! Use ISAKMP to establish the phase 1 SA to the second peer.
crypto map VPN 20 ipsec-isakmp
! Apply protection to any traffic specified in this access-list
crypto map VPN 20 match address 102
! Define the second crypto peer.
crypto map VPN 20 set peer 192.168.7.2
! Use transform-set Portland for the first peer.
crypto map VPN 20 set transform-set Portland
! Bind the crypto map to operate on the Outside interface.
crypto map VPN interface outside
! Bind IKE to operate on the Outside interface.
isakmp enable outside.
! Define the pre-shared keys to use for both peers.
isakmp key cisco123 address 192.168.8.2 netmask 255.255.255.255
isakmp key cisco456 address 192.168.7.2 netmask 255.255.255.255
! IKE will use IP addresses to define crypto peers.
isakmp identity address
! IKE will use pre-shared keys to authenticate crypto peers.
isakmp policy 10 authentication pre-share
! IKE will protect the phase 1 SA with 3DES.
isakmp policy 10 encryption 3DES
! IKE will send the pre-shared key to its crypto peers as a sha hash.
isakmp policy 10 hash sha
! IKE will use a 1024-bit prime number to generate the Symmetric encryption key.
isakmp policy 10 group 2
! IKE will require re-authentication of its crypto peer once a day.
isakmp policy 10 lifetime 86400
```

Example 11-22 *PIX Configuration for Seattle*

```
hostname Seattle
access-list 101 permit ip 10.0.8.0 255.255.255.0 10.0.7.0 255.255.255.0
access-list 102 permit ip 10.0.8.0 255.255.255.0 10.0.9.0 255.255.255.0
access-list 103 permit ip 10.0.8.0 255.255.255.0 10.0.7.0 255.255.255.0
access-list 103 permit ip 10.0.8.0 255.255.255.0 10.0.9.0 255.255.255.0
ip address outside 192.168.8.2 255.255.255.0
ip address inside 10.0.8.1 255.255.255.0
global (outside) 1 192.168.8.20-192.168.8.254 netmask 255.255.255.0
nat (inside) 0 access-list 103
nat (inside) 1 10.0.8.0 255.255.255.0 0 0
conduit permit icmp any any echo-reply
route outside 0.0.0.0 0.0.0.0 192.168.8.1 1
sysopt connection permit-ipsec
crypto ipsec transform-set Seattle esp-3des
crypto map VPN 10 ipsec-isakmp
crypto map VPN 10 match address 101
crypto map VPN 10 set peer 192.168.7.2
crypto map VPN 10 set transform-set Seattle
```

continues

Example 11-22 *PIX Configuration for Seattle (Continued)*

```
crypto map VPN 20 ipsec-isakmp
crypto map VPN 20 match address 102
crypto map VPN 20 set peer 192.168.9.2
crypto map VPN 20 set transform-set Seattle
crypto map VPN 103 ipsec-isakmp
crypto map VPN interface outside
isakmp enable outside
isakmp key cisco123 address 192.168.9.2 netmask 255.255.255.255
isakmp key cisco123 address 192.168.7.2 netmask 255.255.255.255
isakmp identity address
isakmp policy 10 authentication pre-share
isakmp policy 10 encryption 3des
isakmp policy 10 hash sha
isakmp policy 10 group 2
isakmp policy 10 lifetime 86400
```

Example 11-23 *PIX Configuration for San Jose*

```
hostname San_Jose
access-list 101 permit ip 10.0.7.0 255.255.255.0 10.0.8.0 255.255.255.0
access-list 102 permit ip 10.0.7.0 255.255.255.0 10.0.9.0 255.255.255.0
access-list 103 permit ip 10.0.7.0 255.255.255.0 10.0.8.0 255.255.255.0
access-list 103 permit ip 10.0.7.0 255.255.255.0 10.0.9.0 255.255.255.0
ip address outside 192.168.7.2 255.255.255.0
ip address inside 10.0.7.1 255.255.255.0
global (outside) 1 192.168.7.20-192.168.7.254 netmask 255.255.255.0
nat (inside) 0 access-list 103
nat (inside) 1 10.0.7.0 255.255.255.0 0 0
conduit permit icmp any any echo-reply
route outside 0.0.0.0 0.0.0.0 192.168.7.1 1
sysopt connection permit-ipsec
crypto ipsec transform-set San_Jose esp-3des
crypto map VPN 10 ipsec-isakmp
crypto map VPN 10 match address 101
crypto map VPN 10 set peer 192.168.8.2
crypto map VPN 10 set transform-set San_Jose
crypto map VPN 20 ipsec-isakmp
crypto map VPN 20 match address 102
crypto map VPN 20 set peer 192.168.9.2
crypto map VPN 20 set transform-set San_Jose
crypto map VPN interface outside
isakmp enable outside
isakmp key cisco456 address 192.168.9.2 netmask 255.255.255.255
isakmp key cisco123 address 192.168.8.2 netmask 255.255.255.255
isakmp identity address
isakmp policy 10 authentication pre-share
isakmp policy 10 encryption 3des
isakmp policy 10 hash sha
isakmp policy 10 group 2
isakmp policy 10 lifetime 86400
```

Summary

This section summarizes the main points of this chapter:

- Determine the types of traffic that will be encrypted and the hosts or networks that will be protected, and specify the IPSec gateways that will terminate the tunnels as part of planning for IPSec.

- You use the **isakmp policy** command to specify pre-shared keys for authentication and to configure IKE policy parameters.

- Some IPSec transforms require you to make trade-offs between high performance and stronger security.

- IPSec transforms are grouped into sets, and the sets can be grouped into supersets in crypto maps, where you place the strongest security transform sets first.

- Crypto access lists act like outgoing access lists, where permit means encrypt. Crypto access lists also check to see whether incoming traffic *should* have been encrypted but wasn't.

- Crypto access lists should mirror each other between peers.

- Crypto maps pull together all IPSec details and are applied to interfaces, enabling IPSec SA setup.

- The PIX Firewall can terminate IPSec tunnels on any interface from traffic coming in on that interface.

- The **show crypto map** command shows a summary of all IPSec parameters used to set up IPSec SAs.

Review Questions

To test what you have learned in this chapter, answer the following questions and then refer to Appendix F for the answers.

1 Name an advantage and a disadvantage to using pre-shared keys for authentication.

2 What command do you use to enter a pre-shared key?

3 How do you view IKE policies in the PIX's configuration?

4 How many transforms can be defined in a transform set?

5 How do you configure IPSec security association lifetimes on the PIX Firewall?

6 What command do you use to define the traffic flows to be protected?

7 How can you view IKE events as they occur between IPSec peers?

8 Why does IKE fail for pre-shared keys in the following sample configurations?

```
PIX1
isakmp policy 100 authentication rsa-sig
isakmp policy 100 group 1
isakmp policy 100 lifetime 5000
isakmp policy 200 hash md5
isakmp policy 200 authentication pre-share
```

```
PIX2
isakmp policy 100 authentication rsa-sig
isakmp policy 100 group 2
isakmp policy 100 lifetime 5000
isakmp policy 200 authentication rsa-sig
isakmp policy 200 lifetime 10000
isakmp policy 300 hash sha
isakmp policy 300 authentication pre-share
```

References

The topics considered in this chapter are complex and should be studied further to fully understand them and put them to use. Use the following references to learn more about the topics in this chapter.

Refer to the *Configuration Guide for the Cisco Secure PIX Firewall, PIX Firewall Release 5.3*, to learn how to configure IPSec on the PIX Firewall. You will find the following chapters most informative:

- **Configuring IPSec**—Presents an overview and procedure of how to configure IPSec. An IPSec-specific command reference is included.

- **Command Reference**—Contains details on each PIX Firewall command.

- **Configuration Examples**—Shows sample configurations for PIX Firewall IPSec.

Recommended reading for IPSec:

- *Applied Cryptography*, by Bruce Schneier

- *Managing Cisco Network Security*, by Michael Wenstrom

- *IPSec—The New Security Standard for the Internet, Intranets and Virtual Private Networks*, by Naganand Doraswamy & Dan Harkins

- The IPSec Request for Comment papers can be found at: www.antioffline.com/ipsec/rfc

- RFC 2401: "Security Architecture for the Internet Protocol"

- RFC 2403: "The Use of HMAC-MD5-96 within ESP and AH"

- RFC 2404: "The Use of HMAC-SHA-1-96 within ESP and AH"

- RFC 2405: "The ESP DES-CBC Cipher Algorithm With Explicit IV"

- RFC 2406: "IP Encapsulating Security Payload (ESP)"

- RFC 2407: "The Internet IP Security Domain of Interpretation for ISAKMP"
- RFC 2408: "Internet Security Association and Key Management Protocol (ISAKMP)"
- RFC 2409: "The Internet Key Exchange (IKE)"
- RFC 2412: "The OAKLEY Key Determination Protocol"
- RFC 2451: "The ESP CBC-Mode Cipher Algorithms"

This chapter covers the following key topics:

- The Cisco IOS Firewall Context-Based Access Control Configuration
- Introduction to the Cisco IOS Firewall
- Context-Based Access Control
- Audit Trail and Alert
- Port-to-Application Mapping
- Define Inspection Rules
- Apply Inspection Rules and ACLs to Router Interfaces
- Test and Verify

CHAPTER 12

Cisco IOS Firewall Context-Based Access Control

Introduction to the Cisco IOS Firewall

This section introduces the features of the Cisco IOS Firewall.

The Cisco IOS Firewall is a security-specific option for Cisco IOS Software. It integrates robust firewall functionality (CBAC), Authentication Proxy, and intrusion detection for every network perimeter, and enriches existing Cisco IOS security capabilities. It adds greater depth and flexibility to existing Cisco IOS security solutions, such as authentication, encryption, and failover, by delivering state-of-the-art security features such as stateful, application-based filtering; dynamic per-user authentication and authorization; defense against network attacks; Java blocking; and real-time alerts. When combined with Cisco IOS IPSec software and other Cisco IOS Software–based technologies, such as Layer 2 Tunneling Protocol (L2TP) tunneling and quality of service (QoS), the Cisco IOS Firewall provides a complete, integrated virtual private network (VPN) solution.

Context-Based Access Control

The Cisco IOS Firewall Context-Based Access Control (CBAC) engine provides secure, per-application access control across network perimeters. CBAC enhances security for TCP and UDP applications that use well-known ports, such as FTP and e-mail traffic, by scrutinizing source and destination addresses. CBAC allows network administrators to implement firewall intelligence as part of an integrated, single-box solution.

For example, sessions with an extranet partner involving Internet applications, multimedia applications, or Oracle databases would no longer need to open a network doorway accessible through weaknesses in a partner's network. CBAC enables tightly secured networks to run today's basic application traffic, as well as advanced applications such as multimedia and videoconferencing, securely through a router.

CBAC intelligently filters TCP and UDP packets based on application layer protocol session information. It can inspect traffic for sessions that originate on any interface of the router. CBAC inspects traffic that travels through the firewall to discover and manage state information for TCP and UDP sessions. This state information creates temporary openings in the firewall's access lists to allow return traffic and additional data connections for permissible sessions.

Inspecting packets at the application layer, and maintaining TCP and UDP session information, provides CBAC with the capability to detect and prevent certain types of network attacks, such as SYN flooding. CBAC also inspects packet sequence numbers in TCP connections to see if they are within expected ranges—CBAC drops any suspicious packets. Additionally, CBAC can detect unusually high rates of new connections and issue alert messages. CBAC inspection can help protect against certain Denial of Service (DoS) attacks involving fragmented IP packets. Even though the firewall prevents an attacker from making actual connections to a given host, the attacker can disrupt services provided by that host. This is done by sending many non-initial IP fragments or by sending complete fragmented packets through a router. Because router ACLs only check the initial fragment in a chain (offset=0), a large number of non-initial fragments can tie up resources on the target host as it tries to reassemble the incomplete packets.

As with any nondedicated function device, there are significant tradeoffs to consider when weighing whether to use CBAC in place of a PIX Firewall:

- **Memory**—CBAC requires 600 bytes of DRAM for each object it maintains state for. In high-load environments on routers with limited maximum DRAM, memory exhaustion can occur.

- **CPU Usage**—To enforce stateful packet filtering, the router is forced to look much deeper into a packet, checking the validity of many parameters. High traffic loads can overwhelm the CPU and cause performance degradation.

Authentication Proxy

Network administrators can create specific security policies for each user with Cisco IOS Firewall LAN-based, dynamic, per-user authentication and authorization. Previously, user identity and related authorized access were determined by a user's fixed IP address, or a single security policy had to be applied to an entire user group or subnet. Now, per-user policy can be downloaded dynamically to the router from a TACACS+ or RADIUS authentication server using Cisco IOS Software authentication, authorization, and accounting (AAA) services.

With the Authentication Proxy feature, users log in to the network or access the Internet through Hypertext Transfer Protocol (HTTP), and their specific access profiles are automatically retrieved and applied from a Cisco Secure Access Control Server (ACS), or other RADIUS or TACACS+ authentication server. The user profiles are active only when there is active traffic from the authenticated users.

The Authentication Proxy is compatible with other Cisco IOS security features, such as Network Address Translation (NAT), IP Security (IPSec) encryption, and VPN client software.

Intrusion Detection

Intrusion detection systems (IDS) provide a level of protection beyond the firewall by protecting the network from internal and external attacks and threats. Cisco IOS Firewall IDS technology enhances perimeter firewall protection by taking appropriate action on packets and flows that violate the security policy or represent malicious network activity.

Cisco IOS Firewall intrusion detection capabilities are ideal for providing additional visibility at intranet, extranet, and branch-office Internet perimeters. Network administrators now enjoy more robust protection against attacks on the network and can automatically respond to threats from internal or external hosts.

The Cisco IOS Firewall's IDS identifies 59 common attacks by using signatures to detect patterns of misuse in network traffic. The intrusion detection signatures available in the new release of the Cisco IOS Firewall were chosen from a broad cross-section of intrusion detection signatures. The signatures represent severe breaches of security and the most common network attacks and information-gathering scans.

NOTE	While IOS supports intrusion detection, it should be noted that the signature coverage is limited. Also, new signatures cannot be added on the fly to support new applications. Signatures are only added or modified by upgrading to a newer version of IOS. There have been no recent additions.

Table 12-1 documents the 59 intrusion detection signatures supported as of IOS version 12.1.

Table 12-1   *Intrusion Detection Signatures Supported by IOS Version 12.1 and Later*

Sig ID	Signature Name	Sig Type	Description
1000	IP options-Bad Option List	Info, Atomic	Triggers upon receipt of an IP datagram where the list of IP options in the IP datagram header is incomplete or malformed. The IP options list contains one or more options that perform various network management or debugging tasks.
1001	IP options-Record Packet Route	Info, Atomic	Triggers upon receipt of an IP datagram where the IP option list for the datagram includes option 7 (Record Packet Route).
1002	IP options-Timestamp	Info, Atomic	Triggers upon receipt of an IP datagram where the IP option list for the datagram includes option 4 (Timestamp).

continues

Table 12-1 *Intrusion Detection Signatures Supported by IOS Version 12.1 and Later (Continued)*

Sig ID	Signature Name	Sig Type	Description
1003	IP options-Provide s,c,h,tcc	Info, Atomic	Triggers upon receipt of an IP datagram where the IP option list for the datagram includes option 2 (Security options).
1004	IP options-Loose Source Route	Info, Atomic	Triggers upon receipt of an IP datagram where the IP option list for the datagram includes option 3 (Loose Source Route).
1005	IP options-SATNET ID	Info, Atomic	Triggers upon receipt of an IP datagram where the IP option list for the datagram includes option 8 (SATNET stream identifier).
1006	IP options-Strict Source Route	Info, Atomic	Triggers upon receipt of an IP datagram in which the IP option list for the datagram includes option 2 (Strict Source Routing).
1100	IP Fragment Attack	Attack, Atomic	Triggers when any IP datagram is received with the "more fragments" flag set to 1 or if there is an offset indicated in the offset field.
1101	Unknown IP Protocol	Attack, Atomic	Triggers when an IP datagram is received with the protocol field set to 101 or greater. These protocol types are undefined or reserved and should not be used.
1102	Impossible IP Packet	Attack, Atomic	Triggers when an IP packet arrives with a source equal to the destination address. This signature will catch the so-called Land Attack.
2000	ICMP Echo Reply	Info, Atomic	Triggers when an IP datagram is received with the "protocol" field in the IP header set to 1 (ICMP) and the "type" field in the ICMP header set to 0 (Echo Reply).
2001	ICMP Host Unreachable	Info, Atomic	Triggers when an IP datagram is received with the "protocol" field in the IP header set to 1 (ICMP) and the "type" field in the ICMP header set to 3 (Host Unreachable).

Table 12-1   *Intrusion Detection Signatures Supported by IOS Version 12.1 and Later (Continued)*

Sig ID	Signature Name	Sig Type	Description
2002	ICMP Source Quench	Info, Atomic	Triggers when an IP datagram is received with the "protocol" field in the IP header set to 1 (ICMP) and the "type" field in the ICMP header set to 4 (Source Quench).
2003	ICMP Redirect	Info, Atomic	Triggers when an IP datagram is received with the "protocol" field in the IP header set to 1 (ICMP) and the "type" field in the ICMP header set to 5 (Redirect).
2004	ICMP Echo Request	Info, Atomic	Triggers when an IP datagram is received with the "protocol" field in the IP header set to 1 (ICMP) and the "type" field in the ICMP header set to 8 (Echo Request).
2005	ICMP Time Exceeded for a Datagram	Info, Atomic	Triggers when an IP datagram is received with the "protocol" field in the IP header set to 1 (ICMP) and the "type" field in the ICMP header set to 11 (Time Exceeded for a Datagram).
2006	ICMP Parameter Problem on Datagram	Info, Atomic	Triggers when an IP datagram is received with the "protocol" field in the IP header set to 1 (ICMP) and the "type" field in the ICMP header set to 12 (Parameter Problem on Datagram).
2007	ICMP Timestamp Request	Info, Atomic	Triggers when an IP datagram is received with the "protocol" field in the IP header set to 1 (ICMP) and the "type" field in the ICMP header set to 13 (Timestamp Request).
2008	ICMP Timestamp Reply	Info, Atomic	Triggers when an IP datagram is received with the "protocol" field in the IP header set to 1 (ICMP) and the "type" field in the ICMP header set to 14 (Timestamp Reply).
2009	ICMP Information Request	Info, Atomic	Triggers when an IP datagram is received with the "protocol" field in the IP header set to 1 (ICMP) and the "type" field in the ICMP header set to 15 (Information Request).

continues

Table 12-1 *Intrusion Detection Signatures Supported by IOS Version 12.1 and Later (Continued)*

Sig ID	Signature Name	Sig Type	Description
2010	ICMP Information Reply	Info, Atomic	Triggers when an IP datagram is received with the "protocol" field in the IP header set to 1 (ICMP) and the "type" field in the ICMP header set to 16 (ICMP Information Reply).
2011	ICMP Address Mask Request	Info, Atomic	Triggers when an IP datagram is received with the "protocol" field in the IP header set to 1 (ICMP) and the "type" field in the ICMP header set to 17 (Address Mask Request).
2012	ICMP Address Mask Reply	Info, Atomic	Triggers when an IP datagram is received with the "protocol" field in the IP header set to 1 (ICMP) and the "type" field in the ICMP header set to 18 (Address Mask Reply).
2150	Fragmented ICMP Traffic	Attack, Atomic	Triggers when an IP datagram is received with the "protocol" field in the IP header set to 1 (ICMP) and either the more fragments flag is set to 1 (ICMP) or there is an offset indicated in the offset field.
2151	Large ICMP Traffic	Attack, Atomic	Triggers when an IP datagram is received with the "protocol" field in the IP header set to 1 (ICMP) and an IP length greater than 1024.
2154	Ping of Death Attack	Attack, Atomic	Triggers when an IP datagram is received with the "protocol" field in the IP header set to 1 (ICMP), the Last Fragment bit is set, and (IP offset $\times$ 8) + (IP data length) is greater than 65,535.
			In other words, the IP offset (which represents the starting position of this fragment in the original packet, and which is in 8-byte units) plus the rest of the packet is greater than the maximum size for an IP packet.
3040	TCP—no bits set in flags	Attack, Atomic	Triggers when a TCP packet is received with no bits set in the flags field.

Table 12-1   *Intrusion Detection Signatures Supported by IOS Version 12.1 and Later (Continued)*

Sig ID	Signature Name	Sig Type	Description
3041	TCP—SYN and FIN bits set	Attack, Atomic	Triggers when a TCP packet is received with both the SYN and FIN bits set in the flag field.
3042	TCP—FIN bit with no ACK bit in flags	Attack, Atomic	Triggers when a TCP packet is received with the FIN bit set but with no ACK bit set in the flags field.
3050	Half-open SYN Attack/SYN Flood	Attack, Compound	Triggers when multiple TCP sessions have been improperly initiated on any of several well-known service ports. Detection of this signature is currently limited to FTP, Telnet, HTTP, and e-mail servers (TCP ports 21, 23, 80, and 25 respectively).
3100	Smail Attack	Attack, Compound	Triggers on the very common smail attack against SMTP-compliant e-mail servers (frequently sendmail).
3101	Sendmail Invalid Recipient	Attack, Compound	Triggers on any mail message with a pipe (I) symbol in the recipient field.
3102	Sendmail Invalid Sender	Attack, Compound	Triggers on any mail message with a pipe (I) symbol in the From: field.
3103	Sendmail Reconnaissance	Attack, Compound	Triggers when **expn** or **vrfy** commands are issued to the SMTP port.
3104	Archaic Sendmail Attacks	Attack, Compound	Triggers when **wiz** or **debug** commands are issued to the SMTP port.
3105	Sendmail Decode Alias	Attack, Compound	Triggers on any mail message with :decode@ in the header.
3106	Mail Spam	Attack, Compound	Counts number of Rcpt to: lines in a single mail message and alarms after a user-definable maximum has been exceeded (default is 250).
3107	Majordomo Execute Attack	Attack, Compound	A bug in the Majordomo program will allow remote users to execute arbitrary commands at the privilege level of the server.
3150	FTP Remote Command Execution	Attack, Compound	Triggers when someone tries to execute the FTP SITE command.

continues

Table 12-1 *Intrusion Detection Signatures Supported by IOS Version 12.1 and Later (Continued)*

Sig ID	Signature Name	Sig Type	Description
3151	FTP SYST Command Attempt	Info, Compound	Triggers when someone tries to execute the FTP SYST command.
3152	FTP CWD ~root	Attack, Compound	Triggers when someone tries to execute the CWD ~root command.
3153	FTP Improper Address Specified	Attack, Atomic*	Triggers if a port command is issued with an address that is not the same as that of the requesting host.
3154	FTP Improper Port Specified	Attack, Atomic*	Triggers if a port command is issued with a data port specified that is less than 1024 or greater than 65,535.
4050	UDP Bomb	Attack, Atomic	Triggers when the UDP length specified is less than the IP length specified.
4100	Tftp Passwd File	Attack, Compound	Triggers on an attempt to access the passwd file (typically /etc/passwd) through TFTP.
6100	RPC Port Registration	Info, Atomic*	Triggers when attempts are made to register new RPC services on a target host.
6101	RPC Port Unregistration	Info, Atomic*	Triggers when attempts are made to unregister existing RPC services on a target host.
6102	RPC Dump	Info, Atomic*	Triggers when an RPC dump request is issued to a target host.
6103	Proxied RPC Request	Attack, Atomic*	Triggers when a proxied RPC request is sent to the portmapper of a target host.
6150	ypserv Portmap Request	Info, Atomic*	Triggers when a request is made to the portmapper for the YP server daemon (ypserv) port.
6151	ypbind Portmap Request	Info, Atomic*	Triggers when a request is made to the portmapper for the YP bind daemon (ypbind) port.
6152	yppasswdd Portmap Request	Info, Atomic*	Triggers when a request is made to the portmapper for the YP password daemon (yppasswdd) port.
6153	ypupdated Portmap Request	Info, Atomic*	Triggers when a request is made to the portmapper for the YP update daemon (ypupdated) port.

Table 12-1   *Intrusion Detection Signatures Supported by IOS Version 12.1 and Later (Continued)*

Sig ID	Signature Name	Sig Type	Description
6154	ypxfrd Portmap Request	Info, Atomic*	Triggers when a request is made to the portmapper for the YP transfer daemon (ypxfrd) port.
6155	mountd Portmap Request	Info, Atomic*	Triggers when a request is made to the portmapper for the mount daemon (mountd) port.
6175	rexd Portmap Request	Info, Atomic*	Triggers when a request is made to the portmapper for the remote execution daemon (rexd) port.
6180	rexd Attempt	Info, Atomic*	Triggers when a call to the rexd program is made. The remote execution daemon is the server responsible for remote program execution. This may be indicative of an attempt to gain unauthorized access to system resources.
6190	statd Buffer Overflow	Attack, Atomic*	Triggers when a large statd request is sent. This could be an attempt to overflow a buffer and gain access to system resources.
8000	FTP Retrieve Password File	Attack, Atomic*	Triggers on string passwd issued during an FTP session. May indicate someone attempting to retrieve the password file from a machine in order to crack it and gain unauthorized access to system resources.

Context-Based Access Control in Action

This section describes the limitations of Cisco IOS access control lists (ACLs) and explains how CBAC better protects users from attack. It also lists the protocols supported by CBAC and describes the added alert and audit trail features. Finally, the CBAC configuration tasks are listed.

Before delving into CBAC, some basic ACL concepts need to be covered briefly. An ACL provides packet filtering: There's an implied **deny all** at the end of the ACL, and if an ACL is not configured or applied to an interface, it permits all connections. Without CBAC, traffic filtering is limited to access list implementations that examine packets at the network layer, or at most, the transport layer.

NOTE	Access lists are not considered strong security. ACLs are static in nature. Any inbound access you configure is a permanent hole in your security. The dynamically created/deleted ACLs that CBAC creates to allow access are superior and where possible, CBAC should be used to secure your network.

With CBAC, you bind protocol-specific inspection rules and an access list to the "inside" interface, specifying the address ranges you want to protect with CBAC. On the interface acting as the "outside" (Ethernet, serial, Token Ring, etc.), an access list is created that— ideally—blocks all inbound traffic. In most environments, however, you will probably need to allow your routing protocol and ICMP. The access list on the external interface is dynamically modified to allow return traffic. These dynamic access lists are created when needed to allow return traffic and immediately deleted when a session is torn down.

Figure 12-1 illustrates the operation of Context-Based Access Control.

Figure 12-1 *Context-Based Access Control Operation*

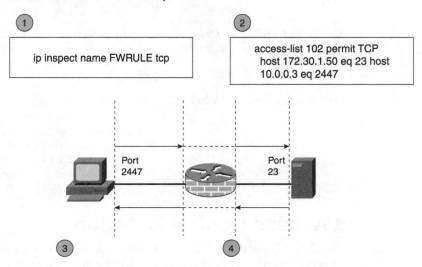

The operation indicated by the numbers in Figure 12-1 is as follows:

1 Control traffic is inspected by the CBAC rule.

2 CBAC creates a dynamic ACL, allowing return traffic back.

3 CBAC continues to inspect control traffic and dynamically creates and removes ACLs as required by the application. It also monitors and protects against application-specific attacks.

4 CBAC detects when an application terminates or times out and removes all dynamic ACLs for that session.

5 CBAC inspects and monitors all TCP and UDP sessions but only performs application-specific level inspection on the control channels of connections; the data channels are not inspected. For example, during FTP sessions, both the control and data channels (which are created when a data file is transferred) are monitored for state changes, but only the control channel is inspected (that is, the CBAC software parses the FTP commands and responses).

CBAC inspection recognizes application-specific commands in the control channel and detects and prevents certain application-level attacks. CBAC inspection tracks sequence numbers in all TCP packets and drops those packets with sequence numbers that are not within expected ranges. CBAC inspection recognizes application-specific commands (such as illegal Simple Mail Transfer Protocol [SMTP] commands) in the control channel and detects and prevents certain application-level attacks. When CBAC suspects an attack, the DoS feature can take several actions:

- Generate alert messages.

- Protect system resources that could impede performance.

- Block packets from suspected attackers.

CBAC uses timeout and threshold values to manage session state information, helping to determine when to drop sessions that do not become fully established. Setting timeout values for network sessions helps prevent DoS attacks by freeing up system resources, dropping sessions after a specified amount of time. Setting threshold values for network sessions helps prevent DoS attacks by controlling the number of half-open sessions, which limits the amount of system resources applied to half-open sessions. When a session is dropped, CBAC sends a reset message to the devices at both endpoints (source and destination) of the session. When the system under DoS attack receives a reset command, it releases, or frees up, processes and resources related to that incomplete session.

CBAC provides three thresholds against DoS attacks:

- The total number of half-open TCP or UDP sessions

- The number of half-open sessions based on time

- The number of half-open TCP-only sessions per host

If a threshold is exceeded, CBAC has two options, shown here:

- Send a reset message to the endpoints of the oldest half-open session, making resources available to service newly arriving SYN packets.

- In the case of half-open TCP-only sessions, CBAC blocks all SYN packets temporarily for the duration configured by the threshold value. When the router blocks a SYN packet, the TCP three-way handshake is never initiated, which prevents the router from using memory and processing resources needed for valid connections.

DoS detection and prevention requires you to create a CBAC inspection rule and apply that rule on an interface. The inspection rule must include the protocols that you want to monitor against DoS attacks. For example, if you have TCP inspection enabled on the inspection rule, CBAC can track all TCP connections to watch for DoS attacks. If the inspection rule includes FTP protocol inspection but not TCP inspection, CBAC tracks only FTP connections for DoS attacks.

A state table maintains session state information. Whenever a packet is inspected, a state table is updated to include information about the state of the packet's connection. Return traffic will be permitted back through the firewall only if the state table contains information indicating that the packet belongs to a permissible session. Inspection controls the traffic that belongs to a valid session and drops traffic it does not know. When return traffic is inspected, the state table information is updated as necessary.

UDP sessions are approximated. With UDP, there are no actual sessions, so the software approximates sessions by examining the information in the packet and determining if the packet is similar to other UDP packets (for example, similar source or destination addresses and port numbers), and if the packet was detected soon after another, similar UDP packet. "Soon" means within the configurable UDP idle timeout period.

Access list entries are dynamically created and deleted. CBAC dynamically creates and deletes access list entries at the firewall interfaces, according to the information maintained in the state tables. These access list entries are applied to the interfaces to examine traffic flowing back into the internal network. These entries create temporary openings in the firewall to permit only traffic that is part of a permissible session. The temporary access list entries are never saved to non-volatile RAM (NVRAM.)

You can configure CBAC to inspect the following types of sessions:

- All TCP sessions, regardless of the application-layer protocol (sometimes called single-channel or generic TCP inspection)
- All UDP sessions, regardless of the application-layer protocol (sometimes called single-channel or generic UDP inspection)

You can also configure CBAC to specifically inspect certain application-layer protocols. The following application-layer protocols can all be configured for CBAC:

- RPC (Sun RPC, not DCE RPC)
- FTP
- TFTP
- UNIX R-commands (such as **rlogin**, **rexec**, and **rsh**)
- SMTP
- HTTP (Java blocking)
- SQL*Net

- RTSP (Real Time Streaming Protocol Ex: RealNetworks)
- Real Audio
- H.323 (Ex: NetMeeting, ProShare, CUseeMe [only the White Pine version])
- Microsoft NetShow
- StreamWorks
- VDOLive

When a protocol is configured for CBAC, the control channel of that protocol traffic is inspected, state information is maintained, and in general, packets are allowed back through the firewall only if they belong to a permissible session.

CBAC also generates real-time alerts and audit trails based on events tracked by the firewall. Enhanced audit trail features use Syslog to track all network transactions: recording timestamps, source host, destination host, ports used, and the total number of transmitted bytes, for advanced, session-based reporting.

Real-time alerts send Syslog error messages to central management consoles upon detection of suspicious activity. Using CBAC inspection rules, you can configure alerts and audit trail information on a per-application protocol basis. For example, if you want to generate audit trail information for HTTP traffic, you can specify that in the CBAC rule covering HTTP inspection.

Configuring CBAC

The following are the tasks needed to configure CBAC:

- Set audit trails and alerts.
- Set global timeouts and thresholds.
- Define Port-to-Application Mapping (PAM).
- Define inspection rules.
- Apply inspection rules and ACLs to interfaces.
- Test and verify.

Setting Audit Trails and Alerts

This section discusses how to configure an audit trail and alert.

Turn on logging and audit trails to provide a record of network access through the firewall, including illegitimate access attempts, and inbound and outbound services.

Use the **ip inspect audit-trail** and **no ip inspect alert-off** commands to enable audit trail and alert, respectively.

The syntax for the **ip inspect audit-trail** commands is as follows:

```
ip inspect audit-trail
no ip inspect audit-trail
```

The syntax for the **ip inspect alert-off** commands is as follows:

```
ip inspect alert-off
no ip inspect alert-off
```

No other arguments or keywords are used with either command.

Setting Global Timeouts and Thresholds

This section discusses how to configure the following global timeouts and thresholds:

- TCP, SYN, and FIN wait times

- TCP, UDP, and Domain Name System (DNS) idle times

- TCP flood DoS protection

CBAC uses timeouts and thresholds to determine how long to manage state information for a session and to determine when to drop sessions that do not become fully established. These timeouts and thresholds apply globally to all sessions.

You can use the default timeout and threshold values, or you can change to values more suitable to your security requirements. You should make any changes to the timeout and threshold values before you continue configuring CBAC.

To define how long the software will wait for a TCP session to reach the established state before dropping the session, use the **ip inspect tcp synwait-time** *global configuration* command. Use the **no** form of this command to reset the timeout to the default.

The syntax of the **ip inspect tcp synwait-time** command is as follows:

```
ip inspect tcp synwait-time seconds
no ip inspect tcp synwait-time
```

where the *seconds* parameter specifies how long the software will wait for a TCP session to reach the established state before dropping the session. (The default is 30 seconds.)

To define how long a TCP session will still be managed after the firewall detects a FIN exchange, use the **ip inspect tcp finwait-time** global configuration command. Use the **no** form of this command to reset the timeout to default.

The syntax of the **ip inspect tcp finwait-time** command is as follows:

```
ip inspect tcp finwait-time seconds
no ip inspect tcp finwait-time
```

where the *seconds* parameter specifies how long a TCP session will be managed after the firewall detects a FIN exchange. (The default is 5 seconds.)

To specify the TCP idle timeout (the length of time a TCP session will still be managed after no activity), use the **ip inspect tcp idle-time** global configuration command. Use the **no** form of this command to reset the timeout to default.

To specify the UDP idle timeout (the length of time a UDP session will still be managed after no activity), use the **ip inspect udp idle-time** global configuration command. Use the **no** form of this command to reset the timeout to default.

The syntax for the **ip inspect** {**tcp** I **udp**} **idle-time** commands is as follows:

```
ip inspect {tcp | udp} idle-time seconds
no ip inspect {tcp | udp} idle-time
```

The *seconds* parameter specifies the length of time a TCP or a UDP session will still be managed after no activity. For TCP sessions, the default is 3600 seconds (1 hour). For UDP sessions, the default is 30 seconds.

To specify the DNS idle timeout (the length of time a DNS name lookup session will still be managed after no activity), use the **ip inspect dns-timeout** *global configuration* command. Use the **no** form of this command to reset the timeout to default. Setting this parameter lower can help mitigate UDP-based DoS attacks directed against DNS.

The syntax for the **ip inspect dns-timeout** command is as follows:

```
ip inspect dns-timeout seconds
no ip inspect dns-timeout
```

where the *seconds* parameter specifies the length of time a DNS name lookup session will still be managed after no activity. (The default is 5 seconds.)

An unusually high number of half-open sessions (either absolute or measured as the arrival rate) could indicate that a DoS attack is in progress. For TCP, half-open means that the session has not reached the established state—the TCP three-way handshake has not yet been completed. For UDP, half-open means that the firewall has detected no return traffic.

CBAC measures both the total number of existing half-open sessions and the rate of session establishment attempts. Both TCP and UDP half-open sessions are counted in the total number and rate measurements. Measurements are made once a minute.

When the number of existing half-open sessions rises above a threshold (the max-incomplete high number), CBAC will go in to *aggressive mode* (also called *clamping*) and delete half-open sessions as required to accommodate new connection requests. The software continues to delete half-open requests as necessary until the number of existing half-open sessions drops below another threshold (the **max-incomplete low** number).

To define the number of existing half-open sessions that will cause the software to start deleting half-open sessions, use the **ip inspect max-incomplete high** command in global configuration mode. Use the no form of this command to reset the threshold to default.

The syntax for the **ip inspect max-incomplete high** command is as follows:

```
ip inspect max-incomplete high number
no ip inspect max-incomplete high number
```

where *high number* specifies the number of existing half-open sessions that will cause the software to start deleting half-open sessions. (The default is 500 half-open sessions.)

To define the number of existing half-open sessions that will cause the software to stop deleting half-open sessions, use the **ip inspect max-incomplete low** command in global configuration mode. Use the **no** form of this command to reset the threshold to default.

The syntax for the **ip inspect max-incomplete low** command is as follows:

```
ip inspect max-incomplete low number
no ip inspect max-incomplete low number
```

where *low number* specifies the number of existing half-open sessions that will cause the software to stop deleting half-open sessions. (The default is 400 half-open sessions.)

When the rate of new connection attempts rises above a threshold (the one-minute high number), the software will delete half-open sessions as required to accommodate new connection attempts. The software continues to delete half-open sessions, as necessary, until the rate of new connection attempts drops below another threshold (the one-minute low number). The rate thresholds are measured as the number of new session connection attempts detected in the last one-minute sample period. The firewall router reviews the one-minute rate on an ongoing basis; therefore, the router reviews the rate more frequently than one minute and does not keep deleting half-open sessions for one minute after a DoS attack has stopped—it will be less time.

To define the rate of new unestablished sessions that will cause the software to start deleting half-open sessions, use the **ip inspect one-minute high** command in global configuration mode. Use the **no** form of this command to reset the threshold to default.

The syntax for the **ip inspect one-minute high** command is as follows:

```
ip inspect one-minute high number
no ip inspect one-minute high
```

where *high number* specifies the rate of new unestablished TCP sessions that will cause the software to start deleting half-open sessions. (The default is 500 half-open sessions.)

To define the rate of new unestablished TCP sessions that will cause the software to stop deleting half-open sessions, use the **ip inspect one-minute low** command in global configuration mode. Use the **no** form of this command to reset the threshold to the default.

The syntax for the **ip inspect one-minute low** command is as follows:

```
ip inspect one-minute low number
no ip inspect one-minute low
```

where *low number* specifies the number of existing half-open sessions that will cause the software to stop deleting half-open sessions. (The default is 400 half-open sessions.)

An unusually high number of half-open sessions with the same destination host address could indicate that a DoS attack is being launched against the host. Whenever the number of half-open sessions with the same destination host address rises above a threshold specified in the **tcp max-incomplete host** command, the software will delete half-open sessions according to one of the methods described for **block-time** settings later in the text.

The software also sends Syslog messages whenever the **max-incomplete host** number is exceeded, and when blocking of connection initiations to a host starts or ends.

The global values specified for the threshold and blocking time apply to all TCP connections inspected by CBAC.

Use the **ip inspect tcp max-incomplete host** *global configuration* command to specify threshold and blocking time values for TCP host-specific DoS detection and prevention. Use the **no** form of this command to reset the threshold and blocking time to the default values.

The syntax for the **ip inspect tcp max-incomplete host** command is as follows:

```
ip inspect tcp max-incomplete host number block-time seconds
no ip inspect tcp max-incomplete host
```

where the *host number* specifies how many half-open TCP sessions with the same host destination address can exist at a time before the software starts deleting half-open sessions to the host. Use a number from 1 to 250. (The default is 50 half-open sessions.)

block-time seconds specifies how long the software will continue to delete new connection requests to the host. (The default is 0 seconds). Some guidelines about **block-time** settings include the following:

- **If the block-time seconds timeout is 0 (the default)**—The software deletes the oldest existing half-open session for the host for every new connection request to the host. This ensures that the number of half-open sessions to a given host will never exceed the threshold.

- **If the block-time seconds timeout is greater than 0**—The software deletes all existing half-open sessions for the host and then blocks all new connection requests to the host. The software will continue to block all new connection requests until the block time expires.

CAUTION   Setting the **block-time** to a value *greater* than 0 can potentially block legitimate traffic.

Defining Port-to-Application Mapping (PAM)

This section discusses the configuration of port numbers for application protocols.

Port-to-Application Mapping (PAM) allows you to customize TCP or UDP port numbers for network services or applications. PAM uses this information to support network environments that run services using ports that are different from the registered or well-known ports associated with an application.

Using the port information, PAM establishes a table of default PAM information at the router. The information in the PAM table enables CBAC-supported services to run on nonstandard ports. Previously, CBAC was limited to inspecting traffic using only the well-known or registered ports associated with an application. Now, PAM allows network administrators to customize network access control for specific applications and services.

PAM also supports host or subnet-specific port mapping, which allows you to apply PAM to a single host or subnet using standard ACLs. Host- or subnet-specific port mapping is done using standard ACLs.

System-Defined Port Mapping

PAM creates a table, or database, of system-defined mapping entries using the well-known or registered port-mapping information set up during the system startup. The system-defined entries comprise all the services supported by CBAC, which requires system-defined mapping information to function properly.

NOTE   While you can add *nonstandard* port mappings to applications, hosts, and networks, the system-defined mapping information cannot be deleted or changed; that is, you cannot map HTTP services to port 21 (FTP) or FTP services to port 80 (HTTP). If you try to map an application to a system-defined port, a message appears warning you of a mapping conflict.

Table 12-2 lists the default system-defined services and applications in the PAM table.

Table 12-2   *PAM Table: Default System-Defined Services/Applications*

Application	Port
cuseeme	7648
exec	512
ftp	21
http	80
h323	1720
login	513
mgcp	2427
msrpc	135
netshow	1755
realmedia	7070
rtsp	554
rtsp	8554
shell	514
sip	5060
smtp	25

Table 12-2   *PAM Table: Default System-Defined Services/Applications (Continued)*

Application	Port
sql-net	1521
streamworks	1558
sunrpc	111
telnet	23
tftp	69*
vdolive	7000

*Port 69 is a UDP port. All other ports in Table 12-2 are TCP ports.

Network services or applications that use nonstandard ports require user-defined entries in the PAM table. For example, your network might run HTTP services on the nonstandard port 8000 instead of on the system-defined default port 80. In this case, you can use PAM to map port 8000 with HTTP services. If HTTP services run on other ports, use PAM to create additional port-mapping entries. After you define a port mapping, you can overwrite that entry at a later time by simply mapping that specific port with a different application.

User-defined port-mapping information can also specify a range of ports for an application by establishing a separate entry in the PAM table for each port number in the range.

User-defined entries are saved with the default mapping information when you save the router configuration.

To establish PAM, use the **ip port-map** configuration command. Use the **no** form of this command to delete user-defined PAM entries.

The syntax for the **ip port-map** command is as follows:

```
ip port-map appl_name port port_num [list acl_num]
```

Table 12-3 describes the arguments for the **ip port-map** command.

Table 12-3   **ip port-map** *Command Arguments*

Arguments	Description
appl_name	Specifies the name of the application with which to apply the port mapping. Use one of the following application names: cuseeme, dns, exec, finger, ftp, gopher, http, h323, imap, kerberos, ldap, login, lotusnote, mgcp, msrpc, ms-sql, netshow, nfs, nntp, pop2, pop3, realmedia, rtsp, sap, shell, sip, smtp, snmp, sql-net, streamworks, sunrpc, sybase-sql, tacacs, telnet, tftp, or vdolive.
port *port_num*	Identifies a port number in the range 1 to 65,535.
list *acl_num*	Identifies the standard ACL number used with PAM for host- or network-specific port mapping.

Host- or Network-Specific Port Mapping

User-defined entries in the mapping table can include host- or network-specific mapping information, which establishes port-mapping information for specific hosts or subnets. In some environments, it might be necessary to override the default port mapping information for a specific host or subnet.

With host-specific port mapping, you can use the same port number for different services on different hosts. This means that you can map port 8000 with HTTP services for one host, while mapping port 8000 with Telnet services for another host.

Host-specific port mapping also allows you to apply PAM to a specific subnet when that subnet runs a service that uses a port number that is different from the port number defined in the default mapping information. For example, hosts on subnet 192.168.0.0 might run HTTP services on nonstandard port 8000, while other traffic through the router uses the default port 80 for HTTP services.

Host or network-specific port mapping allows you to override a system-defined entry in the PAM table. For example, if CBAC finds an entry in the PAM table that maps port 25 (the system-defined port for SMTP) with HTTP for a specific host, CBAC identifies port 25 as HTTP protocol traffic on that host.

NOTE   If the host-specific port-mapping information is the same as existing system or user-defined default entries, host-specific port changes have no effect.

Use the **list** option of the **ip port-map** command to specify an ACL for a host or subnet that uses PAM.

Monitoring PAM

To display the PAM information, use the **show ip port-map** privileged EXEC command, the syntax for which is as follows:

```
show ip port-map [appl_name | port port_num]
```

appl_name specifies the application to display information for.

port *port_num* specifies the alternative port number that maps to the application to display information for.

Configuring CBAC

This section discusses how to configure the rules used to define the application protocols for inspection.

Defining Inspection Rules

Inspection rules must be defined to specify what IP traffic (which application-layer protocols) will be inspected by CBAC at an interface. Normally, you define only one inspection rule. The only exception might occur if you want to enable CBAC in two directions at a single firewall interface. In this case, you must configure two rules, one for each direction.

An inspection rule should specify each desired application-layer protocol, as well as generic TCP or generic UDP, if desired. The inspection rule consists of a series of statements, each listing a protocol and specifying the same inspection rule name.

Inspection rules include options for controlling alert and audit trail messages and for checking IP packet fragmentation.

To define a set of inspection rules, use the **ip inspect name** command in global configuration mode. Use the **no** form of this command to remove the inspection rule for a protocol or to remove the entire set of inspection rules.

The syntax for the **ip inspect name** command is as follows:

```
ip inspect name inspection-name protocol [alert {on | off}] [audit-trail {on | off}]
[timeout seconds]
no ip inspect name inspection-name protocol
no ip inspect name
```

Table 12-4 describes the arguments for the **ip inspect name** command.

Table 12-4   ip inspect name *Command Arguments*

Arguments	Description
name *inspection-name*	Names the set of inspection rules. If you want to add a protocol to an existing set of rules, use the same inspection-name.
protocol	The protocol to inspect. Uses the following keywords: **tcp, udp, cuseeme, ftp, http, h323, netshow, rcmd, realaudio, rpc, smtp, sqlnet, streamworks, tftp, rtsp, fragment** or **vdolive**.
alert {**on** | **off**}	(Optional) For each inspected protocol, the generation of alert messages can be set on or off. If no option is selected, alerts are generated based on the setting of the **ip inspect** *alert-off* command.
audit-trail {**on** | **off**}	(Optional) For each inspected protocol, audit-trail can be set on or off. If no option is selected, audit trail messages are generated based on the setting of the **ip inspect** *audit trail* command.
timeout *seconds*	(Optional) To override the global TCP or UDP idle timeouts for the specified protocol, specify the number of seconds for a different idle timeout. This timeout overrides the global TCP and UDP timeouts but will not override the global DNS timeout.

Applying Java Filtering

Java inspection enables Java applet filtering at the firewall. Java applet filtering distinguishes between trusted and untrusted applets by relying on a list of external sites that you designate as friendly. If an applet is from a friendly site, the firewall allows it through. If the applet is not from a friendly site, it will be blocked. Alternately, you could permit applets from all sites except for those specifically designated as hostile.

NOTE   If you do not configure an access list, but use a "placeholder" access list in the **ip inspect name inspection-name http** command, all Java applets will be blocked.

NOTE   CBAC neither detects nor blocks encapsulated Java applets. Therefore, Java applets that are wrapped or encapsulated, such as applets in *.zip* or *.jar* format, are not blocked at the firewall. CBAC also does not detect or block applets loaded via FTP, gopher, or HTTP on a nonstandard port.

NOTE   CBAC will block Java applets on nonstandard ports if the **ip port-map** command is used to map a nonstandard port to HTTP. See the section on Port-to-Application Mapping (PAM) for more details.

The syntax for the **ip inspect name** command for Java applet filtering inspection is as follows:

```
ip inspect name inspection-name http java-list acl-num [alert {on | off}]
  [audit-trail {on | off}] [timeout seconds]
no ip inspect name inspection-name http
```

NOTE   If you call an access list with the **java-list** option, the access list must be a standard IP access list (1–99).

Table 12-5 describes the arguments for the **ip inspect name** command for Java applet filtering.

Table 12-5   *ip inspect name Command Arguments for Java Applet Filtering Inspection*

Arguments	Description
name *inspection-name*	Names the set of inspection rules. If you want to add a protocol to an existing set of rules, use the same inspection-name as in the existing set of rules.
http	Specifies the HTTP protocol for Java applet blocking.
java-list *acl-num*	Specifies the access list (name or number) used to determine friendly sites. This keyword is available only for the HTTP protocol, for Java applet blocking. Java blocking only works with standard access lists.
**alert {on	off}**	(Optional) For each inspected protocol, the generation of alert messages can be set on or off. If no option is selected, alerts are generated based on the setting of the **ip inspect** *alert-off* command.
**audit-trail {on	off}**	(Optional) For each inspected protocol, audit-trail can be set on or off. If no option is selected, audit trail messages are generated based on the setting of the **ip inspect** *audit-trail* command.
timeout *seconds*	(Optional) To override the global TCP or UDP idle timeouts for the specified protocol, specify the number of seconds for a different idle timeout. This timeout overrides the global TCP and UDP timeouts but will not override the global DNS timeout.

Remote Procedure Call (RPC)

Remote Procedure Call (RPC) inspection allows the specification of various program numbers. You can define multiple program numbers by creating multiple entries for RPC inspection, each with a different program number. If a program number is specified, all traffic for that program number will be permitted. If a program number is not specified, all traffic for that program number will be blocked. For example, if you created an RPC entry with the NFS program number, all NFS traffic will be allowed through the firewall.

The syntax of the **ip inspect name** command for RPC applications is as follows:

```
ip inspect name inspection-name rpc program-number number [wait-time minutes]
   [alert {on | off}] [audit-trail {on | off}] [timeout seconds]
no ip inspect name inspection-name protocol
```

Table 12-6 describes the arguments for the **ip inspect name** command for RPC applications.

Table 12-6   **ip inspect name** *Command Arguments for RPC Applications*

Arguments	Description
inspection-name	Names the set of inspection rules. If you want to add a protocol to an existing set of rules, use the same inspection-name as the existing set of rules.

continues

Table 12-6 **ip inspect name** *Command Arguments for RPC Applications (Continued)*

Arguments	Description
rpc program_number *number*	Specifies the program number to permit.
wait-time *minutes*	(Optional) Specifies the number of minutes to keep the connection opened in the firewall, even after the application terminates to allow subsequent connections from the same source address and to the same destination address and port. The default wait time is zero minutes.
alert {on | off}	(Optional) For each inspected protocol, the generation of alert messages can be set on or off. If no option is selected, alerts are generated based on the setting of the **ip inspect** *alert-off* command.
audit-trail {on | off}	(Optional) For each inspected protocol, audit-trail can be set on or off. If no option is selected, audit trail messages are generated based on the setting of the **ip inspect** *audit-trail* command.
timeout *seconds*	(Optional) To override the global TCP or UDP idle timeouts for the specified protocol, specify the number of seconds for a different idle timeout. This timeout overrides the global TCP and UDP timeouts but will not override the global DNS timeout.

Mail Guard

SMTP inspection causes SMTP commands to be inspected for illegal commands. Any packets with illegal commands are dropped, and the SMTP session hangs and eventually times out. An illegal command is any command except for the following legal commands: **DATA, EXPN, HELO, HELP, MAIL, NOOP, QUIT, RCPT, RSET, SAML, SEND, SOML, and VRFY**.

The syntax for the **ip inspect name** command for SMTP application inspection is as follows:

```
ip inspect name inspection-name  smtp [alert {on | off}]
  [audit-trail {on | off}] [timeout seconds]
no ip inspect name inspection-name smtp
```

Table 12-7 describes the arguments for the **ip inspect name** command for SMTP application inspection.

Table 12-7 **ip inspect name** *Command Arguments for SMTP Application Inspection*

Arguments	Description
name *inspection-name*	Names the set of inspection rules. If you want to add a protocol to an existing set of rules, use the same inspection-name as in the existing set of rules.

Table 12-7   **ip inspect name** *Command Arguments for SMTP Application Inspection (Continued)*

Arguments	Description
smtp	Specifies the SMTP protocol for inspection.
alert {on | off}	(Optional) For each inspected protocol, the generation of alert messages can be set on or off. If no option is selected, alerts are generated based on the setting of the **ip inspect** *alert-off* command.
audit-trail {on | off}	(Optional) For each inspected protocol, audit-trail can be set on or off. If no option is selected, audit trail messages are generated based on the setting of the **ip inspect** *audit-trail* command.
timeout *seconds*	(Optional) To override the global TCP or UDP idle timeouts for the specified protocol, specify the number of seconds for a different idle timeout. This timeout overrides the global TCP and UDP timeouts but will not override the global DNS timeout.

Fragmentation Guard

CBAC inspection rules can help protect hosts against certain DoS attacks involving fragmented IP packets. Even though the router keeps an attacker from making actual connections to a given host, the attacker may still be able to disrupt services provided by that host. This is done by sending many non-initial IP fragments to a router running access lists, because router access lists can't filter non-initial fragments. These fragments can tie up resources on the target host as it tries to reassemble the incomplete packets.

Using fragmentation inspection, the firewall maintains an inter-fragment state (structure) for IP traffic. Non-initial fragments are discarded unless the corresponding initial fragment was permitted to pass through the firewall. Non-initial fragments received before the corresponding initial fragments are discarded.

CAUTION   In certain cases, fragmentation inspection can have undesirable effects, including the router discarding any packet whose fragments arrive out of order. There are many circumstances that can cause out-of-order delivery of legitimate fragments. Applying fragmentation inspection in situations where legitimate fragments are likely to arrive out of order might have a severe performance impact.

Because routers running Cisco IOS Software are used in a variety of networks, and because the CBAC feature is often used to isolate parts of internal networks from one another, the fragmentation inspection feature is not enabled by default. Fragmentation detection must be explicitly enabled for an inspection rule using the **ip inspect name** (global) command. Unfragmented traffic is never discarded because it lacks a fragment state. Even when the system is under heavy attack with fragmented packets, legitimate fragmented traffic, if any, will still get some fraction of the router's fragment state resources, and legitimate, unfragmented traffic can flow through the firewall unimpeded.

The syntax of the **ip inspect name** command for IP packet fragmentation is as follows:

```
ip inspect name inspection-name fragment max  number timeout seconds
no ip inspect name inspection-name fragment
```

Table 12-8 describes the arguments for the **ip inspect name** command for IP packet fragmentation detection.

Table 12-8 **ip inspect name** *Command Arguments for IP Packet Fragmentation Detection*

Arguments	Description
inspection-name	Names the set of inspection rules. If you want to add a protocol to an existing set of rules, use the same inspection-name as in the existing set of rules.
fragment	Specifies fragment inspection for the named rule.
max *number*	Specifies the maximum number of unassembled packets for which state information (structures) is allocated by the software. Unassembled packets are packets that arrive at the router interface before the initial packet for a session. The acceptable range is 50 through 10,000. The default is 256 state entries.
	Memory is allocated for the state structures, and setting this value to a larger number may cause memory resources to become exhausted.
timeout *seconds*	Configures the number of seconds that a packet state structure remains active. When the timeout value expires, the router drops the unassembled packet, freeing that structure for use by another packet. The default timeout value is one second.
	If this number is set to a value greater than one second, it will be automatically adjusted by the software when the number of free state structures goes below certain thresholds. When the number of free states is less than 32, the timeout will be divided by 2. When the number of free states is less than 16, the timeout will be set to 1 second.

Inspection Rules and ACLs Applied to Router Interfaces

To apply a set of inspection rules to an interface, use the **ip inspect** interface configuration command. Use the **no** form of this command to remove the set of rules from the interface. This command is applied in interface configuration mode.

The syntax for the **ip inspect** command is as follows:

```
ip inspect name inspection-name {in | out }
no ip inspect name inspection-name {in | out}
```

Table 12-9 describes the arguments for the **ip inspect name** command to apply inspection rules to an interface.

Table 12-9   **ip inspect name** *Command Arguments to Apply Inspection Rules to an Interface*

Arguments	Description
inspection-name	Names the set of inspection rules
in	Applies the inspection rules to inbound traffic
out	Applies the inspection rules to outbound traffic

For the Cisco IOS Firewall to be effective, both inspection rules and ACLs must be strategically applied to all the router's interfaces.

Follow these three general rules when evaluating your IP access lists at the firewall:

- Start with a basic configuration.

  If you try to configure access lists without a good understanding of how they work, you might inadvertently introduce security risks to the firewall and the protected network. You should be sure you understand what access lists do before you configure your router as a firewall.

  A basic initial configuration allows all network traffic to flow from the protected networks to the unprotected networks, while blocking network traffic from any unprotected networks.

- Permit CBAC traffic to leave the network through the firewall.

  All access lists that evaluate traffic leaving the protected network should permit traffic that will be inspected by CBAC. For example, if Telnet will be inspected by CBAC, Telnet traffic should be permitted on all access lists that apply to traffic leaving the network.

- Use extended access lists to deny CBAC return traffic entering the network through the firewall.

  For temporary openings to be created in an access list, the list must be extended. So wherever you have access lists that will be applied to returning traffic, you must use extended access lists. The access lists should deny CBAC return traffic because CBAC will open up temporary holes in them. (You want traffic to be normally blocked when it enters your network.)

Access List Guidelines When Configuring CBAC on External Interfaces

If you have an outbound IP access list at the external interface, the access list can be standard or extended. This outbound access list should permit traffic that you want to be inspected by CBAC. If traffic is not permitted, it will not be inspected by CBAC but will be simply dropped.

The inbound IP access list at the external interface must be an extended access list. This inbound access list should deny traffic that you want to be inspected by CBAC. Then CBAC will create temporary openings in this inbound access list as appropriate to permit only return traffic that is part of a valid, existing session.

For complete information about how to configure IP access lists, refer to the "Configuring IP Services" chapter of the *Cisco IOS IP and IP Routing Configuration Guide*.

Access List Guidelines When Configuring CBAC on Internal Interfaces

If you have an inbound IP access list at the internal interface or an outbound IP access list at external interface(s), these access lists can be either standard or extended. They should permit traffic that you want to be inspected by CBAC. If traffic is not permitted, it will not be inspected by CBAC, but will be simply dropped.

The outbound IP access list at the internal interface and the inbound IP access list at the external interface must be extended access lists. These outbound access lists should deny traffic that you want to be inspected by CBAC. Then CBAC will create temporary openings in these outbound access lists as appropriate to permit only return traffic that is part of a valid, existing session. You do not necessarily need to configure an extended access list at both the outbound internal interface and the inbound external interface, but at least one is necessary to restrict traffic flowing through the firewall into the internal protected network.

Two-Interface Firewall Example

Configure the router to be a firewall between two networks: inside and outside.

The security policy to implement is as follows: Allow all general TCP and UDP traffic initiated on the inside (outbound) from network 10.0.0.0 to access the Internet. ICMP traffic will also be allowed from the same network. Other networks on the inside, which are not defined, must be denied. For traffic initiated on the outside (inbound), allow everyone to access only ICMP and HTTP to host 10.0.0.3. Any other traffic must be denied. You will translate this policy into a working CBAC configuration, as follows.

Outbound Traffic Policy

Step 1   Write a rule to inspect outbound TCP and UDP traffic:

```
Router(config)# ip inspect name OUTBOUND tcp
Router(config)# ip inspect name OUTBOUND udp
```

Step 2   Write an ACL that permits IP traffic from the 10.0.0.0 network to any destination:

```
Router(config)# access-list 101 permit ip 10.0.0.0 0.255.255.255.0 any
```

Step 3   Apply the inspection rule and ACL to the inside interface on the inward direction:

```
Router(config)# interface e0/0
Router(config-if)# ip inspect OUTBOUND in
Router(config-if)# ip access-group 101 in
```

Inbound Traffic Policy

Step 1   Write an ACL that permits ICMP- and HTTP-only traffic from the Internet to the 10.0.0.3 host:

```
Router(config)# access-list 102 permit icmp any host 10.0.0.3
Router(config)# access-list 102 permit tcp any host 10.0.0.3 eq www
```

Step 2   Apply the ACL to the outside interface in the inward direction:

```
Router(config)# interface e0/1
Router(config-if)# ip access-group 102 in
```

Three-Interface Firewall

Refer to Figure 12-2. Configure the router to be a firewall between three networks: inside, outside, and DMZ. The security policy to implement is as follows: Allow all general TCP and UDP traffic initiated on the inside (outbound) from network 10.0.0.0 to access the Internet and the DMZ host 172.16.0.2. ICMP traffic will also be allowed from the same network to the Internet and the DMZ host. Other networks on the inside, which are not defined, must be denied. For traffic initiated on the outside (inbound), allow everyone to only access ICMP and HTTP to DMZ host 172.16.0.2. Any other traffic must be denied.

Outbound Traffic

Step 1   Write a rule to inspect TCP and UDP traffic:

```
Router(config)# ip inspect name OUTBOUND tcp
Router(config)# ip inspect name OUTBOUND udp
```

Step 2   Write an ACL that permits IP traffic from the 10.0.0.0 network to any destination:

```
Router(config)# access-list 101 permit ip 10.0.0.0 0.255.255.255 any
```

Step 3   Apply the inspection rule and ACL to the inside interface in the inward direction:

```
Router(config)# interface e0/0
Router(config-if)# ip inspect OUTBOUND in
Router(config-if)# ip access-group 101 in
```

Figure 12-2 *Three-Interface Firewall Policy*

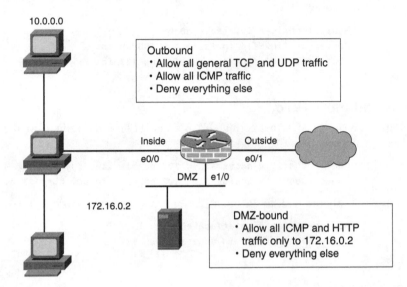

Inbound Traffic

Step 1 Write a rule to inspect TCP traffic:

```
Router(config)# ip inspect name INBOUND tcp
```

Step 2 Write an ACL that permits ICMP- and HTTP-only traffic from the Internet to the 172.16.0.2 host:

```
Router(config)# access-list 102 permit icmp any host 172.16.0.2
Router(config)# access-list 102 permit tcp any host 172.16.0.2 eq www
```

Step 3 Apply the inspection rule and ACL to the outside interface in the inward direction:

```
Router(config)# interface e0/1
Router(config-if)# ip inspect INBOUND in
Router(config-if)# ip access-group 102 in
```

DMZ-Bound Traffic

Step 1 Write an ACL to permit only ICMP traffic to initiate from the DMZ host and to respond to an HTTP request:

```
Router(config)# access-list 103 permit icmp host 172.16.0.2 any
Router(config)# access-list 103 permit tcp host 172.16.0.2 eq www any
```

Step 2 Write an ACL that permits ICMP- and HTTP-only traffic from any
network to the 172.16.0.2 host:

```
Router(config)# access-list 104 permit icmp any host 172.16.0.2
Router(config)# access-list 104 permit tcp any host 172.16.0.2 eq www
```

Step 3 Apply the ACLs to the DMZ interface:

```
Router(config)# interface e1/0
Router(config-if)# ip access-group 103 in
Router(config-if)# ip access-group 104 out
```

Test, Verify, and Monitor CBAC

All aspects of CBAC operation and configuration can be viewed and tested with the **show
ip inspect** and **debug** commands.

The syntax for the **show ip inspect** command is as follows:

```
show ip inspect name inspection-name | config | interfaces | session [detail] | all
```

Table 12-10 describes the arguments for the **show ip inspect** command.

Table 12-10 **show ip inspect** *Command Arguments*

Arguments	Description
inspection-name	Shows the configured inspection rule for *inspection-name*.
config	Shows the complete CBAC inspection configuration.
interfaces	Shows interface configuration with respect to applied inspection rules and access lists.
session [detail]	Shows existing sessions that are currently being tracked and inspected by CBAC. The optional **detail** keyword shows additional details about these sessions.
all	Shows the complete CBAC configuration and all existing sessions that are currently being tracked and inspected by CBAC.

To display messages about CBAC events, use the **debug ip inspect** EXEC command. The
no form of this command disables debugging output.

NOTE Enable Mode privileges are required to issue any **debug** commands.

The syntax for the **debug ip inspect** command is as follows:

```
debug ip inspect {function-trace | object-creation | object-deletion |
  events | timers | protocol | detail }
```

Table 12-11 describes the arguments for the **debug ip inspect** command.

Table 12-11   **show ip inspect name** *Command Arguments*

Arguments	Description
function-trace	Displays messages about software functions called by CBAC.
object-creation	Displays messages about software objects being created by CBAC. Object creation corresponds to the beginning of CBAC-inspected sessions.
object-deletion	Displays messages about software objects being deleted by CBAC. Object deletion corresponds to the closing of CBAC-inspected sessions.
events	Displays messages about CBAC software events, including information about CBAC packet processing.
timers	Displays messages about CBAC timer events, such as when a CBAC idle timeout is reached.
protocol	Displays messages about CBAC-inspected protocol events, including details about the protocol's packets.
detailed	Use this form of the command in conjunction with other CBAC debugging commands. This displays detailed information for all other enabled CBAC debugging.

Use the **no ip inspect** command to remove the entire CBAC configuration, reset all global timeouts and thresholds to their defaults, delete all existing sessions, and remove all associated dynamic access lists. This command has no other arguments, keywords, default behavior, or values.

Review Questions

To test what you have learned in this chapter, answer the following questions and then refer to Appendix F for the answers.

1 I have CBAC running on my perimeter router but my inside users can't ftp to a remote site. They authenticate, but their session hangs when they issue a "dir". Can this be fixed?

2 Is the protection afforded by CBAC as strong as the PIX?

3 Do the CBAC-specific **debug** commands generate a lot of information to the console?

4 Do the Intrusion Detection signatures provided in IOS offer me complete protection against hackers?

5 Are there any good resources on CCO—for example, CBAC configurations?

6 What command applies an inspection rule to an interface?

7 Is there a way to globally erase the entire CBAC configuration?

8 How much DRAM is used to track the state of each session object?

This chapter introduces the information required to understand and successfully configure Cisco IOS Firewall Authentication Proxy, specifically covering the following areas:

- AAA Server Configuration
- AAA Configuration
- Authentication Proxy Configuration
- Testing and Verifying the Configuration

CHAPTER 13

Cisco IOS Firewall Authentication Proxy Configuration

Introduction to the IOS Authentication Proxy

CAUTION Authentication Proxy requires you to activate the IOS **ip http server service**. There are two Cisco Security Advisories pertaining to this service. In certain instances, it's possible to crash a Cisco router by exploiting the **ip http server** service. To determine if your version of Cisco IOS Software suffers from this defect, please refer to the following Service Advisories:

www.cisco.com/warp/public/707/ioshttpserverquery-pub.shtml

www.cisco.com/warp/public/707/IOS-httplevel-pub.html

NOTE The Authentication Proxy service requires the use of the **ip http authentication aaa** command. This command is a workaround for the defects in the previous Security Advisories.

The Cisco IOS Firewall Authentication Proxy feature allows network administrators to apply specific security policies on a per-user basis. Previously, user identity and related authorized access were associated with a user's IP address, or a single security policy had to be applied to an entire user group or subnet. Now, users can be identified and authorized on the basis of their per-user policy, and access privileges can be tailored on an individual basis, as opposed to a general policy applied across multiple users.

With the Authentication Proxy feature, users log into the network or access the Internet with their Web browser, and their specific access profiles are automatically retrieved and applied from a Cisco Secure Access Control Server (CSACS), or a RADIUS or TACACS+ authentication server. The user profiles are active only when there is active traffic from the authenticated users.

The Authentication Proxy is compatible with other Cisco IOS security features, such as Network Address Translation (NAT), Context-Based Access Control (CBAC), IP Security (IPSec) encryption, and VPN client software.

When a user initiates an HTTP session through the router, it triggers the Authentication Proxy. If a valid authentication entry exists for the user, the session is allowed and no further intervention is required by the Authentication Proxy. The Authentication Proxy first checks to see if the user has been authenticated. If no entry exists, the Authentication Proxy responds to the HTTP connection request by prompting the user for a username and password, as shown in Figure 13-1.

Figure 13-1 *User Authentication Screen*

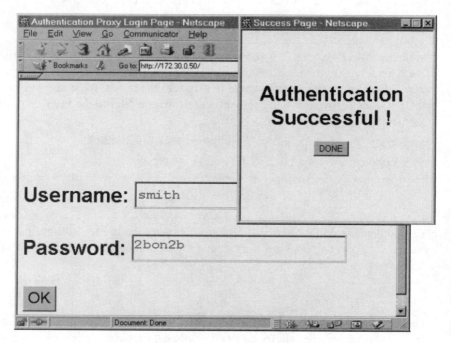

Users must successfully authenticate with the authentication server by entering a valid username and password. If the authentication succeeds, the user's authorization profile is retrieved from the authentication, authorization, and accounting (AAA) server. The Authentication Proxy uses the information in this profile to create dynamic access control entries (ACEs) and add them to the inbound (input) access control list (ACL) of an input interface, and to the outbound (output) ACL of an output interface if an output ACL exists at the interface. By doing this, the router allows authenticated users access to the network as permitted by the authorization profile. For example, a user can initiate a Telnet connection through the router if Telnet is permitted in the user's profile.

If the authentication fails, the Authentication Proxy reports the failure to the user and prompts the user with multiple retries. If the user fails to authenticate after five attempts, the user must wait two minutes and initiate another HTTP session to trigger the Authentication Proxy.

The Authentication Proxy sets up an inactivity (idle) timer for each user profile. As long as there is activity through the firewall, new traffic initiated from the user's host does not trigger the Authentication Proxy, and all authorized user traffic is permitted access through the firewall.

If the idle timer expires, the Authentication Proxy removes the user's profile information and dynamic access list entries. When this happens, traffic from the client host is blocked. The user must initiate another HTTP connection to trigger the Authentication Proxy.

The Cisco IOS Firewall Authentication Proxy supports the following AAA protocols and servers:

- Terminal Access Controller Access Control System Plus (TACACS+)
    - Cisco Secure Access Control Server (CSACS) for Windows NT (CSACS-NT)
    - Cisco Secure ACS for UNIX (CSACS-UNIX)
    - TACACS+ Freeware
- Remote Authentication Dial-In User Service (RADIUS)
    - Cisco Secure ACS for Windows NT (CSACS-NT)
    - Cisco Secure ACS for UNIX (CSACS-UNIX)
    - Livingston
    - Ascend
    - Funk Software's Steel Belted RADIUS

NOTE   TACACS Freeware is not supported by Cisco. You can obtain a gziped binary distribution and/or source code at: http://smc.vnet.net/solaris_2.5_nof.html#xtacacsd

---

Apply the Authentication Proxy in the inward direction at any interface on the router where you want per-user authentication and authorization. Applying the Authentication Proxy inward at an interface causes it to intercept a user's initial connection request before that request is subjected to any other processing by the router. If the user fails to authenticate with the AAA server, the connection request is dropped.

How you apply the Authentication Proxy depends on your security policy. For example, you can block all traffic through an interface, and enable the Authentication Proxy feature to require authentication and authorization for all user-initiated HTTP connections. Users are authorized for services only after successful authentication with the AAA server. The Authentication Proxy feature also allows you to use standard access lists to specify a host or group of hosts whose initial HTTP traffic triggers the proxy.

Authentication Proxy Configuration Tasks

The tasks for authentication proxy configuration (illustrated by Figure 13-2) are as follows:

- Task 1: AAA server configuration.
- Task 2: AAA configuration on the router.
  - Enable AAA.
  - Specify AAA protocols.
  - Define AAA servers.
  - Allow AAA traffic.
  - Enable the router's HTTP server for AAA.
- Task 3: Authenticate proxy configuration on the router.
  - Set default idle time.
  - Create and apply Authentication Proxy rules.
- Task 4: Verify the configuration.

Figure 13-2 *Authentication Proxy Configuration*

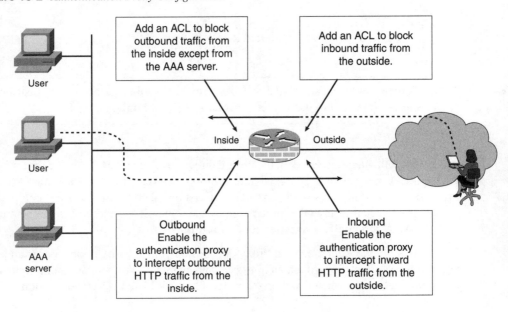

AAA Server Configuration

This section discusses how to configure the AAA server to provide authentication and authorization for the Cisco IOS Firewall Authentication Proxy.

To support the Authentication Proxy, configure the AAA authorization service *auth-proxy* on the AAA server. This defines a separate section of authorization in the Group Setup section of the AAA for auth-proxy to specify the user profiles. This does not interfere with other types of services that the AAA server may have.

Complete the following steps to add authorization rules for specific services in CSACS. The first five steps define the new auth-proxy service used by the group configuration.

Step 1 In the navigation bar, click the **Interface Configuration** button. The Interface Configuration frame opens.

Step 2 Scroll down in the Interface Configuration frame until you find the **New Services** frame.

Step 3 Select the first checkbox in the Service column.

Step 4 Enter **auth-proxy** in the first empty Service field next to the checkbox you just selected.

Step 5 Click **Submit** when finished. Figure 13-3 shows the Interface configuration frame you navigate through for the first five steps.

Figure 13-3 *Adding a New Service to CSACS*

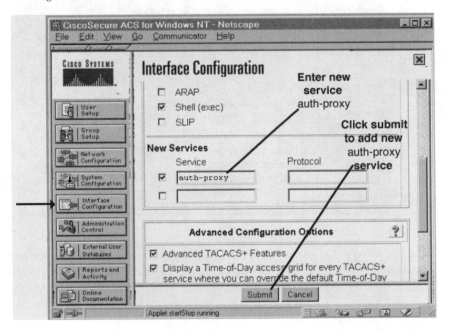

Step 6 In the navigation bar, click **Group Setup**. The Group Setup frame opens.

Step 7 Scroll down in the Group Setup frame until you find the newly created **auth-proxy** service.

Step 8 Select the **auth-proxy** checkbox.

Step 9 Select the **Custom attributes** checkbox.

Step 10 Enter Proxy ACLs in the field below the Custom Attributes checkbox to apply after the user authenticates using the format from the following page.

Step 11 Enter the privilege level of the user (must be 15 for all users) using the format from the following page.

Step 12 Click **Submit + Restart** when finished.

Figure 13-4 shows the new auth-proxy service and a *proxyacl* applied to the default group in the ACS Admin interface.

Figure 13-4 *Create and Apply the auth-proxy Authorization Profile*

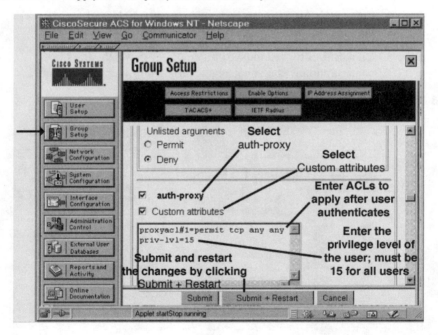

Use the **proxyacl#n** attribute when configuring the access lists in the profile. The **proxyacl#n** attribute is for both RADIUS and TACACS+ attribute-value pairs. The access lists in the user profile on the AAA server must have permit access commands only. Set the source address to **any** in each of the user profile access list entries. The source address in the access lists is replaced with the source IP address of the host making the Authentication Proxy request when the user profile is downloaded to the firewall.

The following is the format for the ACLs used to enter in the Custom attributes box:

```
proxyacl#n=permit protocol any any | host ip_addr | ip_addr wildcard_mask [eq
auth_service]
proxyacl#1=permit ftp any host 192.168.111.1
```

Table 13-1 describes the arguments and options for this ACL.

Table 13-1   *ACL Arguments/Options*

Argument	Description
protocol	Keyword indicating the protocol to allow users to access. This can be **tcp**, **udp**, or **icmp**.
any	Indicates any hosts. The first **any** after protocol is mandatory. This indicates any source IP address, which is actually replaced with the IP address of the user that requests authorization in the ACL applied in the router.
host *ip_addr*	IP address of a specific host users can access.
ip_addr wildcard mask	IP address and wildcard mask for a network that users can access.
eq *auth_service*	Specific service that users are allowed to access.

Use **priv-lvl=15** to configure the privilege level of the authenticated user. The privilege level must be set to 15 for all users.

AAA Configuration

This section discusses how to configure the Cisco IOS Firewall to work with an AAA server and enable the Authentication Proxy feature.

Use the **aaa new-model** global configuration command to enable the AAA access-control system. Use the **no** form of this command to disable the AAA access-control model.

NOTE After you have enabled AAA, TACACS and extended TACACS commands are no longer available. TACACS and extended TACACS are older implementations of AAA and are not compatible with **aaa new-model**. If you initialize AAA functionality and later decide to use TACACS or extended TACACS, issue the **no** version of this command and then enable the version of TACACS that you want to use.

The syntax of the **aaa new-model** command is as follows:

```
aaa new-model
no aaa new-model
```

This command has no arguments.

By default, **aaa new-model** is not enabled.

To define various AAA authentication methods, use the **aaa authentication login** global configuration command. Use the **no** form of this command to disable AAA authentication.

The syntax of the **aaa authentication login** command is as follows:

```
aaa authentication login default group method1 [method2]
no aaa authentication login default group method1 [method2]
```

where the *method1* and *method2* parameters represent the authentication protocols to use: **tacacs+**, **radius**, or both.

To enable AAA authorization for proxy authentication requests, use the **aaa authorization auth-proxy** global configuration command. Use the **no** form of this command to disable AAA authorization.

The syntax of the **aaa authorization auth-proxy** command is as follows:

```
aaa authorization auth-proxy default group method1 [method2]
no aaa authorization auth-proxy default group method1 [method2]
```

where the *method1* and *method2* parameters represent the authorization protocols to use: **tacacs+**, **radius**, or both.

To specify the IP address of a TACACS+ server, use the **tacacs-server host** global configuration command. Use the **no** form of this command to delete the specified IP address. You can use multiple **tacacs-server host** commands to specify additional servers. The Cisco IOS Firewall software searches for servers in the order in which you specify them.

NOTE Each TACACS+ server you define can use a different key.

The syntax of the **tacacs-server host** command is as follows:

```
tacacs-server host ip_addr
no tacacs-server host ip_addr
```

where *ip_addr* is the IP address of the TACACS+ server.

To set the authentication encryption key used for all TACACS+ communications between the Cisco IOS Firewall router and the AAA server, use the **tacacs-server key** global configuration command. Use the **no** form of this command to disable the key.

NOTE   The key entered must match the key used on the AAA server. All leading spaces are ignored; spaces within and at the end of the key are not ignored. If you use spaces in your key, do not enclose the key in quotation marks unless the quotation marks themselves are part of the key.

The syntax of the **tacacs-server key** command is as follows:

```
tacacs-server key string
no tacacs-server key string
```

where *string* represents the key used for authentication and encryption.

To specify the IP address of a RADIUS server, use the **radius-server host** global configuration command. Use the **no** form of this command to delete the specified IP address. You can use multiple radius-server host commands to specify additional servers. The Cisco IOS Firewall software searches for servers in the order in which you specify them.

NOTE   Each RADIUS server you define can use a different key.

The syntax of the **radius-server host** command is as follows:

```
radius-server host ip_addr
no radius-server host ip_addr
```

where *ip_addr* is the IP address of the RADIUS server.

To set the authentication encryption key used for all RADIUS communications between the Cisco IOS Firewall router and the AAA server, use the **radius-server key** global configuration command. Use the **no** form of this command to disable the key.

NOTE   The key entered must match the key used on the AAA server. All leading spaces are ignored; spaces within and at the end of the key are not. If you use spaces in your key, do not enclose the key in quotation marks unless the quotation marks themselves are part of the key.

The syntax of the **radius-server key** command is as follows:

```
radius-server key string
no radius-server key string
```

where *string* represents the key used for authentication and encryption.

At this point, you need to configure and apply an ACL to permit TACACS+ and RADIUS traffic from the AAA server to the firewall. If you have already configured CBAC on your router, there should already be an input access list configured on your router. In this case, all you need to do is add another line to the existing access list allowing the ACS server access to the router.

Use the following guidelines when writing the ACL:

- Source address = AAA server.
- Destination address = the router interface where the AAA server resides.
- You may want to permit ICMP.
- Deny all other traffic.
- Apply the ACL to the interface on the side where the AAA server resides in the "in" direction.

To enable the Authentication Proxy, use the **ip http server** command to enable the HTTP server on the router and the **ip http authentication aaa** command to make the HTTP server use AAA for authentication.

The syntax of the **ip http server** command is as follows:

```
ip http server
```

This command has no arguments.

The syntax of the **ip http authentication aaa** command is as follows:

```
ip http authentication aaa
```

This command has no arguments.

Authentication Proxy Configuration

This section discusses how to configure the Authentication Proxy settings on a Cisco router.

To set the Authentication Proxy idle timeout value (the length of time an authentication cache entry, along with its associated dynamic user ACL, is managed after a period of inactivity), use the **ip auth-proxy auth-cache-time** global configuration command. To set the default value, use the **no** form of this command.

NOTE   Set the auth-cache-time option for any Authentication Proxy rule to a higher value than the idle timeout value for any CBAC inspection rule. When the Authentication Proxy removes an authentication cache along with its associated dynamic user ACL, there might be some idle connections monitored by CBAC, and removal of user-specific ACLs could cause those idle connections to hang. If CBAC has a shorter idle timeout, CBAC resets these connections when the idle timeout expires; that is, before the Authentication Proxy removes the user profile.

The syntax of the **ip auth-proxy auth-cache-time** command is as follows:

```
ip auth-proxy auth-cache-time min
no ip auth-proxy auth-cache-time
```

where *min* specifies the length of time, in minutes, that an authentication cache entry, along with its associated dynamic user ACL, is managed after a period of inactivity. Enter a value in the range of 1 to 2,147,483,647. The default value is 60 minutes.

To create an Authentication Proxy rule, use the **ip auth-proxy name** global configuration command. To remove the Authentication Proxy rules, use the **no** form of this command.

NOTE   The **ip auth-proxy** command was introduced in Cisco IOS Release 12.0.5.T.

The syntax of the **ip auth-proxy name** command is as follows:

```
ip auth-proxy name auth-proxy-name http [auth-cache-time min]
no ip auth-proxy name auth-proxy-name
```

where *auth-proxy-name* associates a name with an Authentication Proxy rule. Enter a name of up to 16 alphanumeric characters.

The optional **auth-cache-time** *min* overrides the global Authentication Proxy cache timer for a specific Authentication Proxy name, offering more control over timeout values. Enter a value in the range of 1 to 2,147,483,647. The default value is equal to the value set with the **ip auth-proxy auth-cache-time** command.

You can associate an Authentication Proxy rule with an ACL, providing control over which hosts use the Authentication Proxy. To create an Authentication Proxy rule with ACLs, use the **ip auth-proxy name** global configuration command with the **list** *std-acl-num* option. To remove the Authentication Proxy rules, use the **no** form of this command.

The syntax of the **ip auth-proxy name** with ACLs command is as follows:

```
ip auth-proxy name auth-proxy-name http list std-acl-num
no ip auth-proxy name auth-proxy-name
```

where *auth-proxy-name* associates a name with an Authentication Proxy rule. Enter a name of up to 16 alphanumeric characters.

list *std-acl-num* specifies a standard access list to use with the Authentication Proxy. With this option, the Authentication Proxy is applied only to those hosts in the standard access list. If no list is specified, all connections initiating HTTP traffic arriving at the interface are subject to authentication.

To apply an Authentication Proxy rule at a firewall interface, use the **ip auth-proxy** interface configuration command. To remove the Authentication Proxy rules, use the **no** form of this command.

The syntax of the **ip auth-proxy** command is as follows:

```
ip auth-proxy auth-proxy-name
no ip auth-proxy auth-proxy-name
```

where *auth-proxy-name* specifies the name of the Authentication Proxy rule to apply to the interface configuration. The Authentication Proxy rule is established with the **authentication proxy name** command.

Testing and Verifying the Configuration

All aspects of Authentication Proxy operation and configuration can be viewed and tested with the **show ip** inspect and debug commands.

Use the **show ip auth-proxy** command to display the Authentication Proxy entries, the running Authentication Proxy configuration, or the Authentication Proxy statistics.

The syntax of the **show ip auth-proxy** command is as follows:

```
show ip auth-proxy {cache | configuration | statistics}
```

Table 13-2 describes the options for the **show ip auth-proxy** command.

Table 13-2   **show ip auth-proxy** *Command Options*

Option	Description
cache	Lists the host IP address, the source port number, the timeout value for the Authentication Proxy, and the state for connections using authentication proxy. If the Authentication Proxy state is HTTP_ESTAB, the user authentication was successful.
configuration	Displays all Authentication Proxy rules configured on the router.
statistics	Displays all the router statistics related to the Authentication Proxy.

The syntax of the **debug ip auth-proxy** command is as follows:

```
debug ip auth-proxy ftp | function-trace | http | object-creation | object-deletion |
tcp | telnet | timer
```

Table 13-3 describes the options for the **debug ip auth-proxy** command.

Table 13-3   **debug ip auth-proxy** *Command Options*

Option	Description
ftp	Displays FTP events related to the Authentication Proxy
function-trace	Displays the Authentication Proxy functions
http	Displays HTTP events related to the Authentication Proxy
object-creation	Displays additional entries to the Authentication Proxy cache
object-deletion	Displays deletion of cache entries for the Authentication Proxy
tcp	Displays TCP events related to the Authentication Proxy
telnet	Displays Telnet-related Authentication Proxy events
timer	Displays Authentication Proxy timer-related events

The syntax of the **clear ip auth-proxy cache** command is as follows:

```
clear ip auth-proxy cache * | ip_addr
```

Table 13-4 describes the options for the **clear ip auth-proxy cache** command.

Table 13-4   **clear ip auth-proxy cache** *Command Options*

Argument/ Option	Description
*	Clears all Authentication Proxy entries, including user profiles and dynamic access lists
ip_addr	Clears the Authentication Proxy entry, including user profiles and dynamic access lists, for the specified IP address

Sample Authentication Proxy Service Configuration

Now that you understand the mechanics of the Authentication Proxy service, let's take a look at sample implementation. Figure 13-6 illustrates the network topology used in Example 13-1.

The security policy is as follows:

- Allow only the server running CSACS to access the router without authentication.
- Force all other inside users to authenticate against AAA to determine what they have access to on the Internet.

Figure 13-5 *Authentication Proxy Sample Topology*

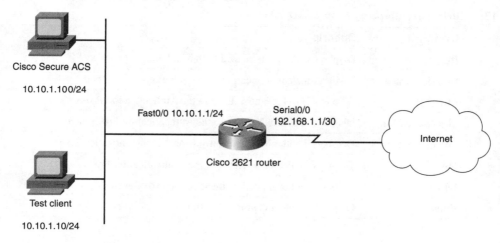

Example 13-1 *Sample IOS Firewall Authentication Proxy Configuration*

```
hostname Auth-Proxy-2621
!
! Globally enable AAA on the router
aaa new-model
!
! Define what will be authenticated, authorized and Accounted for.
!
aaa authentication login default group tacacs+
aaa authorization auth-proxy default group tacacs+
enable secret 5 g70@3*7340jh9dsf987fg87
!
! Force dynamically created access-list entries to timeout after 10 minutes.
!
ip auth-proxy auth-cache-time 10
!
! Define the auth-proxy name that will be associated with the protected interface.
!
ip auth-proxy name APRULE http
!
process-max-time 200
! Interface FastEthernet0/0 is our "Inside"interface.
interface FastEthernet0/0
 ip address 10.10.1.1 255.255.255.0
 !
 ! Block everything except the ACS Server.  All other traffic is forced to
authenticate.
 ip access-group 116 in
no ip directed-broadcast
 !
 !Apply the auth-proxy rule.
```

Example 13-1   *Sample IOS Firewall Authentication Proxy Configuration (Continued)*

```
!
 ip auth-proxy APRULE
 ! Interface Serial1/0 acts as the "Outside"interface
interface Serial1/0
 ip address 192.168.1.1 255.255.255.252
no ip directed-broadcast
!
ip route 0.0.0.0 0.0.0.0 192.168.1.2
!
! Enable the http server with AAA authentication.
!
ip http server
ip http authentication aaa
!
!
! This is our auth-proxy access list.
! This ACL allows the ACS server to communicate with the router
! but blocks everyone else, thus forcing them to Authenticate.
!
access-list 116 permit tcp host 10.10.1.100 host 10.10.1.1 eq tacacs
!
! We define the server(s).
!
tacacs-server host 10.10.1.100
tacacs-server key cisco
!
!
end
```

Review Questions

To test what you have learned in this chapter, answer the following questions and then refer to Appendix F for the answers.

1   What must be configured on the ACS Server for the Authentication Proxy to operate?

2   When I use the **show ip auth-proxy cache** command, what tells me whether authentication was successful?

3   If I use the auth-proxy service to authenticate users from the Internet, are their usernames and passwords protected?

4   Are there any good configuration examples on CCO?

5   Does the auth-proxy service offer protection against denial-of-service attacks?

6   Is there a risk of spoofed addresses getting through the firewall?

Configuring the PIX for Intrusion Detection

Before you begin this appendix, it is important to recognize that the Intrusion Detection System (IDS) feature of the PIX is very limited in its scope within the larger context of Cisco's best-in-class Cisco Secure IDS. The PIX IDS feature should not be considered a complete solution but is meant more to augment the effectiveness of a more holistic approach to intrusion detection. For those of you who are new to intrusion detection, many of the terms in this appendix will be unfamiliar. I would encourage you to spend time reading through the references at the end of the appendix.

Appendix A introduces the information required to understand and successfully configure the PIX Intrusion Detection signatures.

- Introduction to PIX Intrusion Detection
- Intrusion Detection Configuration Elements
- Managing Signatures
- Examples

Introduction to PIX Intrusion Detection

Cisco Secure IDS is an IP-only feature that provides the flexibility for the PIX administrator to customize the type of traffic that needs to be audited, logged, and/or dropped.

The Cisco Secure IDS features provide the following:

- Traffic auditing. Application-level signatures are audited only as part of an active session. The audit must be assigned to an interface.
- Support for different audit policies. Traffic matching a signature triggers a range of configurable actions.
- Capability to disable the signature audit.
- Capability to enable IDS and selectively disable actions of a signature class (informational, attack).

Auditing is performed by looking at IP packets as they arrive at an input interface. If a packet triggers a signature and the configured action does not drop the packet, then the same packet can trigger other signatures.

The PIX Firewall supports auditing at the input of all interfaces. Interfaces can be individually configured with different signatures and default actions to be taken upon matching a configured signature.

Intrusion Detection Configuration Elements

The basis of the PIX IDS system is the **ip audit** command. The **ip audit** command is used to create the *global audit policy* for the PIX firewall. The two forms of the global **ip audit** command are shown here:

```
ip audit attack
ip audit info
```

In each instance, the **ip audit** command specifies the default actions to be taken when an *attack* or *informational* signature is matched. If nothing is configured, the default action for attack and informational signatures is to alarm only and the packet is allowed through or dropped depending on how the PIX is configured. In all of the **ip audit** commands, the **action** can be any combination of **alarm**, **drop**, and **reset**.

The syntax of the **ip audit attack** command is

```
ip audit attack [[action [alarm] [drop] [reset]]
```

The syntax of the **ip audit info** command is

```
ip audit info [[action [alarm] [drop] [reset]]
```

Table A-1 explains the options for both of these commands.

Table A-1   **ip audit attack** *and* **ip audit info** *Command Options*

Options	Description
action	Available actions are **alarm**, **drop**, **reset**.
alarm	Generate syslog message to the configured **logging host.**
drop	The interface on which the signature was triggered drops the offending packet(s).
reset	The PIX sends a TCP reset to both the target IP address and the attacker IP address.

Configuring Audit Policies on a Per-Interface Basis

To begin auditing, you must configure audit policies on a per-interface basis. Each PIX interface can have up to two audit policies bound to it, one policy for informational signatures and one for attack signatures.

First, use the **ip audit name** command to define your audit policy for attack and informational signatures. Use the **no ip audit name** command to disable an audit policy.

NOTE	The **action** specified in the **ip audit name** command overrides the *global audit policy* of the **ip audit attack** and **ip audit info** commands. If no actions are specified in the **ip audit name attack** and **ip audit name info** commands, those **ip audit names** will inherit the action specified by the *global audit policy*.

The syntax of the **ip audit name attack** command

```
ip audit name audit_name attack [action [alarm] [drop] [reset]]
```

Table A-2 explains the options for this command.

Table A-2 **ip audit name attack** *Command Options*

Options	Description
audit_name	The user-defined name of the audit policy.
attack	Defines this as a policy for attack signatures.
action	Available actions are **alarm**, **drop**, **reset**.
alarm	Generate syslog message to the configured **logging host.**
drop	The interface on which the signature was triggered drops the offending packet(s).
reset	The PIX sends a TCP reset to both the target IP address and the attacker IP address.

The syntax of the **ip audit name info** command is

```
ip audit name audit_name info [action [alarm] [drop] [reset]]
```

Table A-3 explains the options for this command.

Table A-3 **ip audit name info** *Command Options*

Options	Description
audit_name	The user-defined name of the audit policy.
info	Defines this as a policy for informational signatures.
action	Available actions are **alarm**, **drop**, **reset**.
alarm	Generate syslog message to the configured **logging host.**
drop	The interface on which the signature was triggered drops the offending packet(s).
reset	The PIX sends a TCP reset to both the target IP address and the attacker IP address.

Now that you've created the audit policies, use the **ip audit interface** command to bind them to the interface(s) you want to protect. Use the **no ip audit interface** command to disable policy processing on that interface.

The syntax of the **ip audit interface** command is

```
ip audit interface if_name audit_name
```

Table A-4 explains the options for this command.

Table A-4   **ip audit interface** *Command Options*

Options	Description
if_name	The interface protected by the **ip audit name** command.
audit_name	Specifies what audit policy is applied to the protected interface.

Selectively Disabling IDS Signatures from the Audit Policy

There may be a need in your environment to selectively disable IDS signatures from your audit policy. Use the **ip audit signature disable** command to disable signatures by signature number. Use the **no ip audit signature** *signature_number* to re-enable a previously disabled signature.

The syntax of the **ip audit signature** command is

```
ip audit signature signature_number disable
```

Use the **show ip audit signature** command to display a list of disabled IDS signatures. Example A-1 illustrates a sample output of the **show ip audit signatures** command.

Example A-1   *Display Disabled IDS Signatures*

```
Pixfirewall (config)# show ip audit signature
ip audit signature 6180 disable
ip audit signature 6190 disable
```

PIX IDS Configuration Examples

Now that you understand the basic building blocks, let's get our feet wet by translating different audit policies into actual configurations. Each illustration policy will have two elements—attack and informational. Refer to Example A-1 for a listing of signatures and their associated *signature_id*'s for use in the **ip audit signature** command. Table A-5 shows the informational and attack signatures for IDS Policy 1 for this example's purposes.

Table A-5   *IDS Policy 1*

Informational Signatures	Policy
Outside Interface	Enable informational signatures, but disable all ICMP signatures.

Table A-5 *IDS Policy 1 (Continued)*

Informational Signatures	Policy
Action	Drop.
Inside Interface	Same as Outside Interface.
Action	Drop and send alert to the syslog server.

Attack Signatures	Policy
Outside Interface	All attack signatures enabled.
Action	Drop the packet(s), send a syslog message, and generate TCP resets in both directions.
Inside Interface	Same as Outside Interface.
Action	Drop and send alert to the syslog server.

Example A-2 shows the configuration built from Policy 1. The **ip audit name Outbound** refers to the inside interface and the **ip audit name Inbound** refers to the outside interface.

Example A-2 *PIX Configuration Built from IDS Policy 1*

```
ip audit name Outbound-Info info action alarm drop
ip audit name Outbound-Attack attack action alarm drop
ip audit name Inbound-Info info action drop
ip audit name Inbound-Attack attack action alarm drop reset
ip audit interface outside Inbound-Info
ip audit interface outside Inbound-Attack
ip audit interface inside Outbound-Info
ip audit interface inside Outbound-Attack
ip audit info action alarm
ip audit attack action alarm
ip audit signature 2000 disable
ip audit signature 2001 disable
ip audit signature 2002 disable
ip audit signature 2003 disable
ip audit signature 2004 disable
ip audit signature 2005 disable
ip audit signature 2006 disable
ip audit signature 2007 disable
ip audit signature 2008 disable
ip audit signature 2009 disable
ip audit signature 2010 disable
ip audit signature 2011 disable
ip audit signature 2012 disable
```

IDS Policy 2 reduces the number of log entries by eliminating all informational signatures from the Inside interface yet still maintaining an aggressive posture for both attack and informational signatures on the Outside interface. Table A-6 shows the informational and attack signatures for IDS Policy 1 for this example's purposes.

Table A-6 *IDS Policy 2*

Informational Signatures	Policy
Outside Interface	Enable all informational signatures.
Action	Drop and send a message to the syslog server.
Inside Interface	No policy defined.
Action	None.
Attack Signatures	**Policy**
Outside Interface	All attack signatures enabled.
Action	Drop the packet(s), send a syslog message, and generate TCP resets in both directions.
Inside Interface	Same as Outside Interface.
Action	Drop and send alert to the syslog server.

Example A-3 illustrates the resulting PIX IDS configuration.

Example A-3 *PIX Configuration Built from IDS Policy 2*

```
ip audit name Outbound-Attack attack action alarm drop
ip audit name Inbound-Info info action alarm drop
ip audit name Inbound-Attack attack action alarm drop reset
ip audit interface outside Inbound-Attack
ip audit interface inside Outbound-Info
ip audit interface inside Outbound-Attack
ip audit info action alarm
ip audit attack action alarm
```

PIX IDS Signatures

For detailed information on the syslog messages generated by the PIX IDS Signatures, please refer to the *System Log Messages for the Cisco Secure PIX Firewall Version 5.3*. You can view this document online at the following site:

www.cisco.com/univercd/cc/td/doc/product/iaabu/pix/pix_v53/syslog/index.htm

If you require detailed information about each individual signature, please refer to the Network Security Database. The NSDB is included with Cisco Secure Scanner. You can order an evaluation CD of Cisco Secure Scanner from the following site:

www.cisco.com/public/sw-center/internet/netsonar.shtml

Frequently Asked Questions

Q. Do I have to make changes to the *global audit policy* set with the **ip audit attack** and **ip audit info** commands to make IDS work?

A. No. The actions set with the **ip audit name attack** and **ip audit attack** *override* the actions set with the **ip audit info** command.

Q. What actions does the **ip audit name** command use if I don't specify any?

A. Again, if no action is specified, the **ip audit name** command will *inherit* the action specified in the **ip audit attack** and **ip audit info** commands. The actions from the global audit policy will appear in the **ip audit name** entries in the PIX configuration.

Q. Will I be able to re-enable a signature I have disabled?

A. Yes. Use the **no ip audit signature** *signature_id* command to re-enable the signature.

Q. Will the use of the PIX IDS features have a negative impact on the performance of the PIX?

A. This depends on many factors, including how hard you are being hit by intruders, the speed of your external connection, and what other features are configured on your PIX.

Q. Is it possible to temporarily disable IDS processing without having to change the **ip audit name** commands and disabled signatures configured?

A. Yes. Use the **no ip audit interface** command to remove the binding of the named policy to the interface.

Q. Can I configure Cisco Secure Policy Manager (CSPM) to use the PIX as a sensor?

A. No. This is not currently a feature of CSPM.

Recommended Reading List

"Cisco Secure Intrusion Detection System Documentation Release 2.2.3"—www.cisco.com/univercd/cc/td/doc/product/iaabu/csids/csids7/index.htm

"Network Security Policy: Best Practices White Paper"—www.cisco.com/warp/public/126/secpol.html

"Cisco Secure Intrusion Detection System: Technical Tips"—http://www.cisco.com/warp/public/707/#cs_ids

Northcutt, Steven, Mark Cooper, Matt Fearnow, and Karen Frederick. *Intrusion Signatures and Analysis*. 2001. New Riders Publishing (0735710635)

The purpose of this appendix is to familiarize you with the configuration of SNMP on the PIX Firewall. Topics include the following:

- Understanding PIX SNMP Support
- Retrieving SNMP Data from the PIX
- SNMP v1 MIB-II Inventory
- SNMP References

Configuring Simple Network Management Protocol (SNMP) on the PIX Firewall

Understanding PIX SNMP Support

This appendix assumes that you are familiar with SNMP network management applications and techniques. It is not intended as a tutorial on SNMP network management, which is beyond the scope of the book.

The SNMP is an industry standard protocol used for remote monitoring of network devices. Unlike other network devices you might have worked with, the PIX Firewall supports *read-only* access.

Using SNMP, you can monitor system events on the PIX Firewall. Because SNMP was not designed for high security, SNMP events can be read, but no values on the PIX Firewall can be changed remotely with it.

The following SNMP traps can be sent to an SNMP management station:

- Generic traps:
    - Link up and link down (for example, a cable accidentally unplugged from an interface)
    - Cold start
    - SNMP authentication failure (mismatched community string)
- Security-related events sent via the Cisco Syslog Management Information Base (MIB):
    - Global access denied
    - Failover syslog messages
    - syslog messages

Use CiscoWorks for Windows, CiscoWorks 2000, or any other SNMP v1, MIB-II compliant SNMP manager to receive SNMP traps and browse an MIB. SNMP traps are sent to destination UDP port 162.

Retrieving SNMP Data from the PIX Firewall

There are two ways to get SNMP data from the PIX:

* By using an SNMP MIB Browser
* Via SNMP traps sent by the PIX to a designated trap receiver

MIB Browsing

This is a tool common to SNMP Manager software, such as CiscoWorks 2000, CiscoWorks for Windows or HP OpenView Network Node Manager. Before you can browse a PIX MIB, you will most likely need to compile the PIX MIBs on your SNMP Manager. Please refer to the "Advanced Configuration" section of the *Configuration Guide for the Cisco Secure PIX Firewall Version 5.3* for detailed information on the MIBs available to download and compile. Refer to the documentation of the Network Management platform you use for the steps to compile MIBs.

SNMP Traps

Traps are different from browsing; they are unsolicited "commentaries" from the managed device to the SNMP management station for certain events, such as link up, link down, syslog event generated, and so on.

An SNMP object ID (OID) for the PIX Firewall displays in SNMP event traps sent from the PIX Firewall. OID 1.3.6.1.4.1.9.1.227 was assigned as the PIX Firewall system OID.

Configuring the PIX to Allow MIB Browsing and Send Syslog Traps

Follow these steps to receive requests and send traps from the PIX Firewall to an SNMP management station:

Step 1 If logging is not already enabled, turn it on.

```
percival(config)# logging on
```

Step 2 Set the **snmp-server** options for **location**, **contact**, and the **community** password as required.

```
percival(config)# snmp-server community 1mP0$$1b132gu3$$
percival(config)# snmp-server location Home Office
percival(config)# snmp-server Contact Dave Chapman
dave.chapman@globalknowledge.com
```

If you only want to send SNMP requests on the PIX Firewall, no additional configuration is required.

Note	To secure your PIX from being browsed by unauthorized entities, it is imperative to choose a strong, non-dictionary–based community string, as in the example in Step 2.

Step 3   Add an **snmp-server enable traps** command statement to signal the PIX to send SNMP messages to the designated SNMP Manager you configured with the **snmp-server host** command.

Use the **snmp-server host** command to Identify the IP address of the SNMP management station to send SNMP data to.

```
percival(config)# snmp-server host 192.168.111.7
```

Step 4   The **logging history** command sets the severity level for SNMP syslog messages and starts sending trap messages to the SNMP Server specified in the **snmp-server host** command. Set the logging level with the **logging history** command:

```
percival(config)# logging history debugging
```

Note	Cisco recommends that you use the **debugging** level during initial setup and during testing. Thereafter, set the level from **debugging** to a lower value for production use.

Step 5   To stop the PIX from sending syslog traps, use the **no logging on** command or the **no snmp-server enable traps** command.

Note	The command **no logging on** globally disables *all* logging.

SNMP v1 MIB-II Inventory

The Cisco Firewall MIB and Cisco Memory Pool MIB are available. PIX Firewall does not support the following variables in the Cisco Firewall MIB:

cfwSecurityNotification NOTIFICATION-TYPE

cfwContentInspectNotification NOTIFICATION-TYPE

cfwConnNotification NOTIFICATION-TYPE

cfwAccessNotification NOTIFICATION-TYPE

cfwAuthNotification NOTIFICATION-TYPE

cfwGenericNotification NOTIFICATION-TYPE

Please refer to the "Advanced Configuration" section of the *Configuration Guide for the Cisco Secure PIX Firewall Version 5.3* for detailed information on what MIB variables are available for browsing.

SNMP Resources on the Web

Table B-1 provides a list of SNMP resources and associated URLs for further reading.

Table B-1 *Online SNMP Resources*

SNMP Resource	Web Location
SNMP and MIB RFC's	http://www.hio.hen.nl/rfc/snmp
Configuration Guide for the Cisco Secure PIX Firewall Version 5.3	http://www.cisco.com/univercd/cc/td/doc/product/iaabu/pix/pix_v53/config/index.htm
CiscoWorks 2000	http://www.cisco.com/warp/customer/44/jump/ciscoworks.shtml
CiscoWorks for Windows v5.0	http://www.cisco.com/univercd/cc/td/doc/pcat/wrwi.htm
Advent SNMP MIB browser for Windows NT	http://cswww.vuse.vanderbilt.edu/~natasha/SNMP/software.html
SolarWinds Network Management System	http://www.solarwinds.net

This appendix introduces you to the tasks needed to configure DHCP client and server support on the PIX. It is not our intent to provide an exhaustive explanation of how DHCP operates, but rather to concentrate on the mechanics of configuration on the PIX 506. DHCP references will be provided at the end of this appendix.

In this appendix, you will learn the following:

- DHCP Basics
- DHCP Server
- DHCP Client
- Sample Configurations
- DHCP Resources on the WWW

Configuring Dynamic Host Configuration Protocol (DHCP) on the PIX Firewall

DHCP Basics

The Dynamic Host Configuration Protocol (DHCP) is a mechanism for automating the configuration of computers that use TCP/IP. DHCP can be used to automatically assign IP addresses; to deliver TCP/IP configuration parameters, such as subnet mask and default gateway; and to provide other configuration information, such as the IP addresses for DNS/WINS servers.

NOTE   Cisco introduced DHCP support to the PIX Firewall in version 5.2 of the PIX OS. Although the DHCP feature is available in all PIX models, it was designed solely for the PIX 506 in mind. Because DHCP support was intended for small office/home office (SOHO) environments, there are limitations on the number of hosts supported by the PIX.

DHCP Server

The DHCP server feature of the PIX was designed for use with the PIX 506 in a SOHO environment. As a DHCP server, the PIX Firewall assigns network configuration parameters to DHCP clients. These configuration parameters provide a DHCP client with the elements used to access the network, such as IP address, default gateway, and DNS server.

The PIX Firewall commands used to configure the DHCP server feature are described in detail in the **dhcpd** command page of the "Command Reference" in the *Configuration Guide for the Cisco Secure PIX Firewall Version 5.3*, available online at

www.cisco.com/univercd/cc/td/doc/product/iaabu/pix/pix_v53/config/advanced.htm#xtocid246451.

The number of IP addresses supported by the PIX Firewall depends on the version of the PIX OS. Table C-1 indicates how many hosts can be issued by various PIX models according to the PIX OS version.

Table C-1   *The Number of DHCP Host Addresses by OS Version and Platform*

PIX OS Version	PIX 506	All Other PIX Platforms
5.2	10	10
5.3	32	32
6.0	32	256

DHCP Client

The DHCP client feature of the PIX Firewall is designed for use in SOHO environments where the PIX 506 is directly connected to DSL or a cable modem that supports the DHCP server function. With the DHCP client feature enabled on your PIX, the PIX functions as a DHCP client and is able to obtain and configure the following parameters based on data received from the ISP:

- Default route
- Interface IP address and subnet mask

NOTE   The PIX Firewall DHCP client feature is not supported in failover configurations.

To enable the DHCP *client* feature of the PIX Firewall, the following command enhancements were made to the **ip address** command:

```
ip address if_name dhcp [setroute]
show ip address if_name dhcp
```

New **debug** commands were added, as shown here:

```
debug dhcpc packet
debug dhcpc detail
debug dhcpc error
```

The **ip address dhcp** command enables the DHCP client feature on the specified PIX Firewall interface to dynamically acquire its IP address from an ISP DHCP server. The optional **setroute** argument tells the PIX Firewall to set the default route using the default gateway parameter the DHCP server returns. Use of the **setroute** option is unnecessary if you have manually configured a default route with the **route** command.

The **debug dhcp** commands provide troubleshooting tools for the enabled DHCP client feature. For specific operation characteristics of the **debug dhcp** commands, please refer to the "Command Reference" in the *Configuration Guide for the Cisco Secure PIX Firewall Version 5.3.*

NOTE   The DHCP-acquired IP address of the outside interface can also be used as the PAT global address. This makes it unnecessary to obtain a static IP address from your ISP. (In some cases your ISP will *not* assign you a static IP.) Use the **global** command with **interface** keyword to enable PAT to use the DHCP-acquired IP address of an outside interface. For more information about the **global** command, please refer to the "Command Reference" section of the *Configuration Guide for the Cisco Secure PIX Firewall Version 5.3*

Sample Configurations

In this section you will learn the two most common DHCP configuration scenarios:

- PIX 506 as DHCP Server: Static Outside Address
- PIX 506 as DHCP Client: Dynamically Acquired Outside Address

PIX 506 as DHCP Server: Static Outside Address

```
(Set both interfaces "up" at 10Mb, half-duplex)
interface ethernet0 10baset
interface ethernet1 10baset
(Configure inside and outside interfaces with static IP addresses)
ip address outside 220.26.55.63 255.255.255.0
ip address inside 192.168.111.1 255.255.255.0
(Instruct the PIX to use the IP address of the outside interface for PAT)
global (outside) 1 interface
(Allow all users on the inside to translate to the PAT address)
nat (inside) 1 0.0.0.0 0.0.0.0 0 0
(Tell the PIX where the default gateway is)
route outside 0.0.0.0 0.0.0.0 220.26.55.1 1
(Create a pool of addresses on the inside interface to assign inside users)
dhcpd address 192.168.111.5-192.168.111.10 inside
(Have the PIX specify up to two IP addresses for DNS servers)
dhcpd dns 192.108.254.11 192.108.254.26
dchpd wins 192.108.254.12 192.108.254.27
(Default: Sets the DHCP lease to 3600 seconds)
dhcpd lease 3600
(Have the PIX configure the client's domain name)
dhcpd domain mydomain.com
(Enable the DHCP server on the inside interface)
dhcpd enable inside
```

NOTE   With respect to the **dhcp address** command, the range of IP addresses assigned *must* be part of the subnet assigned to the inside interface.

PIX 506 as DHCP Client: Dynamically Acquired Outside Address

This example builds on the example of configuring DHCP server support and illustrates how to configure the PIX to dynamically acquire its IP address and subnet mask and optionally set the default route.

```
(Set both interfaces "up" at 10Mb, half-duplex)
interface ethernet0 10baset
interface ethernet1 10baset
(Configure the outside interface to get its IP address from an ISP DHCP server and
automatically set the default route based on the ISP gateway)
ip address outside dhcp setroute
(Configures a static IP address for the inside interface)
ip address inside 192.168.111.1 255.255.255.0
(Instruct the PIX to use the DHCP acquired IP address of the outside interface for PAT)
global (outside) 1 interface
(Allow all users on the inside to translate to the PAT address)
nat (inside) 1 0.0.0.0 0.0.0.0 0 0
(Create a pool of addresses on the inside interface to assign inside users)
dhcpd address 192.168.111.5-192.168.111.10 inside
(Have the PIX specify up to two IP addresses for DNS servers)
dhcpd dns 192.108.254.11 192.108.254.26
dchpd wins 192.108.254.12 192.108.254.27
(Default: Sets the DHCP lease to 3600 seconds)
dhcpd lease 3600
(Have the PIX configure the client's domain name)
dhcpd domain mydomain.com
(Enable the DHCP server on the inside interface)
dhcpd enable inside
```

DHCP Resources on the WWW

Resource	URL
dhcp.org – Resources for DHCP	http://www.dhcp.org
RFC 2131 – Dynamic Host Configuration Protocol	http://www.dhcp.org/rfc2131.html
RFC 2132 - DHCP Options and BOOTP Vendor Extensions	http://www.dhcp.org/rfc2132.html

This appendix covers the information needed to understand and configure your PIX firewall for remote management access using SSH. SSH provides a more secure alternative to plain-text Telnet. SSH and IPSec are the *only* supported methods of connecting to the PIX from the outside interface for management.

This chapter provides an overview of the following topics:

- Introduction to Secure Shell (SSH)
- Configuring the PIX to Allow SSH
- Configuring SSH Client Software
- Troubleshooting
- Obtaining an SSH Client for Your Platform

Configuring Secure Shell (SSH) on the PIX Firewall

Introduction to Secure Shell (SSH)

SSH (Secure Shell) is a program to log into another computer over a network, to execute commands in a remote machine, and to move files from one machine to another. It provides strong authentication and secure communications over insecure networks.

—From the SSH Internet Draft at http://www.free.lp.se/fish/rfc.txt

The use of SSH provides a more secure alternative to Telnet, which sends all data in plain text. In an SSH session, all data, including the initial sign-on and password submission, is encrypted using DES or 3DES encryption. The symetric session key is encrypted by the SSH client using RSA encryption and sent securely to the SSH server.

NOTE   The Cisco Secure PIX Firewall implements SSH v1. There are known problems with SSH v1 in some versions of the PIX OS that can lead to an intruder successfully penetrating your PIX. These vulnerabilities are described along with the fixed versions of PIX OS in "Cisco Security Advisory: Multiple SSH Vulnerabilities," which can be found at

www.cisco.com/warp/public/707/SSH-multiple-pub.html

Even if you are currently running a version of the PIX OS that is vulnerable to exploitation, SSH is still far better protection than Telnet.

Configuring the PIX for SSH Access

There are two separate sets of tasks you need to complete to use SSH to access your PIX.

- Configure the PIX to accept SSH connections.
- Configure your SSH client to connect to the PIX.

Configuring PIX to Accept SSH Connections

Step 1   Assign a host name and a domain name to the PIX. This is required to generate the RSA key set.

```
pixfirewall(config)# hostname percival
percival(config)# domain-name cisco.com
```

Step 2   Generate an RSA Key pair and save the keys to Flash memory.

```
percival(config)# ca generate rsa key 2048
For <key_modulus_size> >= 1024, key generation could
    take up to several minutes. Please wait..........
```

Step 3   View your newly created RSA Public Key.

```
percival(config)# sh ca mypubkey rsa

% Key pair was generated at: 15:02:39 May 28 2001

Key name: percival.cisco.com
 Usage: General Purpose Key
 Key Data:
  30820122 300d0609 2a864886 f70d0101 01050003 82010f00 3082010a
02820101
  00b0475a 85bcfce7 91e36431 16c67070 24e4eb09 1b55766c 3588ea87
ba637382
  8e3455a5 a7f71a8f fcd93f25 2bb95484 668ae92d a2175de3 04605fd0
d84f17e4
  70569d26 90ff55d9 3cb91b90 ca4102d5 dc3c9cd1 25692aba f5cabae7
4f066459
  86ecae91 a6e8c032 1e15184d f12f4bf8 18828ca6 6bc61c80 08a1425a
7d767200
  ae68098f 703a972f 59b92239 ed9ae146 ff4a7ea4 6ae2b527 0486c91a
c76bd376
  3093d024 164e6032 c327d9b9 ed7101c8 73030634 defc0848 78a51d04
6995ad8c
  5cbdc0b1 e77091e0 283e5881 407b3639 8a90abba fa559e4b 07a769ab
19b020f4
  ba76301a 09772faa 2920067b be4ca3c0 84e2f7f0 7985eafe 227940e4
c56aea3e
  23020301 0001
```

Step 4   After generating the keys, you *must* save them to Flash memory. Failure to perform this step will result in the erasure of the keys at the next reload.

```
percival(config)# ca save all
```

Step 5   Specify what hosts are allowed to SSH to the PIX and set the SSH inactivity timeout. In this case, you will limit SSH access to a single inside host and kill sessions after one hour of inactivity.

```
percival(config)# ssh 192.168.111.7 255.255.255.255 inside
percival(config)# ssh timeout 60
```

Step 6   Set the enable password and Telnet password. You will be required to enter the Telnet password to authenticate your SSH session.

```
percival(config)# enable password hArd2Gue$$
percival(config)# passwd Ace$$D3n13d
```

NOTE   If you have previously configured a Telnet password and enable password, you do not need to change them for SSH to work.

Configuring the SSH Client to Connect to the PIX

Before you can connect to the PIX using SSH, you need to install an SSH client compatible with your platform. This example uses the SSH client from SSH Communications. Please see the "Obtaining an SSH Client for Your Platform" section for a listing of sites where you can obtain an SSH client.

Step 1   Launch the SSH client software.

Step 2   Select **Settings** from the Edit menu (see Figure D-1).

Step 3   Click on the **Connection** item from the list under Profile Settings on the left side panel. In the **Host Name** field, enter the IP address of the PIX. Enter **pix** in the **User Name** field. Next, in the Authentication Methods pane, click on **Password** (see Figure D-2).

Step 4   Click on the **Cipher List** item, just below the Connection item under Profile Settings in the left side panel. Uncheck all the ciphers *except* the one you will be using. Once your cipher is selected, use the black Up arrow to move your preferred cipher to the top of the list. In the example illustrated in Figure D-3, the user has selected DES.

NOTE   While many SSH Clients support a wide variety of ciphers, the PIX supports DES and 3DES only. You must install the appropriate activation key before using DES or 3DES. For maximum security, Cisco recommends using 3DES to secure SSH and IPSec.

Figure D-1   *Opening the Settings Panel*

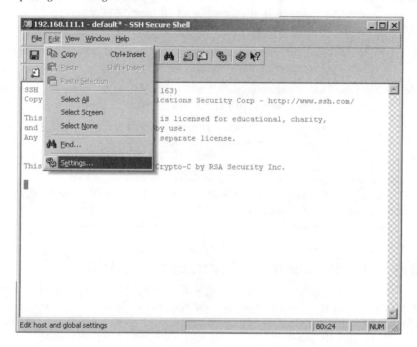

Figure D-2   *Setting Connection Preferences*

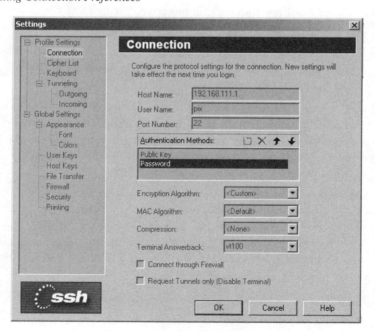

Figure D-3 *Cipher Selection*

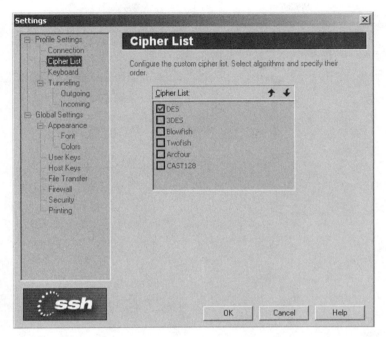

Step 5 To avoid entering this information every time you launch the SSH client, choose **Save Settings** from the **File** menu (see Figure D-4).

Step 6 Open the login pop-up box (see Figure D-5) by clicking on the **Quick Connect** button.

Step 7 Because of the potential vulnerabilities with SSH version 1, this SSH client warns you with the message in Figure D-6. Click the **Yes** button to continue.

Step 8 If this is the first time you have connected to the PIX with SSH, you must exchange Public Keys with each other in order to encrypt the session. The SSH client prompts you to accept the PIX's Public Key. Click on the **Yes** button to save the PIX's Public Key to the local database (see Figure D-7).

Step 9 After you save the PIX's Public Key, your SSH client prompts you for the Telnet password (see Figure D-8).

Step 10 You did it! You have created a secure connection to your PIX Firewall (see Figure D-9). Now, you can perform any configuration and routine maintenance over the SSH connection.

Figure D-4   *Saving Your Preferences to a Profile*

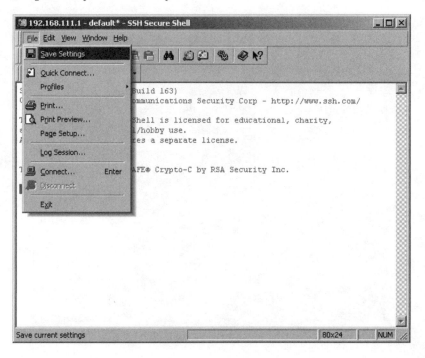

Figure D-5   *Opening the Login Pop-Up*

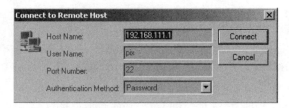

Figure D-6   *SSH Version 1 Warning*

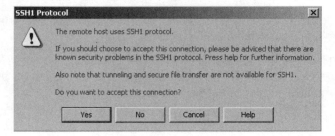

Figure D-7   *Public Key Exchange*

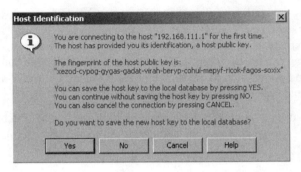

Figure D-8   *Enter Telnet Password*

Figure D-9   *SSH Connection Up*

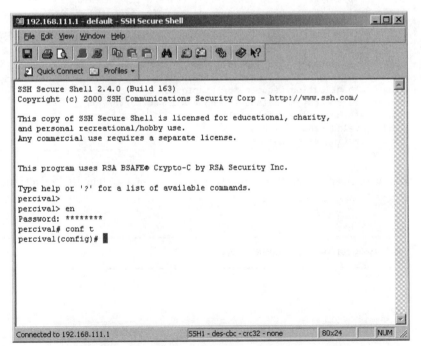

Troubleshooting SSH Client Connection Problems

As with any new remote access client software, there will be a need to figure out why client connections fail. Fortunately, the PIX has **debug ssh** to make life easier on you. If you have previous experience using **debug** commands with Cisco IOS Software, you know that debug output can be very cryptic. I'm pleased to report that the output of **debug ssh** is very readable and points right to the source of the problem. Let's take a look at some common scenarios and how **debug ssh** can make your life easier.

First, what does a normal SSH session look like. Turn on SSH debugging by using the **debug ssh** command. Notice the authentication request for user *pix* was successful.

```
percival(config)# debug ssh
SSH debugging on
```

Example D-1 shows the output for a successful SSH session.

Example D-1   *Successful SSH Session Establishment*

```
Device opened successfully.
SSH: host key initialised
SSH: license supports DES: 1
SSH0: SSH client: IP = '192.168.111.7'  interface # = 1
SSH0: starting SSH control process
SSH0: Exchanging versions - SSH-1.5-Cisco-1.25
SSH0: client version is - SSH-1.5-2.4.0 (compat mode)
SSH0: begin server key generation
SSH0: complete server key generation, elapsed time = 2970 ms
SSH0: declare what cipher(s) we support: 0x00  0x00  0x00  0x04
SSH0: SSH_SMSG_PUBLIC_KEY message sent
SSH0: SSH_CMSG_SESSION_KEY message received - msg type 0x03, length 272
SSH0: client requests  DES cipher: 2
SSH0: keys exchanged and encryption on
SSH: Installing crc compensation attack detector.
SSH0: authentication request for userid pix
SSH(pix): user authen method is 'no AAA', aaa server group ID = 0
SSH0: authentication successful for pix
SSH0: invalid request - 0x22
SSH0: starting exec shell
```

What happens if a user does not use *pix* as the username? The PIX rejects the username cisco in Example D-2.

NOTE   The only acceptable username is *pix*.

Example D-2 *Invalid Username*

```
Device opened successfully.
SSH: host key initialised
SSH0: SSH client: IP = '192.168.111.5'  interface # = 1
SSH0: starting SSH control process
SSH0: Exchanging versions - SSH-1.5-Cisco-1.25
SSH0: client version is - SSH-1.5-2.4.0 (compat mode)
SSH0: begin server key generation
SSH0: complete server key generation, elapsed time = 3050 ms
SSH0: declare what cipher(s) we support: 0x00  0x00  0x00  0x04
SSH0: SSH_SMSG_PUBLIC_KEY message sent
SSH0: SSH_CMSG_SESSION_KEY message received - msg type 0x03, length 272
SSH0: client requests  DES cipher: 2
SSH0: keys exchanged and encryption on
SSH0: authentication request for userid cisco
SSH(cisco): user authen method is 'no AAA', aaa server group ID = 0
SSH0: invalid userid cisco
SSH0: authentication failed for cisco
SSH0: Session disconnected by SSH server - error 0x0d "Rejected by server"
```

Example D-3 illustrates authentication failure due to the user entering the wrong Telnet password.

Example D-3 *Invalid Password*

```
Device opened successfully.
SSH: host key initialised
SSH0: SSH client: IP = '192.168.111.5'  interface # = 1
SSH0: starting SSH control process
SSH0: Exchanging versions - SSH-1.5-Cisco-1.25
SSH0: client version is - SSH-1.5-2.4.0 (compat mode)
SSH0: begin server key generation
SSH0: complete server key generation, elapsed time = 1370 ms
SSH0: declare what cipher(s) we support: 0x00  0x00  0x00  0x04
SSH0: SSH_SMSG_PUBLIC_KEY message sent
SSH0: SSH_CMSG_SESSION_KEY message received - msg type 0x03, length 272
SSH0: client requests  DES cipher: 2
SSH0: keys exchanged and encryption on
SSH0: authentication request for userid pix
SSH(pix): user authen method is 'no AAA', aaa server group ID = 0
SSH0: password authentication failed for pix
SSH0: password authentication failed for pix
SSH0: password authentication failed for pix
SSH0: authentication failed for pix
SSH0: Session disconnected by SSH server - error 0x0d "Rejected by server"
```

Both the SSH client and the SSH server must exchange Public Keys before the session can be encrypted. Example D-4 shows what happens if you forgot to generate an RSA key pair.

Example D-4   *No RSA Key on the PIX*

```
Device opened successfully.
SSH: unable to retrieve host public key for percival.cisco.com', terminate SSH
connection.
SSH-2145046632: Session disconnected by SSH server - error 0x00 "Internal error"
```

Obtaining an SSH Client for Your Platform

The sites in Table D-1 allow you to download a free SSH v1.*x* client. Because SSH versions 1.*x* and 2 are entirely different protocols and are not compatible, be sure to download a client that supports SSH v1.*x*.

Table D-1   *SSH Clients*

Company/ Client	SSH Client Description	URL
*SSH Communications	SSH Communications allows free downloads of its SSH client to academia and to individuals for non-commercial use.	http://commerce.ssh.com/ sshws/ index.html?SshSid=9xXLRLt MNn85ZF24
Tera Term Pro/ SSH	You can download the free Tera Term Pro SSH v1.x client for the following platforms: Windows 3.1, Windows CE, Windows 95, and Windows NT 4.0. **You also need to download the TTSSH security enhancement for Tera Term Pro.	http://hp.vector.co.jp/authors/ VA002416/teraterm.html http://www.zip.com.au/~roca/ ttssh.html
OpenSSH for UNIX/Linux	Download the SSH v1.x client for the following platforms: Linux, Solaris, OpenBSD, AIX, IRIX, HP/UX, FreeBSD, and NetBSD.	http://www.openssh.com
Nifty Telnet for Macintosh	The Nifty Telnet 1.1 SSH client for the Macintosh	http://www.lysator.liu.se/ ~jonasw/freeware/niftyssh/

*All the configuration examples in this appendix are based on the SSH client from SSH Communications.
**You must download TTSSH to use Tera Term Pro with SSH. TTSSH provides a zip file that you copy to your system. Extract the zipped files into the same folder where you installed Tera Term Pro. For a Windows system, the default would be the C:\Program Files\Ttempro folder.

Security Resources

The purpose of this appendix is to provide you with a list of good security resources available on the Internet.

Tables E-1 through E-14 provide information and links to the following related security resources:

- Professional Development/Security Associations
- Legal Resources
- Intrusion Detection (Network-Based)
- Intrusion Detection (Host-Based)
- Reconnaissance Tools (UNIX)
- Reconnaissance Tools (Windows)
- SNMP Discovery Tools (Windows)
- Exploits by OS
- Security Portals
- Cracking Tools
- SSH
- Cisco Links
- Certificate Authority (PKI)
- Recommended Reading

Table E-1 *Professional Development/Security Associations*

Association	URL
(ISC)^2 International Information Systems Security Certifications Consortium, Inc.—CISSP Certification	http://www.isc2.org
Information Systems Security Association (ISSA) (90-day trial membership available)	http://www.issa-intl.org
International Computer Security Association	http://www.icsa.net

continues

Table E-1 *Professional Development/Security Associations (Continued)*

Association	URL
SANS—Certifications in Intrusion Detection and Firewalling (Free Security Poster)	http://www.sans.org
IEEE Computer Society Technical Committee on Security and Privacy	http://ieee-security.org

Table E-2 *Legal Resources*

Legal Resource	URL
Case Law—Hacking/Cracking, Viruses, and Security (Law School web site)	http://www.jmls.edu/cyber/index/hacking.html
Hacking Laws in the 50 States and the UK	http://www.ladysharrow.ndirect.co.uk/Virus%20Information/virus_and_hacking_law.htm
Canadian Hacking Law	http://www.happyhacker.org/hhlist/digest7b5.shtml
Canadian IT Law Index	http://www.it-can.ca/Links.html
The Computer Fraud and Abuse Act (as amended October 3, 1996)	http://206.9.156.15/hacklaw.htm
FindLaw.Com—Searchable Database of Case Law by Court (Use keyword: hacking)	http://laws.findlaw.com
International Law Enforcement Resources	http://www.vaonline.org/law.html

Table E-3 *Network-Based Intrusion Detection*

Resource	URL
Cisco Secure IDS	http://www.cisco.com/warp/customer/cc/pd/sqsw/sqidsz
RealSecure (Download Eval)	http://www.iss.net/cgi-bin/download/evaluation/evaluation-select.cgi
SNORT—FREE Unix Intrusion Detection System	http://www.snort.org

Table E-4 *Host-Based Intrusion Detection*

Resource	URL
BlackICE Pro	http://www.networkice.com
TripWire for NT	http://www.tripwiresecurity.com
FREE Common Security Exploit and Vulnerability Matrix Poster Request Form	http://www.tripwiresecurity.com/promos/poster.cfml

Table E-5 *Reconnaissance Tools (UNIX)*

Tool	URL
SAINT (Formerly SATAN)	http://www.wwdsi.com/saint/archive.html
Network Mapper (nmap)	http://www.insecure.org/nmap

Table E-6 *Reconnaissance Tools (Windows)*

Tool	URL
nMap NT	http://www.eeye.com/html/Research/Tools/nmapNT.html
Cisco Secure Scanner (NetSonar)	http://www.cisco.com/kobayashi/sw-center/internet/netsonar.shtml
eEye Retina	http://www.eeye.com/html
NetCat	http://www.atstake.com/research
Self-Scan (Check your own machine's vulnerabilities)	http://www.cablemodemhelp.com/portscan.htm
DNScape—DNS Dump Tool	http://www.inettools.com

Table E-7 *SNMP Discovery Tools (Windows)*

Tool	URL
SolarWinds	http://www.solarwinds.net

Table E-8 *Exploits by OS*

Rescource	URL
MITRE—CVECommon Vulnerabilities and Exposures	http://www.cve.mitre.org/cve
CERT Advisories	http://www.cert.org

continues

Table E-8 *Exploits by OS (Continued)*

Rescource	URL
Insecure.Org	http://www.insecure.org/sploits.html
BlackCode	http://www.blackcode.com
CyberArmy (Links to Top 50 Hacking Sites)	http://www.cyberarmy.com/t-50/index.shtml

Table E-9 *Security Portals*

Portal	URL
Security Focus	http://www.securityfocus.com
Packet Storm	http://www.packetstormsecurity.org
SearchSecurity.com	http://searchsecurity.techtarget.com
Web Security	http://www.w3.org/Security
Information Security Magazine (FREE Subscription)	http://www.infosecuritymag.com
FREE Protocol Posters (Links to Many Protocol Posters)	http://www.net3group.com/resources.asp
CAIDA	http://www.caida.org/home/index.xml
Center for Internet Security	http://www.cisecurity.org
InfoSysSec	http://www.infosyssec.com

Table E-10 *Cracking Tools*

Tool	URL
L0pht Crack for NT	http://www.atstake.com/research/LC3/index.html
Languard—Free Security Tools	http://www.languard.com/languard/lantools.htm
DMOZ Cracking Tools Index	http://www.dmoz.org/Computers/Hacking/Cracking

Table E-11 *SSH*

Tool	URL
SSH Communications Security	http://www.ssh.com
Tera Term Pro/SSH (Windows 3.1, Windows CE, Windows 95, and Windows NT 4.0)—Download the Free Tera Term Pro SSH v1.x Client	http://hp.vector.co.jp/authors/VA002416/teraterm.html
The TTSSH Security Enhancement for Tera Term Pro	http://www.zip.com.au/~roca/ttssh.html

Table E-12 *Cisco Links*

Resource	URL
Improving Security on Cisco Routers	http://www.cisco.com/warp/public/707/21.html#spoof-rpf
Security Related RFC Index	http://www.cisco.com/warp/public/625/ccie/certifications/security_qual_blueprint.html#24
CCIE—Security	http://www.cisco.com/warp/customer/625/ccie/certifications/security.html
Security Technical Tips: Internetworking	http://www.cisco.com/warp/public/707/index.shtml
Top Issues in VPN	(CCO Login Required) http://www.cisco.com/warp/customer/471/top_issues/vpn/vpn_index.shtml
Enterprise Security Design Implementation Guide	http://www.cisco.com/warp/partner/synchronicd/cc/sol/mkt/ent/secur (Requires PARTNER level CCO access. Speak to your local Cisco SE to download it for you.)
Cisco Secure Encyclopedia (CSEC) Requires CCO Login	http://www.cisco.com/go/csec
Cisco SAFE Architecture (Security Blueprint)	http://www.cisco.com/go/safe
Cisco Password Recovery Techniques	http://www.cisco.com/warp/public/474

Table E-13 *Certificate Authority (PKI) Resources*

Resource	URL
Configuring Microsoft Certificate Server (Windows 2000 Server)	http://www.cisco.com/univercd/cc/td/doc/product/iaabu/csvpnc/csvpnsg/idcmsft.htm

Table E-14 *Recommended Reading*

Resource	Author/Publishing Information/URL
Designing Network Security	Merike Kaeo, 1999, Cisco Press. ISBN: 1578700434
Managing Cisco Network Security	Michael Wenstrom, 2001, Cisco Press. ISBN: 1578701031
Internet Security Protocols: Protecting IP Traffic	Uyless D. Black, 2000, Prentice Hall PTR. ISBN: 0-13-014249-2

continues

Table E-14 *Recommended Reading (Continued)*

Resource	Author/Publishing Information/URL
Hacking Exposed: Network Security Secrets and Solutions, Second Edition	Joel Scambray, George Kurtz, and Stuart McClure, 2000, Osborne (McGraw-Hill Professional Publishing). ISBN: 0-07-212748-1
The Cuckoo's Egg: Tracking a Spy Through the Maze of Computer Espionage	Clifford Stoll, 2000, Pocket Books. ISBN: 0743411463
Take-Down: The Pursuit and Capture of Kevin Mitnick, America's Most Wanted Computer Outlaw	Tsutomu Shimomura and John Markoff, 1996, Hyperion. ISBN: 0786862106
Cyberpunk: Outlaws and Hackers on the Computer Frontier	Katie Hafner and John Markoff, 1995, Touchstone Books. ISBN: 0684818620
Network Intrusion Detection, Second Edition (Be sure to get the NEW Second Edition Edition)	Stephen Northcutt, Donald MacLachlan, and Judy Novak, 2000, New Riders Publishing. ISBN: 0735710082
Intrusion Signatures and Analysis	Stephen Northcutt, et al., 2001, New Riders Publishing. ISBN: 0735710635
Information Security Magazine	Free subscription available at: http://www.infosecuritymag.com
Warriors of the Net (Multimedia Presentation of IP Routing, Proxy Operation and Firewalls)	http://warriorsofthe.net

Answers to Chapter Review Questions

Answers to Chapter 1 Review Questions

1   I want to install a web server and allow Internet users access, but I don't want those users inside my network. How can I accomplish this?

    Answer: Install a firewall with three interfaces. One interface is connected to the Internet. One interface is connected to the inside of your network. One interface is connected to your DMZ network. The DMZ is where the Web server resides.

2   A script kiddie poses what type of network security threat?

    Answer: An unstructured threat.

3   Of all of the different types of threats that exist, which one should I fear most?

    Answer: Because this type of attack is relatively easy and can be performed anonymously, the most feared attack on the Internet is a Denial of Service (DoS) attack.

4   What is used to allow only specified users access to a network?

    Answer: An Identification Authentication System such as Cisco Secure ACS.

Answers to Chapter 2 Review Questions

1   What are the three kinds of Firewall technologies?

    Answer: Packet Filter, Proxy Filter, and Stateful Packet Filter.

2   What type of firewall is a Cisco router?

    Answer: Packet filter

3   Briefly describe the function Adaptive Security Algorithm (ASA).

    Answer: It is the part of the operating system within the PIX that provides the stateful Packet inspection.

4   What is the maximum number of Ethernet interfaces on a PIX model 506?

    Answer: 2

5 What is the maximum number of Ethernet interfaces on a PIX model 535?

Answer: 8 (PIX OS < 6.0) 10 (PIX OS ≥ 6.0)

6 When installing a four-port expansion interface card on a PIX 515, which is the lowest interface number?

Answer: The interface on the left.

7 True or False. The PIX Model 506 supports gigabit Ethernet interfaces.

Answer: False

8 When installing a four-port expansion card on a PIX 520, which is the lowest interface number?

Answer: The interface on top.

Answers to Chapter 3 Review Questions

1 What are the administrative modes that are available to users of the PIX Firewall?

Answer: Unprivileged Mode, Privileged Mode, Configuration Mode, and Monitor Mode.

2 What must be done after changes to the configuration are made to keep those changes?

Answer: Because changes to the PIX are made to the running configuration in RAM, they must be saved to Flash with the write memory command.

3 What is an Ethernet frame called that is less than the minimum frame size required?

Answer: A runt.

4 What command is required to start the process of copying a new OS to Flash, with a PIX running OS version 5.1.1 or later?

Answer: copy tftp flash.

5 How does a PIX get into monitor mode?

Answer: The PIX must be rebooted. Immediately after re-establishing power, press the Escape key or send a break sequence.

6 What command shows a user how long the PIX has been operational since the last reboot?

Answer: show version.

7 What command starts the process of merging a file on a TFTP server with the running configuration in RAM?

Answer: configure net.

Answers to Chapter 4 Review Questions

1 What is the default security level of the *inside* interface?

   Answer: The *inside* interface has a default security level of 100.

2 True or False. Two interfaces cannot have the same security level.

   Answer: False.

3 What is the syntax of the **route** command if I want to configure the PIX with a default route to my perimeter router (IP address 192.168.1.1) and static routes to three internal networks (10.1.1.0, 10.2.0.0, 10.3.0.0), all with a next hop router IP address of 10.1.1.5?

   Answer:

   ```
   route outside 0.0.0.0 0.0.0.0 192.168.1.1 1
   route inside 10.1.1.0 255.255.255.0 10.1.1.5 1
   route inside 10.2.0.0 255.255.0.0 10.1.1.5 1
   route inside 10.3.0.0 255.255.0.0 10.1.1.5 1
   ```

4 What must I also do if I configure the PIX using the **nat (inside) 1 0 0** command to translate all internal addresses when accessing the Internet?

   Answer: There must also be a global statement using the same NAT ID providing one or more addresses to translate into.

5 How do I set the default gateway to 192.168.111.1? That IP address exists on the outside subnet.

   Answer:

   ```
   route outside 0.0.0.0 0.0.0.0 192.168.111.1
   ```

Answers to Chapter 5 Review Questions

1 What is the first thing created in the PIX when a user on the inside establishes an outbound session?

   Answer: A translation (xlate) slot.

2 True or False. TCP and UDP are the only two protocols that are permitted through the PIX?

   Answer: False. Other examples include GRE and ICMP.

3 What is an embryonic connection?

   Answer: An embryonic connection is a half-open TCP session. It becomes an established connection after the "three-way handshake" is completed by the inside host sending an ACK.

4 True or False. If I configure a **static** statement, I must also configure a **conduit** statement.

Answer: False. A static statement may be created to only permit outbound access.

5 What should I do after I make a change to the global range of the **global** command?

Answer: It is good practice to perform a clear xlate after a change is made to the global range of the global command.

6 What command shows all active TCP connections through the PIX?

Answer: show conn.

7 Assuming a NAT ID of 3, build the **global** command necessary to translate all intenal IP addresses to be 172.16.1.1.

Answer: global (outside) 3 172.16.1.1. netmask 255.255.255.255.

8 What is a net static?

Answer: The static command when used to translate an entire (sub)network to another (sub)network, or itself.

For example:

```
pixfirewall# static (inside,outside) 172.16.1.0 192.168.1.0
```

Answers to Chapter 6 Review Questions

1 What is required to allow an HTTP server on the DMZ to retain its assigned IP address when being accessed from the Internet?

Answer: nat (dmz) 0

2 What command is used to create a permanent mapping between a local IP address and a global IP address?

Answer: static

3 What is the maximum number of interfaces supported by the PIX Firewall model 515?

Answer: Six is the maximum number of interfaces.

4 What does the **fixup** command do?

Answer: The fixup command lets a user view, change, enable, or disable the use of a service or protocol throughout the PIX Firewall. By default, the PIX Firewall is configured to fix up FTP, SMTP, HTTP, RSH, SQ*LNET, and H.323.

5 What are the two ways through the PIX that were discussed in this chapter?

Answer: **The conduit command and a response to a valid request.**

6 It is good practice to issue what command after making a change to the range of addresses specified in the **global** command?

Answer: **clear xlate**

7 True or False. The **nat 0** command will permit access from the outside to the DMZ?

Answer: **False.**

Answers to Chapter 7 Review Questions

1 What kind of system events does the PIX Firewall syslog generate messages for?

Answer: **Security, Resource, System, and Accounting**

2 What protocol does the syslog use to send these messages?

Answer: **The PIX can send messages in UDP to standard syslog servers and use TCP for transport to Cisco's PIX Firewall Syslog Server (PFSS)**

3 What command is used to start generating syslog messages?

Answer: **logging on**

4 How many different levels of syslog messages are there? Can you name three?

Answer: **Eight. 0—emergencies, 1—alerts, 2—critical, 3—errors, 4—warnings, 5—notifications, 6—informational, 7—debugging**

5 What command is used to cause the PIX to send syslog messages to the console screen?

Answer: **logging console** *level*

Answers to Chapter 8 Review Questions

1 If AAA authentication is required for Telnet access through the PIX, how can the authentication challenge message be modified to read "User Authentication Required"?

Answer: **pixfirewall(config)#auth-prompt prompt User Authentication Required.**

2 True or False. A user may Telnet into the PIX from the inside interface only.

Answer: **False. Starting with PIX operating system version 5.0, a user may Telnet into the PIX through any interface. If Telneting into the PIX via the outside interface, IPSec must be used.**

3 What are the three ways to authenticate for a service other than FTP, Telnet, or HTTP?

Answer: Authenticate first by accessing an FTP, Telnet, or HTTP server (through the PIX—with authentication) before accessing other services.

Authenticate to the PIX Firewall virtual Telnet service before accessing other services.

Authenticate to the PIX Firewall virtual HTTP service before accessing other services.

4 What is the command used on the PIX for identifying an AAA server with an IP address of 10.8.1.4, a *group_tag* of NYSERVERS, and a key of *mysecret*?

Answer: pixfirewall(config)# aaa-server NYSERVERS (inside) host 10.8.1.4 mysecret timeout 5.

5 The following scenario exists:

The PIX is configured with AAA commands.

The PIX is using TACACS+.

The server *group_tag* is NYSERVERS.

How is the **aaa-server** command removed from the configuration of the PIX?

Answer: pixfirewall(config)# clear aaa-server NYSERVERS protocol tacacs+

6 When configuring **aaa authorization,** what is the syntax for configuring the service to be authorized?

Answer: If FTP, Telnet, or HTTP, use the service name or the key word any. If any other service, the syntax is protocol/port.

7 What is the correct syntax when configuring **aaa authentication** for the console?

Answer: aaa authentication serial console jamiserver (where jamiserver is the group tag).

Answers to Chapter 9 Review Questions

1 How does a **fixup protocol** command know when to open a conduit for an inbound connection?

Answer: The fixup protocol command monitors the TCP *control* channel of an application protocol for the needed information.

2 My UNIX administrator has asked me to allow rsh access through the PIX Firewall to administer servers from home. Is this a good idea?

Answer: Because many hacking tools target this service, Cisco recommends against allowing rsh from outside sources.

3 If the **fixup protocol rtsp 554** is disabled by default, why are my users able to view content?

Answer: Media players such as the RealPlayer 7 from RealNetworks automatically choose the best available transport. If RealPlayer 7 detects problems with RTSP, it will choose to make either a single-channel TCP connection or in the worst case scenario, a single-channel UDP connection. In single-channel mode, the normal ASA rules are followed and return traffic is permitted.

4 I'm planning to install a PIX Firewall, but I've heard that the MailGuard feature is incompatible with Microsoft Exchange Server. What can be done to overcome this?

Answer: If your Exchange Server configuration requires the use of extended SMTP commands such as EHLO, you will need to disable MailGuard for your Exchange Server to operate correctly on an interface protected by the PIX Firewall. It is possible to configure Exchange Server to operate with MailGuard in place. Refer to your Microsoft Exchange Server documentation.

Answers to Chapter 10 Review Questions

1 What verion of PIX OS do I need to run to use stateful failover?

Answer: Stateful failover was introduced in PIX OS version 5.1.

2 Does the PIX stop forwarding packets when it begins testing to see why it hasn't received two keepalives?

Answer: No. Even while it's testing its interfaces, the PIX continues to pass traffic.

3 Can I upgrade the Standby PIX while it's connected to the primary?

Answer: While it's possible to rely on stateful failover to perform OS upgrades in Production, I don't recommend it. Schedule a maintenance window to perform upgrades on both PIX Firewalls at the same time.

4 Can I run different versions of the PIX OS when they're configured for failover?

Answer: No. When you execute a show failover command, the interface status for the standby PIX appears as unknown and it does not participate in failover.

5 We run IPSec between our HQ PIX and several of our field offices. Does stateful failover preserve IPSec tunnels?

Answer: No. The ISAKMP and IPSec SA table is not synched between the active and the standby. ISAKMP and IPSec SAs must be re-established.

6 Can I run stateful failover on my PIX 515-R?

Answer: To run *any* form of failover requires the Unrestricted License. Speak to your Cisco account manager for pricing.

7 What happens if the primary PIX is powered off?

Answer: The standby PIX would take over for the now powered off primary. Once the primary was powered back on, it would assume the standby role.

8 What is the range of time that can be set for the **failover poll** interval?

Answer: The failover poll interval is between 3 and 15 seconds. Note that if setting this value too low, you run the risk of a failover event occurring not because of a genuine failure but from network latency or the load on the PIX.

9 What is the most common mis-configuration?

Answer: The most common mistake I see is forgetting the failover keyword in the failover ip address command.

Example: If I wanted to set the failover IP address for the inside interface of the standby PIX, I would issue the following command, which correctly sets the failover IP address to 10.0.1.7:

```
Lab-PIX(config)# failover ip address inside 10.0.1.7
```

If we forget the failover keyword, the command overwrites the current IP address of the active inside interface to 10.0.1.7. By doing this, we have just changed the default gateway for the entire organization.

Answers to Chapter 11 Review Questions

1 Name an advantage and a disadvantage of using pre-shared keys for authentication.

Answer: Pre-shared keys are the simplest to configure and maintain but don't scale well to large numbers of crypto peers.

2 What command do you use to enter a pre-shared key?

Answer:

```
isakmp key key address ip_address netmask mask
```

3 How do you view IKE policies in the PIX's configuration?

Answer: show isakmp and show isakmp policy.

4 How many transforms can be defined in a transform set?

Answer: The maximum number of transforms is three: one for AH, one for ESP, and one for ESP-HMAC.

5 How do you configure IPSec security association lifetimes on the PIX Firewall?

Answer: Use the isakmp policy *number* lifetime *seconds* command.

6 What command do you use to define the traffic flows to be protected?

Answer: An access list is used to define what traffic should or should not be encrypted. When this access list is bound to a crypto map, it is referred to as a *crypto access list*.

7 How can you view IKE events as they occur between IPSec peers?

Answer: debug crypto isakmp.

8 Why does IKE fail for pre-shared keys in the following sample configurations?

```
PIX1
isakmp policy 100 authentication rsa-sig
isakmp policy 100 group 1
isakmp policy 100 lifetime 5000
isakmp policy 200 hash md5
isakmp policy 200 authentication pre-share
```

```
PIX2
isakmp policy 100 authentication rsa-sig
isakmp policy 100 group 2
isakmp policy 100 lifetime 5000
isakmp policy 200 authentication rsa-sig
isakmp policy 200 lifetime 10000
isakmp policy 300 hash sha
isakmp policy 300 authentication pre-share
```

Answer: The phase 1 SA will never be formed because the two PIXs don't agree on which DH group to use.

Answers to Chapter 12 Review Questions

1 I have CBAC running on my perimeter router but my inside users can't ftp to a remote site. They authenticate, but their session hangs when they issue a "dir". Can this be fixed?

Answer: Yes. Use the ip inspect name *inspect-name* ftp command. This enables the router to monitor the control channel of the FTP session and create dynamic access lists as needed for the ftp-data connections. These temporary access lists are deleted by CBAC once the connection is no longer needed.

2 Is the protection afforded by CBAC as strong as the PIX?

Answer: The stateful packet filtering performed by CBAC is as effective as the PIX's ASA but with a large price tag in the form of memory and CPU utilization.

3 Do the CBAC-specific **debug** commands generate a lot of information to the console?

Answer: Yes! If you need to run CBAC debug commands, turn off logging to the console and be sure you direct the debug messages to a syslog server. The command to turn off logging to the console is no logging console.

4   Do the Intrusion Detection signatures provided in IOS offer me complete protection against hackers?

Answer: No. The IDS subsystem in the IOS Firewall should be considered "supplemental" and not relied on as front line protection.

5   Are there any good resources on CCO—for example, CBAC configurations?

Answer: Yes. You will find the following URLs useful:

Product Security Advisories: www.cisco.com/warp/customer/707/advisory.html

IOS Firewall (formerly Cisco Secure Integrated Software); www.cisco.com/ warp/public/707/index.shtml#IOS

6   What command applies an inspection rule to an interface?

Answer: ip inspect *inspection-name* in

7   Is there a way to globally erase the entire CBAC configuration?

Answer: Yes. Issuing no ip inspect removes all CBAC-specific commands from the router. It, however, leaves all non-dynamically created access lists in place.

8   How much DRAM is used to track the state of each session object?

Answer: The IOS Firewall uses 600 bytes of memory for each object it maintains state information for.

Answers to Chapter 13 Review Questions

1   What must be configured on the ACS Server for the Authentication Proxy to operate?

Answer: The auth-proxy service needs to be enabled and selected in the group configuration.

2   When I use the **show ip auth-proxy cache** command, what tells me whether authentication was successful?

Answer: In the following example, the state HTTP_ESTAB indicates that the user was authenticated.

```
router# show ip auth-proxy cache
Authentication Proxy Cache

Client IP 192.168.25.215 Port 57882, timeout 1, state HTTP_ESTAB
```

3   If I use the auth-proxy service to authenticate users from the Internet, are their usernames and passwords protected?

Answer: Yes and no. If JavaScript isn't enabled on the user's browser, the username and password are sent in the clear. If JavaScript is enabled on the user's browser, authentication is automatically secured with JavaScript. Even

with the protection of JavaScript, if you intend to use this service to authenticate external users, the use of some on-time password system (such as RSA Secure-ID) is strongly recommended to mitigate the threat of interception.

4 Are there any good configuration examples on CCO?

Answer: Yes. They can be reached at the following URLs:

www.cisco.com/warp/public/707/index.shtml#IOS

www.cisco.com/univercd/cc/td/doc/product/software/ios120/120newft/120t/ 120t5/iosfw2/iosfw2_1.htm

5 Does the auth-proxy service offer protection against denial-of-service attacks?

Answer: Yes. The Authentication Proxy monitors the level of incoming HTTP requests. For each request, the Authentication Proxy prompts for the user's login credentials. A high number of open requests could indicate that the router is the subject of a denial-of-service (DoS) attack. The Authentication Proxy limits the level of open requests and drops additional requests until the number of open requests has dropped below 40.

6 Is there a risk of spoofed addresses getting through the firewall?

Answer: When the Authentication Proxy is triggered, it creates a dynamic opening in the firewall by temporarily reconfiguring an interface with user access privileges. While this opening exists, another host might spoof the authenticated user's address to gain access behind the firewall. The Authentication Proxy does not cause the address spoofing problem; the problem is only identified here as a concern to the user. Spoofing is a problem inherent to all access lists, and the Authentication Proxy does not specifically address this problem.

INDEX

Numerics

A

Q–R

U–V

W–X

IF YOU'RE USING CISCO PRODUCTS, YOU'RE QUALIFIED TO RECEIVE A FREE SUBSCRIPTION TO CISCO'S PREMIER PUBLICATION, *PACKET*™ MAGAZINE.

Packet delivers complete coverage of cutting-edge networking trends and innovations, as well as current product updates. A magazine for technical, hands-on Cisco users, it delivers valuable information for enterprises, service providers, and small and midsized businesses.

Packet is a quarterly publication. To start your free subscription, click on the URL and follow the prompts:
www.cisco.com/go/packet/subscribe

☐ **YES!** I'm requesting a **free** subscription to *Packet*™ magazine.

☐ No. I'm not interested at this time.

☐ Mr.
☐ Ms.

First Name (Please Print) _____ Last Name _____

Title/Position (Required) _____

Company (Required) _____

Address _____

City _____ State/Province _____

Zip/Postal Code _____ Country _____

Telephone (Include country and area codes) _____ Fax _____

E-mail _____

Signature (Required) _____ Date _____

☐ I would like to receive additional information on Cisco's services and products by e-mail.

1. Do you or your company:
A ☐ Use Cisco products   C ☐ Both
B ☐ Resell Cisco products   D ☐ Neither

2. Your organization's relationship to Cisco Systems:
A ☐ Customer/End User   E ☐ Integrator   J ☐ Consultant
B ☐ Prospective Customer   F ☐ Non-Authorized Reseller K ☐ Other (specify):
C ☐ Cisco Reseller   G ☐ Cisco Training Partner
D ☐ Cisco Distributor   I ☐ Cisco OEM   _____

3. How many people does your entire company employ?
A ☐ More than 10,000   D ☐ 500 to 999   G ☐ Fewer than 100
B ☐ 5,000 to 9,999   E ☐ 250 to 499
C ☐ 1,000 to 4,999   F ☐ 100 to 249

4. Is your company a Service Provider?
A ☐ Yes   B ☐ No

5. Your involvement in network equipment purchases:
A ☐ Recommend   B ☐ Approve   C ☐ Neither

6. Your personal involvement in networking:
A ☐ Entire enterprise at all sites   F ☐ Public network
B ☐ Departments or network segments at more than one site   D ☐ No involvement
C ☐ Single department or network segment   E ☐ Other (specify):
                                                            _____

7. Your Industry:
A ☐ Aerospace   G ☐ Education (K–12)   K ☐ Health Care
B ☐ Agriculture/Mining/Construction   U ☐ Education (College/Univ.) L ☐ Telecommunications
C ☐ Banking/Finance   H ☐ Government—Federal   M ☐ Utilities/Transportation
D ☐ Chemical/Pharmaceutical   I ☐ Government—State   N ☐ Other (specify):
E ☐ Consultant   J ☐ Government—Local   _____
F ☐ Computer/Systems/Electronics

CPRESS

PACKET

Packet magazine serves as the premier publication linking customers to Cisco Systems Inc. Delivering complete coverage of cutting-edge networking trends and innovations, *Packet* is a magazine for technical, hands-on users. It delivers industry-specific information for enterprise, service provider, and small and midsized business market segments. A toolchest for planners and decision makers, *Packet* contains a vast array of practical information, boasting sample configurations, real-life customer examples, and tips on getting the most from your Cisco Systems' investments. Simply put, *Packet* magazine is straight talk straight from the worldwide leader in networking for the Internet, Cisco Systems, Inc.

We hope you'll take advantage of this useful resource. I look forward to hearing from you!

Cecelia Glover
Packet Circulation Manager
packet@external.cisco.com
www.cisco.com/go/packet

PACKET